The New Sociology of Economic Behaviour

BSA *New Horizons in Sociology*

The British Sociological Association is publishing a series of books to review the state of the discipline at the beginning of the millenium. New Horizons in Sociology also seeks to locate the contribution of British scholarship to the wider development of sociology. Sociology is taught in all the major institutions of higher education in the United Kingdom as well as throughout North America and the Europe of the former western bloc. Sociology is now establishing itself in the former eastern bloc. But it was only in the second half of the twentieth century that sociology moved from the fringes of UK academic life into the mainstream. British sociology has also provided a home for movements that have renewed and challenged the discipline; the revival of academic Marxism, the renaissance in feminist theory, the rise of cultural studies, for example. Some of these developments have become sub-disciplines whilst yet others have challenged the very basis of the sociological enterprise. Each has left their mark. Now therefore is a good time both to take stock and to scan the horizon, looking back and looking forward.

Series Editor: Bridget Fowler, *University of Glasgow*

Recent volumes include:

Nationalism and Social Theory
Gerard Delanty and Patrick O'Mahoney

Interactionism
Paul Atkinson and William Housley

Feminist Sociology
Sara Delamont

The New Sociology of Economic Behaviour

Ralph Fevre

SAGE Publications

London • Thousand Oaks • New Delhi

© 2003 Ralph Fevre

First published 2003

SAGE Publications Ltd
6 Bonhill Street
London EC2A 4PU

SAGE Publications Inc
2455 Teller Road
Thousand Oaks, California 91320

SAGE Publications India Pvt Ltd
B-42 Panchsheel Enclave
Post Box 4109
New Delhi 100 017

British Library Cataloguing in Publication data

A catalogue record for this book is available from the British Library

ISBN 0 7619 6662 5
ISBN 0 7619 6663 3

Library of Congress Control Number Available

Printed and bound in Great Britain by TJ International Ltd, Padstow, Cornwall

contents

preface

It seems a very long time since I struggled through my undergraduate degree in economics and sociology. No doubt a large part of the struggling was due to my lack of sympathy with calculus but I also felt that the two halves of my degree were contradictory rather than complementary. It seemed to me that the basic assumptions of economics undermined the whole idea of sociology and vice versa. That early experience gave me an itch that I have been wanting to scratch ever since. When I finally gave in to the urge to scratch I wrote this book. It explains to me, and hopefully to you, exactly why I found the basic assumptions of my joint honours disciplines so inimical, but it does several other things as well.

Since I got my degree – it was not a brilliant performance but I *did* get it – a whole academic industry has taken root, particularly in the US, which is dedicated to bridging the gap that I found so challenging. I actually read some of its product – the early work of the 'radical economists' – while I was a student but the industry did not really start to grow until later. By this time there were other developments in economics and, of course, the rise of economic sociology had begun. Although its inspiration lies further back, this book has to put these more recent developments at the heart of the story it tells. It also has to take account of the way sociology as a whole has developed since I was an undergraduate. Frankly I have been quite dispirited by much, if not most, of it. It has very often made me wonder what sociology is for and whether it has any point. Less frequently, I have even been given cause to wonder whether sociology is really the sort of thing that sensible populations and governments should spend their money on. For a long time I could not find answers to my questions about what sociology should really be doing if it were not producing the stuff I read in books and journals and sometimes even had to teach (through gritted teeth). I think I have found the answer to most of my questions in this book.

It also has to make room for discussion of a number of fields in which I have undertaken research. These include the early factory system, labour migration, industries that rely on cheap labour, outsourcing in manufacturing, the privatization of state owned enterprises, the effect of deindustrialization on localities and education and training systems. I have also relied on my own theoretical interests in the sociology of labour markets, the development of classical sociological theory, social identity, demoralization and social capital. Of course I have also relied on the research and thinking of hundreds of other scholars and there are two particular groups that deserve a mention. First, there are my colleagues in the Cardiff School of Social Sciences whose publications provide some of the key examples of sociological work which I think is developing in the right way. Second, I must mention all those involved with Work Employment and Society, the journal on whose editorial board I served for a number of years. I am particularly grateful to the editors during my time on the board – first Paul Edwards and then Theo Nichols – and to the contributors whose work I refereed. Many of their papers also figure here as examples of the right way to develop sociology.

Quite a few people have read this book, in whole or in part, in its several versions and I am extremely grateful to all of them: Robert Moore, Chris Rojek, Keith Grint, Barry Smart, Bill Jordan and Andrew Sayer, and, from the Cardiff School of Social Sciences, Theo Nichols, Finn Bowring, Phil Brown, Ken Prandy, Tom Hall and Huw Beynon. Some of these people, in particular Finn Bowring and Theo Nichols, have been extraordinarily generous with their time and written me pages of useful comments. At an early stage of my thinking about Chapter 5 I also had a very useful conversation with Gordon Marshall. All these people have given me courage to continue with what, at times, seemed an outlandish project. All the mistakes that I have made along the way are no responsibility of theirs.

Kay Bridger at Sage has been a great help and very patient. My family has been very patient too, particularly my wife who missed an idyllic day trip somewhere in the South China Sea just so I could finish the damn thing. No doubt you will find this fact curiously at odds with the message I am trying to put across in the book. I am sure my wife does – sorry Mo.

one

the classical renaissance in the sociology of economic behaviour

Something very interesting is going on among sociologists who write about economic behaviour. This book is intended to disseminate knowledge of these important recent developments and to interpret this knowledge in a way that helps people to make better sense of the work they are engaged in. Given what has happened to the sociology of economic behaviour over the past seventy years it is no surprise that interpretation should be required. The sub-discipline has long since lost its sense of purpose and those sociologists who are producing the most important new knowledge often have little idea of the significance of their work.

Ten years ago this book could not have been written. In its place you might have found a slim epitaph to the unfulfilled promise of a bankrupt branch of sociology. This would have been particularly regrettable because the study of economic behaviour had been a preoccupation of all the founders of the discipline, but there would have been no disguising the fact that the sociology of economic behaviour had totally run out of ideas. The orthodoxy appeared to have become a mindless empiricism in pursuit of one academic fad or another in debates that always proved inconclusive (Jones, 2000). Sociologists made a more-or-less arbitrary commitment to these debates because this was necessary if they were legitimately to pursue research funding and publication opportunities. When debates finally ended, this was not because a conclusion was reached but because the boredom thresholds of the least thoughtful sociologists were finally exceeded.

When sociologists of economic behaviour felt the need for a sense of purpose, they turned to popular writers on management and organizations who had their own ideas about how the world was changing and how it ought to change. Given the bankruptcy of ideas within sociology, it was not really surprising that people who seemed to have plenty of ideas were warmly embraced (Casey, 1995: 10). Moreover, many of these writers had authentic social science backgrounds (some in sociology) and seemed to use familiar sorts of evidence and even research. They also offered something of the grand sweep and vision that had been such a feature of the classical period when Marx, Durkheim, Weber, Simmel and others founded the sociology of economic behaviour, however, these new writers did not share the goals of classical sociology. For the most part, they were managerialists who were interested in making organizations more efficient and effective. Sometimes it was also claimed that increased effectiveness or efficiency could be combined with making the people who were managed more fulfilled, and their organizations more egalitarian, or more socially aware, but these could never be ends in themselves which could be pursued at the cost of efficiency and effectiveness.

This is a good point at which to define 'economic behaviour' because a definition will help us to see why there might be something dangerous about letting others define the purpose of the sub-discipline in this way. Your behaviour can be described as economic when you help to produce a good or a service (no matter whether you get paid for it or not) or consume one. It is also economic behaviour when you prepare yourself for your role in production by undergoing training and arranging day-care for your children, and when you compete with others in the labour market to get the best jobs. The sum of people's economic behaviour contributes to the shape of their organizations (especially their corporations) and the level of economic development that pertains in their society.

Thus far, economic behaviour has been defined without reference to the motives people have for engaging in it or the meanings that they give to it. It is *possible* that a great deal of this behaviour is understood by the people who do it to have economic motivation, for example they wish to maximize benefits and minimize costs, accumulate resources and buy the good things in life as cheaply as they can. Similarly, the economic behaviour of managers and others who are given the power to order economic behaviour (like those in government) *might* always be motivated by the desire to move resources from less to more productive uses. This is all theoretically possible but it requires empirical evidence for us to decide whether it is true in fact. We should not jump to the conclusion that just because behaviour takes place in the economic realm, it is economically motivated and only has an economic meaning.

It is dangerous for the sociology of economic behaviour to give up control over its agenda to people who are fundamentally committed to economic motivations and meanings because they are very likely to conclude that economic behaviour should only be understood in such terms. For example, if you think that the whole point of research and scholarship is to help humanity pursue economic motivations, you are quite likely to either ignore alternative aims or, if you do notice them, to try to undermine and marginalize them. But such alternative aims and meanings were very far from marginal to the classical sociology that initiated the study of economic behaviour. Indeed, not only was classical sociology interested in the non-economic meanings of economic behaviour, but it also used those non-economic meanings and values to critique economic behaviour. By this I do not mean simply that it criticized particular kinds of behaviour, showed their short-comings and investigated their unfortunate, and perhaps unintended, consequences. Classical sociology tried to change the perspective from which people looked at economic behaviour so that they could do more than understand it within its own terms. Classical critiques used non-economic meanings and values to uncover the hidden dimensions to economic behaviour which made it possible to appraise this behaviour properly (Anthony, 1977: 315).

What were the other-worldly values and meanings that classical sociology relied upon to underpin this critique? Durkheim (1893/1964, 1897/1952) was able to give the most straightforward answer to this question. He said they were *moral* meanings, by which term he did not mean some very narrow set of prescriptions about behaviour derived from Christianity or, indeed, any religion. He certainly thought morality had a lot to do with belief, but applied the term much more widely to refer to all the precepts about behaviour, and ways of judging behaviour, that stemmed from beliefs about what was right, and what was wrong, for humans to do. These beliefs could be trivial in the extreme (how long should a lunch-break be?) or more weighty (was there ever an occasion when homicide was justified?) but they had in common the quality of moral compulsion that only derives from things that must simply be believed in and cannot be measured or demonstrated (Fevre, 2000b). Thus, when morality determines how people vote on capital punishment, it is not the calculations of re-offending rates and unsafe convictions that settle their opinions.

Moral beliefs were other-worldly in this sense, as in others, because economic meanings derived so clearly from what could be measured and calculated. There was no need to believe in the economic because it was all so obviously tangible. Thus it was the intangible – beliefs about what constituted good character, good actions, a good society – that classical sociology used to critique that which could be easily demonstrated and understood. For Durkheim there was one very obvious place for sociology to begin this critique. While he had no doubt that economic behaviour was suffused with economic meanings and motivations, Durkheim used the vantage point of other-worldly critique to show how these meanings and motivations were displacing the more moral meanings and motivations which he thought necessary to

3

make people and society good. Durkheim used the term *anomie* to describe the way this displacement was experienced by individuals and society, and he discussed the way that the primacy of economic activity was responsible for the *demoralization* of society:

> A form of activity which has assumed such [an anomic] place in social life evidently cannot remain in this unruly state without resulting in the most profound disasters. It is a notable source of demoralization. For, precisely because the economic functions today concern the greatest number of citizens ... it follows that as that world is only feebly ruled by morality, the greatest part of their existence takes place outside the moral sphere ... If in the task that occupies almost all our time we follow no other rules than that of our well-understood interest, how can we learn to depend upon disinterestedness, on self-forgetfulness, on sacrifice? In this way, the absence of all economic discipline cannot fail to extend its effects beyond the economic world, and consequently weaken public morality. (Durkheim, 1893/1964: 3–4)

As every student of sociology knows, Durkheim pointed out that morality, in the shape of the social bonds that preceded contractual ones, was required in order to get industrial capitalism started, but that industrial capitalism would kill off this morality.

According to Durkheim, some new morality would have to be put in place to create solidarity and prevent society breaking down. Whatever might serve this purpose would automatically qualify as morality. The idea that whatever causes solidarity (and moderates our egoism) is moral is familiar to sociologists (Wolfe, 1989) but this is the beginning of the first of many examples of a conceptual wrong-turning that we will encounter in this book. According to Durkheim, the increased division of labour, and particularly the occupational specialization, that occurred with industrial capitalism would provide the new morality because it would create a new ('organic') sense of solidarity. With twenty-first-century hindsight we can pass judgement on Durkheim's prediction that the division of labour would found a new morality. At the end of the nineteenth century Durkheim was quite right to think insufficient time had elapsed for society to adjust to the demoralizing effects of industrial capitalism but it no longer seems sensible to argue that the cause of anomie will also supply its cure (Anthony, 1977). For one thing, we do not seem to suffer from less anomie; but we need to look at Durkheim's ideas in more detail to begin to see where the wrong turning was taken (ibid.).

Durkheim thought the increased division of labour would be the cause of solidarity because it would show each of us how much we depended upon each other. It was not necessary that this mutual dependence be rammed down our throats. Instead we could learn the

4

new morality indirectly by immersing ourselves in our specialized occupations. Our occupational specialization would make us moral, in other words. In order to complete the job of creating a new morality for the new society we needed rules which ensured that 'each individual will have the place he merits, will be rewarded as he deserves, where everybody, accordingly, will spontaneously work for the good of all and of each' (Durkheim, 1893/1964: 408). In the chapters which follow I will show that the assumptions embedded in this statement are highly problematic, but for the moment we need to know that Durkheim thought that, although it would be a difficult task to make this kind of society, we would find

> that what characterizes the morality of organized societies ... is that there is something more human, therefore more rational, about them. It does not direct our activities to ends which do not immediately concern us; it does not make us servants of ideal powers of a nature other than our own, which follow their direction without occupying themselves with the interests of men. It only asks that we be thoughtful of our fellows and that we be just, that we fulfil our duty, that we work at the function we can best execute, and receive the just reward for our services.' (ibid.: 407)

Rationality dealt only in things which were tangible, which could be subject to the measurement and calculation required to show whether a given end had been achieved. What might work for religious observance was totally inappropriate in the marketplace, indeed, perhaps it did not even work for religious observance. It is not a very far step from here to Weber (see below) or to the opinions of the great majority of sociologists who studied economic behaviour in the second half of the twentieth century. In this way sociology came to think of itself as a rational discipline which should deal in the spread of rational understandings and motivations (and the undermining of irrationality).[1]

Economic rationality is the sub-category of rationality which says life is all about economics and economics is all about a particular way of calculating means and ends. Economic rationality is in many ways the ideal type of rationality for social science to deal in (as is witnessed by the popularity of rational action approaches throughout social science). Sociologists espouse economic rationality, yet if Durkheim was wrong about the way increased occupational specialization would produce a new morality, this could be extremely dangerous. As the economic realm expanded, it would spread economic rationality into the rest of social life and yet economic rationality made no space for morality and morality had little purchase on economic behaviour. To the extent that the sociology of economic behaviour was converted to the pursuit of economic ends, it would become part of the process of demoralization

5

which Durkheim feared, marginalizing and undermining alternative (moral) aims and meanings.

If we are to construct a new critique of economic behaviour, we will have to find some way of reintroducing moral considerations (Mestrovic, 1991). Although it has rarely been done systematically, or even consciously, this is exactly what has begun to happen in the sociology of economic behaviour. It is this process of laying the foundations for a new critique that makes the field so exciting and makes it necessary for me to write this book. The reintroduction of morality – both as a possible ingredient in any explanation of human behaviour and a necessary ingredient in any judgement of the effect of social and economic change – was what was required to bring an end to the mindless empiricism and dedication to managerialism that bedevilled the discipline. The first step was to consider the possibility that economic behaviour might have some non-economic meaning or motivation. After this initial step it becomes possible to look at the effect of economic rationality on morality and to use morality in a critique of economic behaviour. This is an enormous task. If, like Durkheim, we wish to make all of the 'present-day utilitarian, rational arrangements' (Mestrovic, 1991: 183) a target for critique, we will find our task much greater than Durkheim's because the spread of these arrangements is much greater and economic rationality has become much more entrenched.

Stimulated by the extension of economic sphere, and the increasing hegemony of economic rationality, the demoralization that Durkheim feared has proceeded apace. Indeed, the idea of demoralization is now slipping into wider use (Fevre, 2000b) as a kind of shorthand used to describe the end product of several tendencies first identified by classical theory: the decay of bourgeois values, anomie and the death of the collective conscience, the disenchantment wrought by rationalization, and the use of money as the source of all value (Anthony, 1977). The term demoralization also allows us to allude to an associated phenomenon: the way affluence appears to diminish human happiness.

The way that social science looked at morality had already begun to change in Durkheim's day, of course. Durkheim was trying to understand the industrial capitalism that he saw taking over France at the end of the nineteenth century, but industrial capitalism had been around for some time by this point. Before Durkheim identified the dangers of anomie and demoralization, people had tended to think that morality could not be affected by anything human kind could do or make, including industrial capitalism. Adam Smith (1976b) saw morality as natural, perhaps God-given, and not susceptible to fundamental change by any cause. For Smith morality was like an environment (the rocks, the trees and the stars) which he took completely for granted. He could explore the intricacies of the new economic rationality sure in the knowledge that nothing could happen to alter this environment (Smith, 1976a). By Durkheim's time it was evident that all of this confidence in the unchanging, given nature of morality was misplaced.

Durkheim showed that morality could be changed, indeed undermined and marginalized, by things that men and women did and thought. It was neither natural nor God-given and what could be made by people could be changed and diminished by them. In effect, industrial capitalism remodelled the moral environment in its own image: blasting rocks, flattening trees and pulling the stars down out of the sky. But this fundamental change in the way morality was understood carried on in ways that Durkheim could not have anticipated. Adam Smith put morality in the category of a natural law, Durkheim saw it as a social fact or construction that could be enfeebled or demolished, but now we frequently find morality appearing as a means to ends defined by economic rationality. This is where the effects of a classical renaissance in the sociology of economic behaviour are most exciting: it would not be possible to recognize any of the more recent changes in the way we look at morality without this revival. Indeed, until this revival began, sociology was accustomed to blithely co-operating with efforts to make morality an instrument of economic rationality with, apparently, no real understanding of what it might be involved in (Kunda, 1992: 227).

A revitalized classical sociology of economic behaviour is beginning to show that morality is increasingly likely to turn up in the category of an instrument which is used to achieve economic ends precisely because demoralization has proceeded so far. The best new sociology in fact suggests that this represents as important a change as the one that Durkheim identified. Within sociology there is widespread agreement that industrial capitalism has changed beyond recognition but there is, as yet, no consensus about what it has changed into. Insights from a revitalized sociology of economic behaviour can help us to clarify what the new form of society is.

To begin this process of clarification we might return to the analogy in which the first commentators on industrial capitalism thought morality as safe and sure as the natural environment. It subsequently became clear how fragile this moral environment really was to all sorts of people as well as Durkheim, including those most involved in spreading economic rationality. After remaking the environment according to this rationality, people gradually discovered that the rocks and trees had, after all, served a purpose and that it was necessary to make substitutes for them: plastic rocks and synthetic stars. This manufacturing of our moral life is a key feature of the way we live now, and it is this process that distinguishes our societies from the ones characterized by industrial capitalism. *If industrial capitalism was all about demoralization, contemporary society is much more about the production of synthetic or instrumental morality.*

How do these manufactured substitutes for morality compare to those solutions Durkheim (1893/1964, 1991) once touted for societies that were affected by anomie? When Durkheim suggested that effort be put into fostering the moral role of professional and occupational associations, he saw these as artificial and, to a degree, instrumental, but the goal he had in mind was to put a stop to the process of demoralization and ameliorate its worst effects. A century later, substitutes for morality are apparently made in the cause of the sales, profits and efficiency which make up the goals and lexicon of economic rationality. The capitalism we have now is radically different from industrial capitalism: it is making not only goods and services for its own ends but morality itself.[2] On the other hand, is this really so different from what Durkheim saw as the moral significance of immersing ourselves in occupational specialization? As Anthony (1977: 150) suggested, Durkheim pointed towards Elton Mayo and the conviction that, with the help of managers, we will find moral meaning in our lives only through our work. We can add that there is also a curious parallel between Durkheim's faith in the division of labour and all the late twentieth-century companies which told their employees that their specialist contribution to the company's mission was what made their lives meaningful (see Chapter 3).

In the remainder of this chapter I am going to support the argument I have just outlined by, first of all, showing how classical concerns – for example, as present in the work of Marx and Simmel as well as Durkheim – were developing into a thorough-going and radical critique of economic behaviour. I will then show how, largely under the influence of Weber – and, particularly in the USA, Weber as interpreted by Parsons (1949, 1951; Parsons and Smelser, 1956) – the sociology of economic behaviour took another fatal wrong turning. The long and slow decline that followed finally brought us to a period in which the classical critique had been watered down to the extent that it was barely visible. The cause of this dilution and marginalization was the wholesale conversion of the sociology of economic behaviour into a sub-discipline devoted to understanding things in the terms of the economic rationality it had been founded to criticize. To signal this change I will use the term 'economic sociology' to describe the sub-discipline. Economic sociology did not just put an end to hopes of critique, it actually helped to spread economic rationality by making it the source of all judgement (and of course placing it beyond judgement itself). Given the central role of the sub-discipline in the

8

history and purpose of sociology, this degradation and colonization necessarily weakened the discipline as a whole. I will show, finally, that this process is now at an end and that a revitalized sociology of economic behaviour is beginning to mount a new critique which can both put economic rationality in perspective and simultaneously lay bare the role of 'economic sociology' – particularly in the version associated with managerialism – in propagating it (Anthony, 1977; Beder, 2000; Kunda, 1992; Shenhav, 1999). As an elaboration of this argument I will suggest that economic sociology has been complicit in the creation of morality substitutes required to replace the real morality which grows scarce with demoralization. When all this has been accomplished I will briefly describe the organization and content of the book's remaining chapters.

CLASSICAL THEORY'S CRITIQUE OF ECONOMIC BEHAVIOUR

When sociology came into being, it did so in order to make sense of economic behaviour because the economic behaviour which distinguished industrial capitalism was so novel and disturbing and had such potentially wide-ranging effects. This new way of organizing human life was so different to its predecessors that a whole new discipline had to be created in order to understand it. To put it crudely, sociologists wanted to find out how widely (and deeply) this new system had been adopted and, crucially, what its implications were going to be for the rest of human life. The key thing about capitalism as a way of organizing behaviour appeared to be that it made that part of life that was understandable in economic terms more important than ever before. It became so important, in fact, that people were gradually accepting the possibility that everything might be reducible to economic terms, and eventually they would come to wonder whether all behaviour might be economic at bottom. The classical sociologists were worried that all moral concerns might somehow be forced out of business by the primacy of economic motivation.

The classical critiques were intended to keep economic rationality in check by shedding new light on it from an other-worldly viewpoint. One common objective of such a critique was to level the playing field so that there could be proper competition between economic rationality and morality. In other words, a classical critique would argue that it was not ridiculous to measure economic behaviour against morality because economic rationality was not a qualitatively different kind of thought system (to morality). Moreover, this critique was intended to show that it is the ideological function of economic rationality to make us believe that this is not so and that economic rationality lies above and beyond out-dated concepts of morality. Thus we are meant to

9

understand that it is the mission of economic rationality to make us believe that it certainly is ridiculous to suggest it can be measured against morality. We can get a short cut to the heart of the critique that was being devised – within classical sociology – to counter this, by making use, once more of the comparison with Adam Smith. In this instance, however, the comparison is between Smith's political economy and the sociology of Karl Marx.[3]

The political economists explained, to the great benefit of Marx and the other early sociologists, how the new system worked (markets were more efficient than alternative methods of distribution, the inefficiency of rent taking, and so on). They may have pointed out that there were one or two disadvantages to the new system but this amounts to criticism, not critique. As I have made clear in the introduction to this chapter, a critique of economic behaviour seeks to problematize it in some fundamental way by opening it up to external judgement (Anthony, 1977). There was nothing of this in Smith (1976a, 1976b), for example. He was, arguably, more interested in understanding how morality worked than anyone (even Durkheim) but he did not see the connection between morality and economy as a way of opening up the critique of economic behaviour.

As Griswold (1999) explains, Smith was an Enlightenment thinker dedicated to directing the light of reason everywhere, including in the face of morality. But like other Enlightenment thinkers who did not realize the full, or personal, implications of their quest, Smith did not understand that morality was in danger. *The Theory of Moral Sentiments* (Smith, 1976b) was not an exploration of the well-springs of morality but a mapping of its structure and functions in a Parsonian manner. Smith did not think the wells of morality would dry up simply because, as noted above, he took it all for granted, as natural and not requiring explanation (Griswold, 1999). Smith therefore had no need to waste a second worrying about the fate of morality in capitalism: it would be as pointless as worrying about whether capitalism might affect the weather. So when Smith wrote in his other great work (Smith 1976a) that it is the self-interest of the baker that makes sure we have bread on our table, there was no intended implication for morality (any more than there was for the weather). Once you see this you understand that Smith was actually being ironic (Griswold, 1999).[4] He was not saying that we should do without morality (how could we?) but that, ironically, the self-interested amorality of the baker turned out to be good for all of us. And that is all: economy and morality can continue on, side by side, never touching and never having implications for each other. No matter how good economic behaviour might become at generating invisible hands which serve the common good, morality would continue to be

10

as safe and sure as the rain. Marx did not agree.

Marx was certainly sure that morality was neither natural nor immortal and he expected capitalism to undermine its very foundations:

> In the conditions of the proletariat, those of old society at large are already virtually swamped. The proletarian is without property; his relation to his wife and children has no longer anything in common with the bourgeois family relations; modern industrial labour, modern subjection to capital, the same in England as in France, in America as in Germany, has stripped him of every trace of national character. Law, morality, religion, are to him so many bourgeois prejudices, behind which may lurk in ambush just as many bourgeois interests. (Marx and Engels, 1848/2002: 231–2)

We should not be confused by the fact that Marx also thought this undermining of morality a good idea, a necessary step on the way to a better society. The most important point for our present purposes is that Marx did not take bourgeois morality for granted as natural and unshakeable but rather thought it was going to disappear altogether! In his critique of economic behaviour, Marx also began to suggest that the way capitalism succeeded in changing so much so quickly involved an enormous illusion or deception (indeed, it entailed some self-deception by the illusionist). Marx said capitalism was not what it seemed, even to the capitalist and, like Smith, he used irony to show us what he meant. The essence of this irony was that the capitalist fools himself and us *about the morality of what he does and, especially, the morality of where his money comes from.*[5] Economic rationality told us his money came from adding value to commodities and exchanging them where Marx would have us see that, in reality, the process by which capital accumulates is horribly immoral.

Even when it was in its infancy, Marx could see that capitalism could not produce an exponential growth of value by moving resources (including labour) from less-productive to more-productive uses. Marx used irony to dispute this, and to present the logic of capitalism as made up entirely of ghostly appearances which had no relationship to fact. In the process, he laid the foundations of the sociology of economic behaviour, but there is more to Marx's critique than this. When Marx said, again and again, that objects, mere things, *stood* outside and against people, and when he said that everything really human was transformed into impersonal material forces, he was not telling us to be content with the way humanity was demoted to a passive role with its creations in charge. Money, for example, became value itself rather than an expression of value.

11

If the logic which accompanied capitalism (as expressed in the political economy which Marx critiqued, in the first instance), was an illusion, then we were left with capital accumulation in the hands of a few and widening inequality. Shorn of deception, this became explicable as the moral goal of one section of society and the playing field between morality and economic rationality was effectively levelled. Once we understood those few were fooling themselves about the amoral quality of their new beliefs and behaviour, we could see that, in fact, their new beliefs had the same qualities as the old moralities and functioned as substitute moralities themselves.

A similarly important contribution to the sociology of economic behaviour was made by Georg Simmel in *The Philosophy of Money* (1900/1990) and his lecture on 'The Metropolis and Mental Life' (Simmel, 1902–3/1971: 324–39). According to Simmel, money obliterated all the differences between people that once defined traditional societies, not just ascribed differences but also personal and subjective qualities of every kind. Money made exchange more impersonal and as money became more important, that impersonality became characteristic of society. Bad character and ascribed character mattered less: they were no longer handicaps to social esteem for example. With money (and the complex division of labour it makes possible) we became more and more dependent on other people but who those people were, what they were really like, mattered less and less. Money intruded deeper and deeper into parts of our life which, a little earlier, no one could have conceived might have anything to do with economic calculation. Even where money was not pre-eminent, we were beginning to look at all aspects of our lives as some form of exchange (cf. Blau, 1964). This fundamentally changed how we felt about others.

Simmel described the way in which irrationality gave way to reason because of the spread of money as the medium of exchange: it flattened cultural differences between peoples as everyone related within and between their societies in this impersonal way. This obviously recalls contemporary anxieties about the cultural homogenization associated with globalization. Simmel would have not been in the least surprised by the way money now allows us to over-ride cultural difference and feel at home everywhere. He understood that this familiarity did not sit well with mystery and magic and that the transparent and rationalized orientation to money contributed to disenchantment. Money was the talisman of modern life in which the whole world and everything in it could be measured against everything else so, in a way, that made us think we knew about the whole world. On the other hand, intriguing new possibilities were created when money became the universal objective standard of personal worth, the yardstick which everyone used to measure themselves against everyone else.

Living in a society where money ruled, rather than religion or kinship for example, gave individuals more freedom because money was neutral. Rather than make you live your life according to a morality, you could use the signs of money to manipulate how people treated you. Money gave individuals control over the way they could appear in the eyes of others in a way that had been impossible in traditional societies (where ascription could not be escaped, for example). But this could seem a very empty victory because men and women were in some danger of becoming simply the impressions they sought to give to others, with no core of things that they believed in, nothing that mattered to them, and no relations with others that were authentic. Simmel was influenced by Schopenhauer who believed that virtues like compassion are much more irrational than rational. Schopenhauer had argued that it was our reason that set us thirsting after novelty and difference. This constant search for stimulation was what served in place of the things we used to believe in. It was what we had to do now we thought we knew everyone had their price.

When money became a generalized mode of exchange we lost our individuality but got the chance to buy it back by, for example, following fashion. According to Simmel, fashion 'renders possible a social obedience, which at the same time is a form of individual differentiation' (1904/1971: 305). Fashion was a necessary prop because, just as we could longer see more value in one person than another, so we were no longer capable of discrimination between one object and another:

> This mood is the faithful subjective reflection of the completely internalised money economy. By being the equivalent to all the manifold things in one and the same way, money becomes the most frightful leveller. For money expresses all qualitative differences of things in terms of 'how much?' Money, with all its colourlessness and indifference, becomes the common denominator of all values: irreparably it hollows out the core of things, their individuality, their specific value and their incomparability. All things float with equal specific gravity in the constantly moving stream of money. (Simmel, 1902–3/1950: 414)

Simmel thought this could not help but spawn a *blasé* attitude which prefigures the attitudes of David Riesman's 'inside dopesters' (Riesman, 1950). There was nothing unknown, no longer anything that could not be tamed with money; indeed, there was nobody who was above money and we all had our price. These are some of the necessary conditions for demoralization.

CLASSICAL THEORY TAKES A WRONG TURNING

There has been general acceptance of the view that when sociologists leave the study of economic life to economists they are forgetting the lessons of Max Weber who taught that economic behaviour should only be seen 'as a special, if important, category of social action' (Granovetter, 1985: 597). Moreover, it was Weber who drew our attention to the process of rationalization – including the spread of bureaucratic and economic rationality – in industrial, capitalist societies and to the unwelcome effects of this process, including disenchantment. It must therefore seem far-fetched to argue that it was in Weber's work that classical theory took a wrong turning yet this is the only way to understand how the promise of classical theory was effectively thrown away.

Many people will have encountered the idea of an intellectual wrong turning in the work of the philosopher, Alasdair MacIntyre, who argued that Western philosophy made this sort of mistake when it turned away from the path of Aristotle (see, for example, MacIntyre, 1985). According to MacIntyre, philosophy, and even Western society as a whole, suffered from the ill-effects of this error in all the centuries that followed. At one level I simply wish to borrow this idea and show that the sociology of economic behaviour made a similar mistake[6] but this is not all that my argument owes to MacIntyre. MacIntyre did not hold Weber responsible for the wrong turn in Western philosophy but he was critical of Weber's approach to bureaucracy and rationalization. To simplify a subtle and complex argument, we could say that MacIntyre argued that Weber identified a key trend of Western society but then (wrongly) convinced himself that this trend was irresistible (MacIntyre, 1985). It is almost as if Weber gave way to an excess of intellectual pessimism. There is much more to MacIntyre's criticism than this – and the role of mistaken notions of the capabilities of rationality, including social science, will be discussed below – but he showed that it was not Weber's original insight that constituted a wrong turning for the classical sociology of economic behaviour, but his pessimism about how far rationalization must go. It was the fact that Weber concluded that there was no alternative to economic rationality that constituted the wrong turning.

Daniel Bell refers to economically rational behaviour as 'economizing'. He describes Weber's rationalization as equivalent to the spread of an 'economizing attitude' (1976: 67) where 'economizing societies ... are organized around a principle of "more for less" and to choose the more "rational" course of action (ibid.: 75–6). Weber, in particular, established the practice of treating morality solely as a means and never as an end. For example, morality could help or hinder economic development but in either argument it was subordinate to (economic) rationality. Where Durkheim saw the importance of pre-contractual solidarity, he did not thereby demote morality to an instrumental role in all other respects. Indeed, the deleterious effects of economy on morality were his initial preoccupation. Similarly, Marx could see the way that capitalism destroyed bourgeois morality *and* the way capitalist sense-making functioned as a kind of smoke-screen and substitute morality rolled into one. This is not to suggest that the Marxist and Durkheimian sociologists who studied economic behaviour in the twentieth century were able to avoid taking the Weberian wrong turning. For the most part they never questioned Weber's pessimism and, indeed, the self-evident supremacy of ration-ality – and the demotion of morality to a supporting role – were sim-ply taken for granted (Anthony, 1977; Shenhav, 1999). The fact that there had ever been another path, another way of developing the soci-ology of economic behaviour, had been forgotten. The consequence of this was that the sociology of economic behaviour was in a very sorry state by the 1990s. It had become repetitive and devoid of inspiration with nothing to offer to the rest of the discipline.

Marxist sociologists did more than most to keep the sociology of economic behaviour in touch with moral ideas but this did not mean they were any more successful at integrating morality into their sociol-ogy than the most Weberian of their colleagues. Careful empirical work might, for example, catalogue the way workers were subject to pres-sures to intensify their labour but the idea that this intensification was wrong, and should be resisted, was not part of the sociology but was imported from outside. Inside the sociology it had to be admitted, indeed it was a core assumption of the methodology, that the intensifi-cation of labour was highly rational economic behaviour on the part of capitalists. So far as the sociology of economic behaviour went, there was not a word to say against it. For this reason many of the Marxist writers did not even mention in their work that they judged speed-up or deskilling to be immoral. Instead they tried to convey this impression by the use of literary technique. In a few cases the results were magnif-icent pieces of literature (see for example, Beynon, 1974) but fell short of the standards of classical critique (Anthony, 1977).[7]

In these respects the Marxist studies of the workplace were really no different from Weberian studies of social stratification which faith-fully documented the stability of patterns of relative social mobility but could only judge this to be wrong if they imported an idea like 'social justice' (Marshall et al., 1997). The heyday of the Marxist soci-ology of economic behaviour in the 1970s – always a more European than American affair – had passed into memory when the intellectual death of Marxism was announced in 1989.[8] Nothing was more indica-tive of the bankruptcy of a Marxist sociology of economic behaviour which took Weber's pessimism about the virtues of 'economizing' as an article of faith than the interminable and completely fruitless 'labour process "debate"' which occurred – it would be stretching

15

credulity to say that it 'raged' – throughout the late 1970s and 1980s (see pp. 111–112). When the journals and publishers of academic books had finally had enough of this (and turned their attention to the equally pointless 'flexibility debate' instead), those sociologists who had managed to retain an interest in this area of research did at least have a clearly defined research agenda. It seemed that, once you decided that your job was to study what bosses did to get ahead, or simply to keep up with their competitors, it was but a small step to doing research in order to decide which of these innovations worked best. From here it was another tiny step to the point at which sociologists started volunteering to employers their knowledge of how best to accomplish what they once used to call 'exploitation'.[9] In fact, this *volte face* became inevitable when the sociology of economic behaviour took its wrong turning. There was apparently nothing in the disposition of Marxist sociologists that could protect them from the same fate that befell all who took the supremacy of economic rationality for granted (Anthony, 1977; Shenhav, 1999).

A sociology of economic behaviour which is so happy to take economic rationality on trust will eventually be confounded by the results of its own empirical research. Thus sociologists who deplored the effects of the rational behaviour of employers and managers spent a great deal of time looking for evidence of 'worker resistance' to this behaviour. Where it was competently conducted, empirical research tended to show that workers' behaviour varied along a continuum between resistance and co-operation (Friedman, 1977; Nichols and Benyon, 1977). Moreover, when workers resisted, they were likely to do it for their own economically rational reasons and the mere fact of their resistance therefore did nothing to support a moral critique of capitalism (Calhoun, 1982).

It is worth citing one further example of the way that sociologists who tried to criticize capitalism without critically examining economic rationality eventually saw their theories being undermined by empirical evidence. In the sociology of economic development it had been axiomatic – in under-development theory, for example – that, at best, capitalism might be good for poorer people in rich countries but could never be good for anyone but a tiny elite in poor countries. In the 1980s the empirical evidence began to suggest otherwise and those who had done most to popularize the theory of under-development soon found themselves recanting every word (Frank, 1998). It is undoubtedly the case in this instance, and all the others like it, that many sociologists of economic behaviour thought they were involved in an intellectual crusade against capitalism, or even 'monopoly capitalism' (Baran and Sweezy, 1966). These sociologists had mistaken the *occasion* for inventing the sociology of economic behaviour (and indeed the discipline as a

16

whole) for its sole function. It might have been stimulated by the development of industrial capitalism but its function was to critique all economic behaviour, not just a particular form of it (Anthony, 1977; Gorz, 1989).

It can readily be understood why sociologists who were committed to the narrow function of the sociology of economic behaviour were confounded by the apparent success of capitalism as evidenced by their empirical studies of workplace behaviour and patterns of industrial development. Sociologists gave up the right to critique any economic behaviour because they accepted the apparent victory of capitalism as complete. In this way the sociology of economic behaviour voluntarily abandoned the critique of economic behaviour and accepted the straitjacket of economic rationality as its regulation dress. In the last quarter of the twentieth century a few sociologists were still being stirred by the thought of the dehumanizing and alienating effects of capitalism but what was generally missing was the sort of fundamental thinking Marx had begun to do. In particular, sociologists had ceased to compare what economic rationality claimed for itself with what it actually accomplished. They therefore denied themselves the chance of judging whether the 'rational' status of economic rationality stood up to scrutiny. Far from following Marx, many sociologists began evangelizing for economic rationality. It was becoming clear that the sociology of economic behaviour had followed the lead of economics and allowed all moral concerns to be subsumed to economic ones.

17

ECONOMIC SOCIOLOGY AND SOCIAL ECONOMICS

The sociology of economic behaviour was invented along with industrial capitalism because economic rationality became more important than it had ever been in this new kind of society (Gorz, 1989). The most important goal of the sub-discipline was to subvert this rationality by setting it against the notion of morality: how was the new relationship that was being established between the moral and the economic to be understood? A century later sociologists appeared to have answered this question: the relationship was an unequal one in which morality was either instrumental, or subservient, to economic aims. The sociology of economic behaviour was invented to critique economic rationality but eventually capitulated to it. By the last quarter of the last century it had been thoroughly contaminated with economic rationality (Shenhav, 1999).

We need to understand this colonization (which occurred as part of the processes of rationalization and demoralization of which classical sociology had warned), if we are to see the enormous significance of the most recent developments in sociology which suggest that the sociology of economic behaviour is, at last, showing signs of turning into the diagnostic tool which classical theory promised it would become. In particular, we need to understand that by the 1980s the sociology of economic behaviour had itself become part of the social and political machinery dedicated to furthering the socio-economic changes that sociology had been invented critique. In this way sociology had itself become an instrument of demoralization (Anthony, 1977). To renew this branch of sociology as a form of classical critique from such a unpromising starting point would seem almost miraculous.

The involvement of sociology in the spread of economic rationality is most clearly visible in the *off-shoots* of sociology which helped to give rise to many of the courses taught in business schools. Under *noms de guerre* such as management theory and the study of organizational behaviour, these off-shoots provided some potent weapons for advancing the sorts of social and economic changes sociology was invented to problematize (Beder, 2000; Shenhav, 1999). These were largely ideological weapons: ways of presenting the changes, and the rationale for making and accepting them, as if they were good for everyone or there was simply no alternative to making them (Kunda, 1992). Through these off-shoots, sociology and the other social sciences created the knowledge that the foot-soldiers of economic rationality, the managers, had to learn before they were allowed to soldier (Anthony, 1977).

Rather less obviously, the colonization of sociology by economic rationality proceeded as an internal process within the sociology of economic behaviour (as it appeared in the most respected sociology journals, for example). Indeed, this branch earned itself a new name: the sociology of economic behaviour that rigorously prosecuted the agenda defined by economic rationality became known as 'economic sociology'. By the 1980s this term was in common use to describe sociology in a variety of substantive areas (Swedberg, 1986). Economic sociology was, for example, informing sociologies of migration, of work, or industrial organization, of education and training, of social mobility and of labour markets.

The term 'economic sociology' was used by both Durkheim and Weber but it was not until Parsons (Parsons, 1949, 1951; Parsons and Smelser, 1956) and Smelser – in various contributions throughout the 1960s – began to interpret Weber that the idea of a separate sub-discipline began to take shape (Smelser and Swedberg, 1994). By the early 1990s some of its practitioners were so proud of its achievements, and so sure of the progress made since Durkheim and Weber, that they preferred their work to be known as the '*new* economic sociology'

(Friedland and Robertson, 1990; Swedberg, 1993; Zukin and DiMaggio, 1990). In the most influential statement of the new economic sociology, Granovetter (1990) defined the scope of the subdiscipline much more widely than Parsons had. Ironically, Granovetter drew his inspiration from Polanyi (see pp. 22–23) but what Granovetter took from Polanyi was the key concept of embeddedness (Granovetter, 1985). In effect, economic rationality had to have a social context but there was more to economic behaviour than economic rationality. Granovetter used the idea of social networks to show how the economy was embedded and the focus on networks become a central focus – along with markets and corporations – of economic sociology (Smelser and Swedborg, 1994).

Economic sociology was not interested in the classical preoccupation with the effects of economic behaviour, and the rise of economic rationality, on the non-economic, more straightforwardly social, parts of our lives. Rather, its interest in economic behaviour was excited by the way in which economic life could also be seen to be social. Economic sociology concerned itself with the investigation of the social context of economic behaviour and considered the idea of a critique of this behaviour unnecessary and, indeed nonsensical (Callon, 1998). Yet sociologists do not always limit themselves to documenting human behaviour without comment just because this behaviour is common. This is not how they have approached the study of racist behaviour, for example. Instead of simply documenting racism, sociologists have mounted a critique of this behaviour showing, for instance, why the world-view on which racism is founded is mistaken and suggesting that race is not a meaningful category for explaining social behaviour. The alternative to economic sociology is a critique which questions the foundations of economic rationality and thus problematizes its goals, capabilities and functions.

The idea that economic behaviour had a social context – as expressed by the idea of embeddedness, for example – gave economic sociology its justification for trespassing on the territory of economics. The search for this justification was its holy grail. Since Parsons and Smelser (1956) it had been clear that economic sociology looked towards the neoclassical economics rather than classical social theory. Indeed, the whole sub-discipline could be understood as a polite plea from sociologists for recognition and validation from neoclassical economics. Such an attitude could not fail to compromise sociology, for example, from the very beginning it committed sociology to a partial view of the rise of economic rationality. Weber's observation that we cannot take economic rationality for granted was developed by Parsons into the proposition that economic rationality was a system of norms that appeared at specific stages of development in the West (Smelser and Swedberg, 1994). In other words, Parsons wished economists to take notice that the things sociologists were interested in (norms) were important after all – since they served economic ends.

It is worth pointing out that the same position can just as easily be reached from the other side of the disciplinary divide, and with barely a reference to Weber (or any other classical social theory). Etzioni invented his own version of economic sociology without ever leaving the economists' side of the fence. A brief discussion of his 'social economics' will serve to highlight all the dangers economic sociology runs by orienting itself towards the concerns of economics. Etzioni argued that neoclassical theory dismissed the idea that morality might affect economic behaviour because to do otherwise undermined the 'article of faith' that collective intervention in the lives of individuals made bad economic sense as well being a blow for tyranny (1988: 10). Not only did morality affect economic behaviour, but morality served economic ends like lower transaction costs, less tax evasion, more savings, better industrial relations and productivity and even higher GNP. Of course there were examples where morality had an inefficient downside but morality was also an efficient way of providing for the commons.

The tendencies of social economics are best summed up by Etzioni's idea that giving workers dignity would make them work harder, reduce turnover and absenteeism and that 'many people work best, and feel less exploited, in contextual relations, in which they work in part out of moral commitment and are treated as human beings, and not merely as commodities' (ibid.: 75). In his conclusions Etzioni argued that companies could save the money they might have put into financial incentives for their workers because 'there is considerable evidence that changing the corporate culture, including its informal moral codes, frequently can deliver a significant part of the desired results, at a much lower cost' (ibid.: 230). Etzioni went on to cite Deal and Kennedy in this passage and by the 1990s economic sociologists were increasingly influenced by writers like Peters, Drucker and Kanter who were explicitly, and unashamedly, concerned with finding ways of making corporations, and the managers of corporations, more successful. In effect, sociology was now turning for its ideas to the off-shoots of the discipline which had been established in the business schools. This was rather like mainlining economic rationality. The ideas being injected into sociology were so thoroughly managerialist that they made economic rationality a combination of a *political* aim and the foundation of a world-view.[10]

In this most recent incarnation of economic sociology we can begin to discern the unrealistic opinion that economic sociology has of its own capabilities. Whereas Granovetter (for example) took Oliver

Williamson to task for naïvely over-estimating the efficacy of managerial authority (Granovetter, 1985), more recent economic sociology shared its false opinion with managerialism. The comments made by Deetz in respect of psychology could apply just as easily to the economic sociology which looked to Kanter, Drucker and Peters (and even Reich and Castells) for its inspiration: '[a]s an academic discipline psychology matches well what Scott (1985: 153) identified as the core beliefs of managerialism: "People are Essentially Defective"; "People are Totally Malleable"' (Deetz, 1992: 42).

Just like the managerialism with which it shares so much in common (Gillespie, 1991), economic sociology had a ridiculous idea of the capabilities of human-knowledge, for example, it took seriously its predictive power (Andreski, 1972; MacIntyre, 1985; Winch, 1990). Whereas Etzioni, for example, recognized the limitations of social science as an aid to policy making (1988: 244), self-deception was surely a major reason why economic sociology failed to recognize its real, but unacknowledged, role in propagating managerial ideology.

The reduction of the sociology of economic behaviour to economic sociology had a negative effect on the whole discipline because, for much of its history, the sociology of economic behaviour had been the discipline's moving spirit (Rose, 1988: 131). Classical sociology came into being to help people to cope with the invention of industrial capitalism. It was meant to act as a diagnostic tool that would provide knowledge that would allow people to recognize and address the problems that industrial capitalism created. Instead, the sociology of economic behaviour became marginal to the discipline. Sociologists found they could ignore it, confident in the knowledge that they were missing nothing that was important. For much of the twentieth century this neglect was justified but during this time economic sociology continued its work – largely consisting in the completely unnecessary duplication of marginalia – and countless opportunities to mount a meaningful critique along the lines suggested by classical theory were missed.

21

THE RENEWAL OF CRITIQUE

While economic sociology had other preoccupations, some thought was given to the renewal of the critique begun by classical sociology among a disparate band of social theorists and philosophers, and one or two sociologists, which included Cooley, Sorokin, Polanyi, Marcuse, Habermas, Fromm, Riesman, Ellul, Bell, Gorz, Bellah, MacIntyre and Bauman. The problem is that none of these efforts have, until very recently, captured the attention of sociologists who study economic behaviour. The most significant example of this is Polanyi.

Early in the twentieth century Cooley discussed some of the ideas which Polanyi elaborated thirty years later. Cooley held to the classical assumption that the market was 'an institution, like another, having important functions but requiring, like all institutions to be brought under control by the aid of a comprehensive sociology, ethics and politics':

> Thus, even if market values were the best possible of their kind, we could not commit the social system to their charge, and still less can we do so when the value institution, owing to rapid and one-sided growth, is in a somewhat confused and demoralized condition. Bearing with it not only the general inheritance of human imperfection but also the special sins of a narrow and somewhat inhuman commercialism, it by no means reflects life in that broad way in which a market, with all its limitations, might reflect it. The higher values remain for the most part untranslated, even though translatable. (Cooley, 1913: 197)

These higher values could not be produced in the 'sphere of pecuniary valuation' but they could be made to apply there. Separating the market from morality was harmful and the market should be in a constant 'process of moral regeneration' (ibid.: 202).

Like Cooley, Polanyi thought the market was the outcome of an historical process driven by a social class rather than a natural institution which spontaneously arose from some abiding characteristics of human nature. His work also exhibited other classical characteristics. He criticized the idea that unlimited commodities solved all human problems and argued that the belief in the virtues of economic rationality was not founded in evidence but in a mystical acceptance of its results as a good thing. Polanyi also explained that economic rationality allowed us to delude ourselves that destitution and suffering were nobody's fault, and that it was much more usual for the economy to be turned to social ends rather than the reverse.[11]

Polanyi's unique contribution was the idea that the political and social impulse to tame markets had grown wherever markets had grown but in nineteenth-century Britain the disastrous experiment of the self-regulating market had been introduced. With economic rationality freed from social oversight, demoralization and environmental degradation would be inevitable:

> Robbed of the protective covering of cultural institutions, human beings would perish from the effects of social exposure; they would die as the victims of acute social dislocation through vice, perversion, crime and starvation. Nature would be reduced to its elements, neighbourhoods and landscapes defiled, rivers polluted, military safety jeopardized, the power to produce food and raw materials destroyed. (Polanyi, 1944/1957: 73)

22

Nineteenth-century Britain invoked all of these calamities and, of those who recognized the dangers, Polanyi singles out Robert Owen who drew attention to the corrosive effects on human character of putting economic rationality in charge and explained how human happiness was being diminished.

By the early twentieth century the pursuit of regulation and the protection of the economy had become the preoccupation of different social classes which 'used and abused' the political and economic sections of society in pursuit of their own interests. What was needed was what Owen had asked for: no separation between economy and society and therefore no power-base for economic rationality, not regulation but proper planning and social control. Society could only cope with industrial capitalism if it was a new kind of society with all the emphasis on morality which Owen had promoted in New Lanark. More than a century later it was again clear that regulation would not work and that what was needed was to take land, labour and money outside the market principle.

As we know, economic sociology took from Polanyi the idea of embeddedness when it might have been reminded to evaluate economic behaviour and bring it to account. More recently there have been similar pleas within a tradition of 'moral economy' – a term which refers to 'both the ways in which economic actions are influenced by moral sentiments and norms, and a standpoint from which we can *evaluate* economic arrangements' (Sayer, 2000b). No matter where it finds its inspiration, a fully-fledged critique of economic rationality will put to use the better understanding of the possibilities of social science that we have reached at the end of the twentieth century (MacIntyre, 1985; Winch, 1990). We know far better than Weber what the limitations of both social science and economic rationality are (Anthony, 1977). In effect, twentieth-century social science served as an unintended, and rather long, complicated and expensive research project which was designed to test whether the claims made for economic rationality would hold up under experimental conditions. The answer is emphatically that they do not: in brief, social science may claim to do what science can and it cannot do so because its subject matter is different. The same conclusion applies to economic rationality and it is thereby demoted to its proper place amongst less reliable, and non-predictive, forms of knowledge like common sense (Shenhav, 1999). In fact, economic rationality is better understood as a more rigorous and sophisticated form of common sense (see Chapter 2 for a definition and discussion).

Once this is clear, we are forced to rethink the source of the appeal of economic rationality and this automatically opens up the possibilities for fundamental critiques of economic behaviour on the classical

23

model. If this appeal was not founded in the ability of economic rationality to deliver the goods in the way it claimed when assuming the status of a science, then where did the secret of its attraction to those who would live their lives by it really lie? If people were not, in fact, judging economic rationality by its results, why was it that they were increasingly likely to apply economic rationality in the course of their everyday lives? Indeed, the greater the intrusion of economic rationality into everyday lives, the more obvious it became that there was no evidence of the extravagant results that were claimed for it.

Since there is no evidential basis to the claim that economic rationality satisfies its own criteria of efficiency and efficacy, we must look for the source of its appeal in actors' interests (Gillespie, 1991). For example, such considerations might go some way towards explaining why management consultants are paid so well when there is so little evidence that they increase efficiency. In this case, as in many others, managerialism launders power into authority, but naked self-interest is never sufficient to account for an ideology, still less a hegemonic one. The missing factor turns out to be the normative appeal made by economic rationality. Daniel Bell points out that 'economizing societies ... are organized around a principle of functional efficiency whose desideratum is to get "more for less" and to choose the more "rational" cause of action' (1976: 75–6). Yet if there is no proof that more has been gained for less by the pursuit of economic rationality, then the appeal of this rationality must be understood as an end in itself. Western societies were not swept by rationalization because it was effective (as Weber imagined) but because it was believed to be a good thing (Gorz, 1989; Shenhav, 1999). In the end, the secret appeal of economic rationality can be found in the way it attaches to the same social 'receptors' as morality does, or did (Anthony, 1977).[12]

These insights provide the basis for a new critique of economic behaviour, something that carries the same power as a classical critique but reworked for new times. The earliest signs of this new critique could be found in work such as that undertaken by Arlie Hochschild (1983; 1989) which began to give us our first glimpses of the way in which contemporary economic behaviour entailed the invention of substitutes for morality. This nascent critique is beginning to show that economy needs morality (of a kind) just as morality undoubtedly needs economy. In the chapters that follow we will suggest that managerialism, and indeed economic sociology, has often been engaged in attempts to engineer morality. Managerialism is heavily implicated in both the spreading of economic rationality and the subsequent re-engineering of ersatz moralities to make up for the demoralization it promoted.

This book is meant to act as midwife to the new sociology of economic behaviour by systematizing the emerging critique. Of course this necessarily entails the abandonment of economic sociology as useless (in respect of its acknowledged aims) and pernicious (in respect of its unacknowledged ones). In its place we need a sociology of economic behaviour which will not join forces with managerialism but, rather, problematizes it. Moreover, we need a sociology of economic behaviour that makes the study of moral economy, and the more complex relationship between demoralization and economy (and particular the emergence of engineered or ersatz moralities), the core of the revitalized sub-discipline that should be at the heart of sociology.

OVERVIEW OF THE BOOK

In order to make this argument, the next six chapters consist of essays on different aspects of the sociology of economic behaviour. The final chapter summarizes and discusses the conclusions of these six chapters after considering the development of this kind of sociology in relation to the history of the societies that spawned it. Chapters 2 to 7 do not give equal weight to the various elements of the argument outlined in this introductory chapter, and different themes receive more emphasis in one chapter than another, but each chapter will give a key example of the way a wrong turning was made which took a particular piece of research in the direction of economic sociology and away from a classical critique. The remainder of each chapter will be devoted to showing, first, how economic sociology has prosecuted the agenda defined by economic rationality on the basis of a mistaken notion of the capabilities of social science. Each chapter will show how morality was subordinated to economic rationality, and there will be examples of economic sociology taking recourse to the approach and concepts of economics[13] in order to deal with morality in an instrumental way.

25

Second, each chapter will set about explaining the possibilities for a much more informative view of the relationship between morality and economy represented by an authentic sociology of economic behaviour. The best examples of this are the ones that make morality endogenous to theory and research and explore the effects on morality as one of its key tasks. The other key task for the sociology of economic behaviour is to show how economic rationality itself functions as a kind of morality. Each chapter will show that when this happens we return to the opportunities opened up by Marx for a critique of economic rationality which exposes the logic which justifies the (otherwise illegitimate) consequences of economic behaviour as surreal and absurd.

NOTES

1 Berlin (1969: 114–15) traces the error of thinking we can do without morality back to Comte, suggesting that the original source of this mistake lies in the positivist tradition of sociology. Anthony (1977) identifies the contribution of Comte and Saint Simon to the promotion of economic rationality.

2 Sometimes the term 'culture' is used in place of morality. This loses the Durkheimian emphasis on the ideas of good and bad underpinning motivation and understanding and I reject this language for this reason; similarly the use of 'normative' instead of moral also loses the original emphasis since a norm need have no moral loading but is simply what we do round here (compare to Margaret Archer, 2000 on 'normative man'). It is probably no coincidence that unreconstructed sociology which is enthralled by economic rationality favours 'norms' and 'culture' to describe the phenomena I am alluding to here. It refuses to be caught seriously talking about morality as a determinant of human behaviour whereas I want to emphasize the real or pretended moral tone of these guidelines to action.

3 Finn Bowring has suggested that I take a rather too charitable view of Marx throughout this text. In particular, he thinks I exaggerate Marx's humanism. There may well be considerable substance to this criticism and it would certainly have been possible to find more examples of sociology taking a wrong turning in Marx's work. In the end I have decided to retain a generous reading of Marx for the benefit of readers who can more clearly distinguish the promise of classical theory from the disappointments of economic sociology.

4 Should any reader wonder whether I am being obtuse, I am also investing the idea that it would be absurd for capitalism to affect the environment or, as here, the weather, with some irony.

5 Francis Wheen's (1999) biography of Marx contains as convincing an account of Marx's uses of irony as can be read anywhere. Wheen's own excursions into satire prepared him to find in Marx what many sociologists appear to have missed.

6 In the anthropology of economic behaviour the same idea of a wrong turning crops up in the work of Davis (1992).

7 As does Engels' *The Condition of the Working Class in England* but it is still one of the most important books of the nineteenth century. Beynon's *Working for Ford* deserves a similar place in the twentieth-century canon.

8 This is not an obvious point to make about the decline of Marxism. The much more obvious one would be that this sort of sociology disappeared because of developments in theory and in the way the world works – postindustrialism, postmodernism, globalization, and so on. It was set up to understand and critique industrialism with grand narratives which are simply past their sell-by dates. My response is that sociology of this kind is not necessarily perishable and that if we could revitalize it by creating new critiques (see below) we would be better able to respond to all these 'posts'.

9 'The labour process debate risks aiding the development of capitalism by offering insights into the problems confronted by employers in motivating workers to internalise organisational goals. Labour process analysis, in short, will be turned against itself and used to formulate more effective control strategies to exploit labour. The recent incorporation of labour process theory into HRM points all too starkly to the problems of political dilution that accompany its movement away from Marxism' (Spencer, 2000: 240).

10 This is the process referred to on p. 1 where I allude to control over the research agenda being renounced.

11 'Instead of economy being embedded in social relations, social relations are embedded in the economic system.' (Polanyi, 1944/1957: 57).

12 By analogy with brain function: for example, the drugs that stimulate the same receptors as serotonin. In an alternative formulation, Bauman (1993) shows how the appeal of scientific rationality lies in the 'close-focusing' which gives the false impression that this rationality can deliver on its promise of producing desirable outcomes.

13 As recommended by Parsons and Smelser (1956).

27

two

living to work?

Durkheim knew the society he lived in was not yet a society in which occupational specialization made people both moral and happy:

> A generation is not enough to cast aside the work of generations, to put a new man in the place of the old. In the present state of our societies, work is not only useful, it is necessary; everyone feels this, and this necessity has been felt for a long time. Nevertheless, those who find pleasure in regular and persistent work are still few and far between. For most men, it is still an insupportable servitude. The idleness of primitive times has not lost its old attractions for them. (Durkheim, 1893/1964: 241)

Some historians would observe that the attractions of the 'idleness of primitive times' were not really so distant to the generation of Durkheim and Weber. Within living memory a great many people had actively resisted the sort of demands that work made on them (Pollard, 1965; Thompson, 1974).

Is it now the case that sufficient generations have toiled and departed for Durkheim's example to be out of date?: are we now so accustomed to work that we no longer think of it 'as a punishment and a scourge' (1893/1964: 242)? Mainstream opinion suggests otherwise: we are so devoted to consumption and leisure that we are quite clearly only doing the work we need to do in order pay for our pleasures. If we need more and more money to spend in this way this is partly because we have so much more time in which we are not at work and are free to pursue those pleasures. We work fewer hours in every day than we used to and we spend a smaller proportion of our lifespan in work: an increasing number of young adults do not engage seriously in the labour market until their late twenties or early thirties and more and more people feel able to retire in their fifties. If work takes up only a quarter of your lifespan and, when you are working, you only work for a third of your waking hours, how could it possibly make sense to say that anyone in this sort of society is living to work? Moreover, for quite some time our culture has encouraged us to brand anyone who seems to be living to work as deviant and possibly mentally ill.

On the face of it, nothing could be more different to the cultural controls and incentives described by Weber in *The Protestant Ethic and the Spirit of Capitalism* (1904–5/1958). Weber discussed the way, at a point in the history of capitalism, people developed an attachment to work (and, even more strongly, to capital accumulation) which was best understood as a moral compulsion. This compulsion was succeeded in time by the economic rationality of 'the spirit of capitalism'. By Weber's own time the moral colouring to the compulsion was no longer necessary, or in evidence. Instead people were compelled to work only by the idea of accumulating possessions, or as Weber put it, their 'care for external goods'.

This chapter seeks to amend the view that the morality of living to work is only of historical interest and it begins by showing how economic sociology took a wrong turning after Weber. Economic sociology assumed that, as described by Weber, the conversion of ascetic Christianity into an ethic of working to accumulate was a settled question but, as I will briefly demonstrate, Weber did not know whether moral issues would be permanently banished from this part of our lives. In economic sociology, by way of contrast, the idea that there might ever be life in a fundamental moral critique of how much we work, or which of us should work, became unthinkable. It simply became routine to assume that work was a necessity which allowed us independence, autonomy and to live well (Przeworski, 1980). So far as moral battles were concerned, they should be fought against the obstacles (unemployment, disadvantage or discrimination) that prevented people from accessing this necessity which underpinned their well-being.

This entirely ignores – or, at least, relegates to the therapists' waiting rooms – the possible persistence of a moral compulsion to work so that people actually want to work rather than feeling compelled to do so in order to be able to buy things. Yet if we were able to explore the continuing relationship between morality and work into our own time, we would open up the possibilities for an authentic critique of current arrangements for work. If people only work to buy things, then the opportunities for critique are limited to unsophisticated exhortations to stop buying so much, wanting so much, to settle for a lower standard of living! Such exhortations are usually ignored, but if we can explore the possibility that people are working because they *want* to, then we can also expose the complex of ideas that give rise to this feeling and critique them – pitting morality against morality.

29

In recent years more attention has been given to the persistence of a moral compulsion to work (Beder, 2000) but Arlie Hochschild deserves recognition as one of those sociologists who first attended to this phenomenon.

In her studies of the work-family balance (1989, 1997) Hochschild showed how economic motivation apparently came into conflict with morality by changing the way in which parenting was accomplished. Moreover, Hochschild explained that economic rationality did not derive its power from its utility (in satisfying our 'care for external goods') but from a compulsion that seemed curiously *like* morality. This chapter includes an extended treatment of Hochschild's work followed by a discussion of the way in which her ideas were developed into what became a research programme for a revitalized sociology of economic behaviour in the area of the work-life balance. This research began to reopen questions about when in our lives we should work, and who amongst us should work.

THE IRON CAGE

Weber found that in the spirit of capitalism – as exemplified in the life and works of Benjamin Franklin – the element of morality in the compulsion to work and accumulate was now a means by which utilitarian ends could be achieved: '[n]ow, all Franklin's moral attitudes are coloured with utilitarianism. Honesty is useful, because it assures credit; so are punctuality, industry, frugality, and that is the reason they are virtues' (Weber, 1904–5/1958: 52).

But there was another sense in which Weber discerned that a moral element remained important to, perhaps even characteristic of, the spirit of capitalism. And in this respect it would be hard to say which element of the moral and the rational was means and which was ends:

> In fact, the *summum bonum* of this ethic, the earning of more and more money, combined with the strict avoidance of all spontaneous enjoyment of life, is above all completely devoid of any eudæmonistic, not to say hedonistic, admixture. It is thought of so purely as an end in itself, that from the point of view of the happiness of, or utility to, the single individual, it appears entirely transcendental and absolutely irrational. Man is dominated by the making of money, by acquisition as the ultimate purpose of his life. Economic acquisition is no longer subordinated to man as the means for the satisfaction of his material needs. This reversal of what we should call the natural relationship, so irrational from a naïve point of view, is evidently a leading principle of capitalism. (Weber, 1904–5/1958: 53)

If people were compelled to accumulate as a duty which, when discharged, brought its own reward, then moral compulsion survived at

30

the apex of the spirit of capitalism. This was, after all, why Weber called the spirit of capitalism an ethos – the spirit of capitalism was itself a new kind of morality.

Yet Europe in the 1900s was not given over to the blind and joy-less pursuit of money as an end in itself and many Europeans were fonder of hedonism than Benjamin Franklin had found them more than a hundred years earlier.[1] If European societies were, nevertheless, capitalist, it was not because they were (any longer) enslaved by the ethos Weber described in his historical study. In the final chapter of *The Protestant Ethic and the Spirit of Capitalism*, Weber reiterates how the renunciation of leisure and the pursuit of pleasure were com-mon to both the teachings of Benjamin Franklin and Puritan ethicists like Richard Baxter. But the space for hedonism, even if this involved spending money, was nowhere near so circumscribed in Weber's own time.[2] Capitalism had now acquired its own momentum and no longer required any kind of ethic to reproduce it:

> This order is now bound to the technical and economic conditions of machine production which to-day determine the lives of all the indi-viduals who are born into this mechanism, not only those directly con-cerned with economic acquisition, with irresistible force. Perhaps it will so determine them until the last ton of fossilized coal is burnt. In Baxter's view the care for external goods should only lie on the shoul-ders of the 'saint like a light cloak which can be thrown aside at any moment'. But fate decreed that the cloak should become an iron cage. (Weber, 1904–5/1958: 181)

In the modern world that Weber saw around him, economic behaviour no longer had anything to do with morality. This world was animated by technical[3] and economic rationalities whose logics would now unfold in an incontrovertible way. It was no longer the world in which monastic asceticism and the spirit of capitalism had shared an elective affinity – the world with which his book had been concerned until this point, five paragraphs from its conclusion, at which Weber began to tell his readers how they lived now. History had brought us to a place in which morality and economic rational-ity could co-exist in the way that cuttlefish and birthdays co-exist and morality would no longer have any effect on economic behaviour. Weber (ibid.: 176) cites Dowden to make his point – 'the isolated eco-nomic man who carries on missionary activities on the side' – that we are now so completely motivated by economic rationality that a bit of religious morality is all the same with us like a hobby cultivating dahlias, but for most of us there is no point in extra-curricular mis-sionary activity. We see no point in it because we have no ethics of any kind; we inhabit a void in which the only reality is the cage: 'material goods have gained an increasing and finally an inexorable power over the lives of men as at no previous period in history' (Weber, 1904–5/1958: 181). In these circumstances we no longer *feel the need to justify why we labour*. If we feel no need to justify, why indeed would we require morality?

The Protestant Ethic and the Spirit of Capitalism is a sort of preface or preamble to our modern culture which is acted out by '[s]pecialists without spirit, sensualists without heart; this nullity imagines that it has attained a level of civilization never before achieved' (ibid.: 182) but Weber does not know whether morality will always be so divorced – or, as he puts it:

> To-day the spirit of religious asceticism – whether finally, who knows? – has escaped from the cage ... No one knows who will live in this cage in the future or whether at the end of this tremendous development entirely new prophets will arise, or there will be a great rebirth of old ideas and ideals, or, if neither, mechanized petrification, embellished with a sort of convulsive self-importance. (ibid.: 181–2)

At this point – and not for the first time in his *œuvre*[4] – Weber refuses to go on: 'this brings us to the world of judgements of value and of faith, with which this purely historical discussion need not be burdened' (ibid.: 182). Economic sociology – starting with Parsons and Smelser (1956) – took its lead directly from Weber[5] and also refused to go down this path. In doing so, it barred sociology from playing a part in lifting the veil on the world of appearances and, ultimately, in helping to change that world.

Economic sociology could not help because it took the world of appearances utterly for granted: whether or not a moral compulsion to work existed was always an empirical question about the motivations in a particular example of economic behaviour. Whereas economics would assume that the motivation to work could be understood entirely in terms of economic rationality, economic sociology was much more likely to look for a moral element in economic behaviour but if this moral motivation was found, it always remained a means to an end. In this, economic sociologists seemed to share the moral attitudes of Benjamin Franklin which Weber had found, I think, a little disgusting: '[h]onesty is useful, because it assures credit; so are punctuality, industry, frugality, and that is the reason they are virtues'.

In almost all respects economic sociology considered economics a more mature, indeed a model, social science but it had one big lesson to teach economics. Whereas economics treated economic rationality as a postulate that made economic theory work, economic sociology considered economic rationality a 'primary empirical feature' of 'the economy as a social system' (Parsons and Smelser, 1956: 175). For

Parsons and Smelser, economic values had to be thought about in two ways, or rather at two different levels.[6] A society had a system of values which told it where to place its various functions. In a society like America the economic function was rated highly, perhaps at the top of that society's hierarchy values. At a lower level, that of the economy, there was a value system appropriate to that a sub-system of the society. This value system was economic rationality:

> Rationality refers to the mode of organization relative to the standard of effective attainment of a system's paramount goal. In the case of the economy this paramount goal is *production* in the technical economic sense. Economic rationality in the value-system sense is thus the valuation of the goals of production and appropriate controls over behaviour in the interest of such goals. (ibid.: 176, emphasis in the original)

Economic rationality was the value system for the economic function but in a society like America economic rationality and the economic values would also be ranked above other value systems and other values in the society as a whole. This remained, however, just an empirical feature of the American case: economic sociology did not assume that economic rationality had any other sort of primacy over other value systems.

Parsons and Smelser did assume that economic rationality was 'a value system appropriate to the economy as a differentiated sub-system of society'. This was why economic rationality was 'institutionalized in the economy and internalized in personalities in their roles as economic agents' (ibid.: 302). But what had actually been institutionalized and internalized? When they wrote about an 'empirical sense' of economic rationality, Parsons and Smelser sometimes seemed to be prepared to admit to the category of economic rationality any values that they happened to find in the economic system, but for the most part they stressed the values of production, achievement and success. Thus in societies where economic rationality was placed high in the hierarchy of values, there was an emphasis on work, and *success* at work, rather than on what the income earned through work could buy (ibid.: 178). Moreover, it was knowing that you had contributed to the organization that you worked for in terms of the (achievement) values of economic rationality that made you feel you had met moral standards. In Parsons and Smelser's interesting formulation, it was the firm that gave the employee and their household moral approval (ibid.: 118).

Parsons and Smelser were able to see economic rationality as a value system but within that value system they saw economic values (production, achievement, success) as ends whereas morality was only a means to an end: individuals would pursue production and success

33

because they would get moral approval for their achievement. This was, after all, appropriate since production values should come first in the economy and morality could only ever be instrumental in achieving them. Morality could never be the equal of the goals of economic rationality within the 'economic sub-system'.

Thus economic sociology was not only condemned to live inside the iron cage but to find the bars of the cage invisible. Economic sociology could never again adopt the viewpoint of Weber when he drew our attention to the sheer absurdity of our total submission to making money. It would never observe how unnatural and irrational our attitudes to work might look from another perspective because it grew up inside the iron cage, with a conviction that ethical thought was inappropriate to its subject matter.[7] It was from inside the iron cage that the research agenda of economic sociology was plotted. For much of this time the moral factors Parsons and Smelser had noted received little if any attention (Portes, 1995a) but even when they did appear in works of economic sociology, they were always considered at the level of means and not ends.

So far as the study of work motivation is concerned, by far the best example of the effects of the wrong turning taken by Parsons and Smelser and others on the research agenda of economic sociology can be found in the way economic sociology set its questions about women and work. Arguably the biggest change that had occurred in economic behaviour for a century (Hochschild calls it 'the major social revolution of our time', 1989: 206) was happening at the very same time as economic sociology was finding its feet in the 1960s: the proportion of women in paid employment was increasing at a staggering rate which was totally unprecedented in peace-time. For the most part, functionalist economic sociology did not ask why this was happening, indeed, it did not appear to know that it was happening. No research projects were undertaken in any of the countries where this upheaval was taking place in order to find out what seismic changes in society and economy were causing it. Indeed, for the most part, sociology ignored the massive increase in female employment altogether. When sociology finally did turn its attention to the phenomenon, the lead was taken by feminist economic sociology whose practitioners showed themselves just as much prisoners of the iron cage as their functionalist predecessors.

According to feminist economic sociology the reason why women had not worked in such numbers (in peace-time) before was because it had not been realized how wrong it was to have women in a dependent and isolated position, subject to patriarchal domination, disadvantage and discrimination (Beechey, 1987; Hartmann, 1979; Siltanen, 1994; Walby, 1986, 1988, 1990). Women had come to realize the extent of their subordination and had begun to resist it, wresting from men the same right to engage in paid work that they enjoyed. Of course, elements of patriarchy remained and this was why there was still job segregation, a glass ceiling, and a gender gap in incomes and other work-related benefits; and why women who were success-ful in their chosen occupations had to work so much harder than men in the same occupations. Even where many barriers to achievement, for example in the education system, had been removed, discrimina-tion still remained a problem as did the unfair share of domestic responsibilities borne by married women.

If feminist economic sociology could not conclusively demonstrate that women had always wished to work in paid employment in the same way as men, this was held to be a further consequence of patri-archal domination. If women were not put off by the hostility they were certain to encounter if they tried to break out of the stereotypi-cal (male) perceptions of their role, they were handicapped by the demands placed on them as care-givers. If women were tasked with all the domestic responsibilities that men shirked, was it any wonder that their 'choices' directed them towards jobs with shorter hours, less training and career prospects, and lower pay? If it were not for these unjust circumstances, it was claimed, women would have wanted to work in the same way as men.

Feminist economic sociology would not deny that there was a change in the way women defined what it was to succeed (as Parsons and Smelser would have put it) as a woman. While women were largely confined to the home, success was defined in terms of domes-tic activity. Once they confronted patriarchy, women freed themselves to embrace other values, including the morality of contributing to production, doing worthwhile work and being self-sufficient. But this change was simply instrumental in the wider sweep of things. It described the changing psychology that was needed if women were to apply for all the new jobs being created for them in the 1960s but (changing) morality remained a means to an end, one of the many changes required to bring about this huge shift in society and econ-omy. This was not so different to the theory of Parsons and Smelser. It was common to both approaches that the way people relate through their morality to economic rationality was a part of a process, no more.

There is some (rather banal) truth in this. After all, if it had not been for changes in labour demand – arising from the industrial and organizational changes that increased the percentage of jobs which could readily be assigned to women – there would have been no mas-sive increase in female employment in the 1960s. But the idea that changes in women's moral attitudes towards what they did with their

35

lives were somehow epiphenomenal was not banal at all. Consider the response provoked by Hakim's (1991, 1995, 1996) suggestion that many women, perhaps the majority, had a range of reasons for wanting not to engage in employment in the same way as men. In effect, Hakim claimed to be able to show that many women still did not have the same priorities as men. Although their values had changed, they were not the same as men's values and this difference was reflected in their different employment patterns.

Hakim's paper was strongly, and repeatedly, criticized (see, for example, Ginn et al., 1996). The gist of the criticism was that the values to which she drew attention simply reflected the situation these women were in – one in which all the important elements of a patriarchy which was only half-dismantled were still in force. If they said they did not care as much as men did about the level of pay or career prospects, and that they wanted part-time rather than full-time work, this all had to be understood in terms of the unequal way in which domestic responsibilities were shared between men and women and the scarcity of affordable childcare and family-friendly employment policies. Moreover, women who made this choice (which was not really a choice) were condemned to take on the greater share of domestic responsibilities in perpetuity. If the jobs they had (or were likely to get) were less important and, crucially, less remunerative, than their partners' jobs, then they would always be in a weak position to argue for their domestic responsibilities to be shared more equally. Hakim had abstracted women's values from this important context.

We now see that the idea of women's values being epiphenomenal is actually crucial to economic sociology. This was why Hakim's statement was attacked in the way that it was. If was not that she was suggesting that these values be taken at face value rather than as evidence of some sort of false consciousness (which did not accord with feminist values). Her heresy was to privilege the morality of actors in her explanation of their economic behaviour. Feminists might have been annoyed by her paper but economic sociologists thought it simply wrong: in the economic field, explanation could never stop at morality.

To illustrate this approach we need only look at some recent examples of research which claims to show the way that both women's behaviour and the way they *think* about their behaviour are conditioned by the lack of suitable day-care facilities for their children. Where they uncover the sort of values and priorities Hakim was taken to task for using to explain economic behaviour, these studies follow the explanation as approved by economic sociology. The *cause* of the behaviour and the values is the shortage of day-care. If there were no shortage, women would not think like they do.

In a study of British social services staff, Ginn and Sandell (1997) showed how having children (and other caring responsibilities) increased the stress reported by working men and women. Having dependent children, the type of work and the hours of work had independent effects on stress levels. Opting for part-time or less demanding work was a way of reducing overall stress for parents and this was one reason why women reported less stress than men. But, when controls were introduced for type and hours of work, women with children reported more stress than men. The authors concluded that 'gender ideology' was still forcing women to assume more responsibility for their children and therefore increasing the strain on them so that they opted for less hours and less demanding (mommy-track) jobs to reduce stress. The answer to this problem was family-friendly policies and better day-care. The authors of this research also assumed (on the basis of no data at all) that family-friendly policies would be better for companies because performance might otherwise be adversely affected. We will return to this interesting piece of speculation below (pp. 43–44).[8]

Four years later Bond and Sales concluded their analysis of a large UK survey in the still obligatory terms of feminist economic sociology: women were 'disadvantaged in the labour market due to their domestic responsibilities and their disadvantaged position in employment leads to a continuation of these domestic responsibilities' (2001: 245). The unfairly distributed domestic work was an encumbrance which prevented women taking their proper part in the labour market, confirmed their economic dependence on men, and underpinned their 'unequal social citizenship' (ibid.: 246).[9] If men would not share domestic work, then one solution was to do without the partners and children who were the source of the additional responsibilities:

> Of course some women do still manage to achieve high status, well-paid positions in the labour market. However, since these women cannot necessarily expect equal sharing of household work, this group of women may shun marriage or permanent relationships. Women's 'dual burden' may also be linked to increasing divorce rates, delayed age of marriage, the increased proportion of babies born outside marriage and increased childlessness. (ibid.: 246)

The solution to all of these social problems was 'a radical change to the present organization of household work'. This could only be brought about by an improvement in women's labour-market position (which would strengthen their hand in dividing domestic responsibilities with their partners), better childcare provision and legislation which encouraged men to take up more of the burden. In this way economic sociology contrived to ignore a series of questions about economic behaviour which were deserving of attention. For example, it assumed that there could be nothing *intrinsically* problematic about combining work with family responsibilities. Any temporary problem in these arrangements was the result of the indolence of men or the state. More particularly, better childcare provision was seen as a perfect substitute for parenting. As in all its other guises, economic sociology could not bring itself to look at the real cost of participation in employment. It was simply that the excuse for not doing so in this case was a feminist one.

Arlie Hochschild (1989, 1997) approached the study of the work-life balance as a feminist but not as an economic sociologist. In her work, economic rationality conflicts with morality, most notably by changing the way parents relate to their children. The material achievements of capitalism are manifest in the lives of the people who populate her books. They have more commodities than ever before, more labour-saving devices, more freedom and autonomy, more interesting work and, for some, more equality. But Hochschild shows that men and women do not have time to enjoy the commodities and need the labour-saving devices simply to accomplish the minimum needed to keep their families functioning. Their freedom and autonomy are only exercised when they choose to escape their children and use their work to inject meaning into their lives. It seems people have been fooled about the nature of the bargain they strike between effort and affluence when they trust to economic progress. Not only do they have to spend their hard-earned money on making up for their absence at work but they lose many of the other things their parents had time for, including civic society and a public life (now it is only retired people who have time for these). Hochschild began to show us the fallacious (and indeed surreal) nature of the economic rationality on which the idea that 'there is no alternative' is always based. This is why the following extended discussion of Hochschild's work is necessary.

ARLIE HOCHSCHILD

Hochschild (1989) described a gender imbalance in the division of labour between men and women. Even though both partners were now in full-time, paid employment most of the 'second shift' required at home was worked by women. She examined in some detail the 'marital economy of gratitude' between these working parents but the term 'economy' was misleading.[10] She made no reference to Homans (1950, 1961) or Blau (1964) but it was clear that she had in mind the sort of exchanges between individuals (services for prestige; asymmetric exchanges involving differences in power) that these utilitarian thinkers had analysed. In her later work Hochschild made far less use of the language of economics (economy, exchange). Indeed, very little of the material she uncovered during her research concerned the calculation of costs and benefits. People described their behaviour and their relationships in non-economic and much more moral language, for example through the idea of sacrifice (also see Nichols and Beynon, 1977, and Chapter 6 below).

In the first place, Hochschild wished to disabuse us of the notion that women worked only out of economic necessity:

> Paid work has come to seem exciting, life at home dull. Although the most acceptable motive for a woman to work is still 'because I have to', most of the working mothers I talked to didn't work just for the money. In this way they have begun to participate in a value system once exclusively male and have developed motivations more like those of men. Many women volunteered to me that they would be 'bored' or would 'go bananas just staying at home all day', that they were not, on any permanent basis, the 'domestic type'. This feeling held true even among women in low-level clerical jobs. (1989: 242)

In her discussion of 'the limits of economic logic' she pointed out that the men who earned less than their wives did not share responsibility for the unpaid work, including parenting, accomplished in the home, whereas sizeable minorities of those who earned more, or the same as, their wives did share some of this work.[11] She analysed this finding as Blau would have done – behind unequal exchange must lie inequalities in power – but Hochschild also described the way men and women engaged in 'balancing' behaviours which were meant to address perceived injustice. In this case, the women who did all the domestic work could be said to be redressing the moral injury their husbands felt they suffered outside the home (Honneth, 1995; 1997). Indeed, Hochschild introduced the idea of a 'moral accounting system' to explain her data (1989: 223). This allowed her to explain how one man who earned more than his wife shared domestic responsibilities with her because he valued the contribution she made to society as an 'extraordinarily gifted' teacher in the public school system. He would not have shared domestic work in this way if she were just doing a job – selling real estate – for the sake of having a job (ibid.: 225). Although Hochschild did not point this out, her respondent was recognizing the moral value of a calling.

Hochschild described the way in which some couples tried to negotiate a division of labour they thought *fair* and *just* and which allowed them to be satisfied that they had discharged their duty. She also began to do her own 'moral accounting'. She showed how men who were sharing domestic work were receiving more thanks than was their due according to her notion of justice (ibid.: 157). Here and

39

elsewhere Hochschild joined her respondents in the task of working out the moral meaning of the changing division of labour.

The negotiation of the morality of relationships with employers and workmates was not a primary concern of the 1989 study but Hochschild did observe that parents

> did not feel very supported in their parenthood ... many parents in the business world felt obliged to hide concerns that related to a child ... Many men feared that their doing anything for family reasons ... would be taken as a sign that they lacked ambition or manliness ...
>
> For all the talk about the importance of children, the cultural climate has become subtly less hospitable to parents who put children first. This is not because parents love children less, but because a 'job culture' has expanded at the expense of a 'family culture'. (ibid.: 231)

The notion that it was shaming to admit that non-work commitments affected work was also shared by many women. Although some women still refused to take their work this 'seriously' (ibid.: 107), Hochschild discovered men and women were prepared to be judged by a work-based morality. Failure to live up to this morality damaged a person's character. The couples in Hochschild's study seemed far less concerned about the potential shaming effects of failing to live up the standards that once pertained to work outside the home.

Much of her findings concerned the way standards – for example, in regard to parenting – were lowered, as women tried to fit in the second shift. Although they did not apparently feel at moral risk, many turned over responsibility for their children to the baby-sitter or to day-care, with heavy hearts. The mothers who wore their parental responsibilities more lightly had tried, unsuccessfully, to get their husbands to share some of their values (ibid.: 119). At the extreme, their relationships had become demoralized with both partners abdicating their responsibilities. They competed with each other to show who cared the least about the housework and pursued their self-interest. Since there was no point in self-sacrifice, the goal was to be away from home more than your partner and leave work in the home to the hired help. Each thought of staying home or caring for the child as a defeat (ibid.: 210). The effects of this demoralization were the predictable battles between self-interested individuals which ended in inevitable marital breakdown.[12] The other inevitable outcome was that both partners spent more and more time at work, even wasting time during the day just so that there would be a legitimate reason for working late.

Hochschild's analysis of the changing moral meanings of the division of labour was remarkably perceptive. She showed how many of her female respondents were learning to look at women who did not work for money as unproductive, and as failing the *moral* test of the world of work. Indeed, there were wives who felt queasy if their husbands failed to show whole-hearted commitment to a job. Among men there were some who recognized the morality of work in the home but could not quite make it theirs. For Hochschild, 'the most important injury to women who work the double day is ... that they can not afford the luxury of unambivalent love for their husbands' (ibid.: 260). These women could not help but harbour resentment about the injustice of the division of domestic labour. Hochschild felt this was a necessary condition for a stable marriage, but couples who attached the same moral meanings to work and family were still unusual enough to feel themselves anomalous; one couple

> felt morally isolated from their conventional relatives in upstate New York, who continued to write letters reflecting puzzlement and disapproval, and from many of Michael's male colleagues, who ran through more wives but seemed to get more work done. Neither the old world of family nor their new world of work fit them easily. But they fit each other, and pulled against the social tide. (ibid.: 180)

But in most couples women were balancing two moralities (of work inside the home and work outside) while men were shaping their behaviour according to the morality of paid work and did not recognize their obligations at home. Because of this moral imbalance, the sacrifices made by each partner were not recognized as such or, at best, were under-valued, with the result that both partners felt 'taken advantage of' (ibid.: 206).

41

Hochschild perceived a real danger in that 'the work of raising a family becomes devalued because women have become equal to men on traditionally male terms' (ibid.: 211). As domestic work is devalued it is 'passed on to low-paid housekeepers, baby-sitters, and day-care workers. Like an ethnic culture in danger of being swallowed up by the culture of the dominant group, the contribution of the traditional home-maker has been devalued first by men and now by more women' (ibid.: 215).[13] Although Hochschild hoped that revalorization would occur when men were seen to be taking an equal share in domestic work she was perfectly well aware that the question of valorizing unpaid work was a *moral* issue (ibid.: 246).[14]

In her second book (Hochschild, 1997) on the work-family balance, Hochschild turned her attention to the employees of 'Amerco', a major American corporation with family-friendly working practices. Once again she was interested in exploring the way men and women were re-negotiating the moral meanings of work and family. In the new study it still fell more to women than to men to 'set limits on commercial "violations" of domestic life' but mothers were continually re-examining the 'moral meanings' attached to their behaviour

(1997: 233). In other respects men and women were converging and the epithet 'family man' was beginning to pick up the negative connotations of 'mommy-track' (ibid.: 132). Moreover, it was now even clearer that women were adopting the working patterns of men: not only were they spending more time at work but more of them were working full-time and their work schedules were less flexible than ever. Fathers were doing little to fill the breach, with some studies reporting that fathers were working as many hours as childless men. Hochschild wanted to know why men and women were working such long hours even when they had an alternative in the form of family-friendly policies that their employer provided but they did not use. In her case study, flexitime – *rearranging* hours – was popular but nobody wanted to cut back on their hours.[15]

Working parents were complaining of never having enough time, especially with their children, but not only were parents with young children refusing to take advantage of the family-friendly policies, they were actually working longer hours than childless employees. Hochschild thought this fairly typical of top American manufacturing firms and of American working parents.[16] As in her earlier research, there were limits to how much of this economic behaviour could be explained by reference to money. Many of the salaried employees who were working long hours received no extra income for working overtime (ibid.: 26). Among 'Amerco' employees, very few men at any level were interested in part-time work or job-sharing, but among women their level of interest was *inversely* related to their pay.[17]

Middle managers might not have been reinforcing the family-friendly message devised by their superiors but employees were not using these policies even when their managers were known to be sympathetic. Hochschild thought they did not reduce their hours because work was too attractive. This attraction contained a moral component:

> The more women and men do what they do in exchange for money and the more their work in the public realm is valued or honored, the more, almost by definition, private life is devalued and its boundaries shrink. For women as well as men, work in the marketplace is less often a simple economic fact than a complex cultural value. (ibid.: 198)
>
> For a substantial number of time-bound working parents, the stripped-down home and the community-denuded neighbourhood are simply losing out to the pull of the workplace ... One reason women have changed more than men is that the 'male' world of work seems more honorable and valuable than the 'female' world of home and children. (ibid.: 247)

Home was no longer a haven but 'another workplace' (ibid.: 37) in which harassed parents lurched from one demand which they dealt with in an unsatisfactory way to another. Home was particularly unattractive for women because they did not feel able to take time off (from domestic work) when they were there. Work was more social and less isolated, more fun and less depressing, more supportive, and rewarding, more ordered and frequently affording parents more opportunity for time they considered their own. They preferred to be at work rather than at home and this was especially true of women: '[w]hen the kids are driving me nuts, I come into the office. In all honesty, I just come in to drink coffee. Work can be a real escape' (ibid.: 223). Work was therefore increasingly seen as a haven as well as the source of personal worth and reward by women.

'Amerco' employed many parents who competed with each other in reducing the amount of time they spent at home: 'time spent at home came to signal weakness, not only to outsiders but within the marriage itself. And the family lost out' (ibid.: 79), 'Denise wanted absolutely nothing to do with flexible or shorter hours. With a gender war on, shorter hours meant surrender' (ibid.: 107). As in her earlier study Hochschild insisted family life was 'succumbing to a cult of efficiency previously associated with the workplace' (ibid.: 46) and observed that '[t]he emotional dirty work of adjusting children to the Taylorized home and making up to them for its stresses and strains is the most painful part of a growing third shift at home' (ibid.: 51).[18] Some of Hochschild's older respondents told her how glad they were that their children were now independent and they no longer felt so conflicted and dissatisfied about the way they responded to the demands made of them. She also suggested some younger parents might be wishing their children would grow up more quickly for the same reason.

Hochschild thought parents were spending non-work time more efficiently than their work time and that better organization at work could release parents to do a better job of parenting and relax a bit more about doing it.[19] If a very broad view were taken, this might even seem logical according to economic rationality, so why was nothing done to use work time more efficiently? Part of the reason was that people preferred to be at work rather than at home but this preference was bolstered by a morality (propagated by management) that obliged people to be at work even if they are not producing anything: 'time on the job was the basis of a moral accounting' (ibid.: 141).

Possibly because the company she studied ended up virtually abandoning its family-friendly policies as part of a cost-cutting operation, Hochschild did not finally decide whether the business case for them

43

was convincing. She described this case in terms of the need to compete for the best women recruits, and effects on absenteeism, time keeping and productivity. While she did not acknowledge it, every part of this case was put in doubt by her own study. If so few women actually intended to use family-friendly arrangements, then family-friendly policies would not help a firm to compete in the labour market except, perhaps, by signalling they were a 'good' employer which might also have other policies a potential recruit might want actually want to make use of. There was no evidence in Hochschild's case study that working hours which were not family-friendly resulted in problems with absenteeism and time-keeping. The observation that work hours were stretched out to keep people at work for reasons which had nothing to do with efficiency undermined the idea that corporations could see advantages to family-friendly policies in terms of productivity, time keeping, and so on.

Hochschild was convinced that the long hours parents devoted to their jobs were not as productive as they might be and that their employers actually condoned this. They valued productivity but they apparently wanted something else even more. According to a handbook for new employees: '[t]ime spent on the job is an indication of commitment. Work more hours', 'More hours indicate you are paying your dues' (ibid.: 19). This message was bolstered by the widespread belief among 'Amerco' employees that people who did not put in long hours did not get promoted. Productivity advantages could not be part of a business case for family-friendly policies if business valued the presence of employees over their efficiency.[20]

Although Hochschild did not always explain it in this way, the commitment that was being demanded of employees had strong moral undertones. As in her earlier research, Hochschild found people who knew they were meant to think it was *shameful* if they contemplated asking to work shorter hours (ibid.: 96) and they knew that having to pick up their children was not 'a good excuse' for leaving work *on time* (ibid.: 120). Even the few employees who did take advantage of the family-friendly policies adjusted their behaviour to take the moral commitment to long hours into account: 'the only way to keep a part-time schedule without violating the unspoken rules of the workplace was, in effect, to work full time' (ibid.: 99).

Many of the workers in Hochschild's study experienced a widening chasm between their own behaviour and what they thought they believed and the result was that 'many parents divided themselves into a real and a potential self, into the person each of them was and the person each of them would be "if only I had time". Often the real self had little time for care at home while the potential one was boundlessly available' (ibid.: 221).

This was one of three strategies that families adopted. Another involved outsourcing the work needed to keep the family going and detaching 'their own identities from acts they might previously have defined as part of being "a good parent" or " a good spouse"' (ibid.: 221). That parents were abandoning the idea that there was a morality – signalled by the adjective 'good' inviting judgement (see also ibid.: 233) – was positive proof of demoralization. The third strategy suggested even deeper demoralization:

> Some developed ideas that minimized how much care a child, a partner or they themselves 'really needed'. In essence, they denied the needs of family members, as they themselves became emotional ascetics. They made do with less time, less attention, less fun, less relaxation, less understanding, and less support at home than they one imagined possible. They emotionally downsized life. (ibid.: 220–1)

In the outsourcing version moral obligations were discharged by paying substitute carers but here human nature was being reinterpreted.

Whereas Hochschild's respondents thought it might be shameful to fail to show the necessary moral commitment to work, they were much less likely to admit that it might be shameful to fail to discharge their obligations to their families. The only point at which this arose the shame was entirely implicit. Hochschild reported that many women who left their young children home alone after school could not even admit they did this. Men, and women who were not senior managers, were much more open about leaving their children home alone. Perhaps these women suspected that this might be the extreme case in which their actions, and particularly the rewards they derived from work as highly successful women, might become morally questionable.[21]

That such questions can even be raised shows how far we have moved away from the certainties of a narrowly focused economic sociology in the direction of a critique of economic rationality which exposes the logic which would justify the consequences of economic behaviour as surreal and absurd. In *The Time Bind* and *The Second Shift* it was clear Hochschild was using her empirical research to mount a critique of economic rationality and to expose its calculus in just the way Marx did. How did sociologists respond to the opportunities for critique opened up by Hochschild?

OTHER RESEARCH ON THE WORK-FAMILY BALANCE

Feminist concerns have featured prominently in research on the work-family balance but there is nevertheless evidence of some dissatisfaction with the approach promoted by economic sociology.

From a study of the working and parenting arrangements of lesbian partners Dunne (1998) concluded there was a much more even balance of responsibilities in the two spheres between partners and a much healthier attitude towards the demands of work than in heterosexual relationships. This suggested that the problem lay in male attitudes and expectations and Dunne concluded that men who experienced parenting as mothers did 'would be as reluctant to prioritize time at work at the expense of time with children' (ibid.: 292).

Crompton and Harris (1998) studied women doctors and bankers in four countries and showed how the occupation which they entered affected the balance between work and family. Doctors scaled down expectations of themselves[22] as both professionals and parents but women bankers did not assume domestic work and childcare responsibilities to anything like the same degree. Some of them were demanding radical changes in their division of labour between themselves and their partners. In a later paper on British and Norwegian bank managers, Crompton found men and women were finding family life more and more difficult to sustain as organizational restructuring and recent innovations in managerial practice, such as Total Quality Management, increased the pressure their employers placed on them. Crompton and her co-researcher concluded that it would be necessary to challenge economic rationality if a case was to be made for readjusting the work-family balance (Crompton and Birkelund, 2000).

The notion of a business case for family-friendly policies was the subject of research by McKee, Mauthner and Maclean (2000) on the UK oil and gas industry. Possible business reasons for family-friendly policies, or at least family-friendly rhetoric, included a contribution to positive public relations and the avoidance of labour shortages and retention problems. Family-friendly policies might give an employer the edge in the labour market, especially the global labour market. In fact legislation and regulation – including some European Union directives – were rather more important influences than any discrete business case for family-friendly employment policies. There was no evidence for the 'new social contract' observed by Gonyea and Googins (1996), and the economic logic remained firmly set against family-friendly employment.

Much of this research adds only a little to what we have already learned from Hochschild, but some new and important findings have emerged in studies of family-friendly policies introduced by *governments*. Hochschild frequently praised the policies of European, and particularly Scandanavian, governments and research on these policies is certainly interesting. Brandth and Kvande (2001) reported a study of Norwegian legislation which was designed to achieve aims which made little sense in terms of economic rationality: '[t]he intention behind the new parental leave scheme in Norway has been to strengthen the father-child relationship and also to facilitate equal sharing of family work between men and women' (ibid.: 264). The key to the success of the Norwegian scheme was an element of compulsion. Whereas the voluntary schemes of employers and governments always failed (Epstein et al., 1999; Lewis 1997), when governments *obliged* fathers to take parental leave the scheme worked. Unless the state weighed in on the fathers' side with this element of compulsion, they would never demand leave of their employers even though the opinion polls said fathers wanted parental leave.

Brandth and Kvande explained that corporations and families made demands on people's voluntary commitments and that legislation offered some relief to men and women squeezed between the two 'greedy institutions' of work and the family. By referring (after Coser, 1974) to work as a 'greedy institution', the researchers recognized that work had a moral pull and that the family was not an effective counterweight to this compulsion. The Norwegian scheme worked because 'the welfare state has taken over from the mothers much of the onus for convincing the fathers. If fathers do not wish to use the paternity quota, they will have to negotiate with the state' (Brandth and Kvande, 2001: 260). The state acted as a 'normative third party' in parents' negotiations with employers (ibid.: 263). In the absence of traditional morality, 'both men and women need the legitimisation that state legislation collectively gives in order to be able to reduce their working hours' (ibid.: 264).

Brandth and Kvande were able to show that a government could alter one aspect of the work-family balance if two conditions were satisfied. First, government had to be prepared to set policy aims without reference to economic rationality. Second, government had to recognize the moral pull of work on fathers who, despite their desire to be more involved with their children, did not take advantage of voluntary schemes, and set an element of compulsion against it as an effective counterweight. Research conducted elsewhere in Europe shows that government policies which fail to satisfy both of these conditions are ineffective.

On the basis of a comparative study of Britain and France, Windebank (2001) showed how government policy had failed to change the domestic division of labour between men and women. The French state had stronger family-friendly legislation and better public provision for childcare than Britain which in this respect is closer to the American model criticized by Hochschild. Yet in France much of the traditional division of labour remained whereas, even though women worked less hours than in France, British men had begun to take on a little more domestic and parenting work.[23] In France men did not share domestic responsibilities even when they had free time but in Britain working couples organized their lives so that they were not both at work at the same time and they could take turns looking after their children. Windebank tried (unsuccessfully) to explain this difference in terms of economic rationality[24] but the contrast between Britain and France simply shows how government policy which fails to address the moral pull of work cannot change economic behaviour.[25] French government policy was effective when it worked *with* the grain of the moral compulsion to work – better childcare provision and increased female participation went hand-in-hand – but the enduring achievement of this policy was to make sure French women worked the same two shifts (at work and at home) that their American sisters worked.

In spite of the evidence produce by Windebank and others, we have already seen (pp. 36–38) that some British sociologists continued to argue for the extension of family-friendly government policy and better childcare (and, in particular, for the extension of French policies to the UK) as solutions to injustice in the domestic division of labour. Without the benefit of a critique of economic rationality, this kind of sociology runs the risk of exacerbating the problems it pretends to solve. No matter whether it is feminist in inspiration, economic sociology which sees the world from inside the iron cage is incapable of changing that world.

We need a critique to understand why family-friendly policies (and even better day-care) do not work (and, actually, employers have nothing to fear from them). If a revitalized sociology of economic behaviour is really going to contribute to social reform, it will need to develop the critique of economic rationality begun by Hochschild and others. Some suggestions as to how this might be done are made in Fevre (2000b: 220–3) as part of a discussion of the ways in which the problems created by demoralization might be overcome. The final section of this chapter develops these suggestions in the direction of a critique of the economic rationality which underpins the work-family balance.

CRITIQUE AND REFORM

A proper critique of economic behaviour would have problematized the conversion of women to economic rationality rather than cheerleading it. From the point of view of a classical sociology of economic behaviour, one of the most interesting things about the second half of the twentieth century was the relationship between the changing morality of women's work and the massive increase in female participation in paid employment. Widespread economic and technological change after the Second World War meant service sector and light manufacturing jobs replaced jobs in smokestack industries. What was needed was a cultural shift – a second incarnation of the work ethic – which would allow women to enter the labour force in large numbers in order to take up these jobs which were thought more suitable to them. Hochschild drew the parallel between the recruitment of women to the labour force in the late twentieth century and other changes in the composition of labour force: '[w]omen want paying jobs, part-time jobs, interesting jobs – but they want jobs, I believe, for roughly the same complex set of reasons peasants in modernizing economies move to the cities' (1989: 243). Weber would surely have written about the way the role of ascetic Protestantism was subsequently passed to feminism?[26]

It may have been a feminist morality that made access to paid work central to self-expression and identity but this was not what we read in the economic sociology literature. Instead the conversion of women to employment was portrayed as self-evidently rational. This was the latest achievement of the engine of progress which the Enlightenment had set rolling and which only fools and mischief-makers would try to arrest. The job of economic sociology was to give a quick cheer for this latest success and move on to the job of getting rid of the discrimination that remained. Feminist economic sociology was not interested in explaining how the moral shift – which made it possible for women to satisfy the demand employers had for their labour – occurred. It therefore had no need to reflect on its own relationship to this shift. Arguably, feminism played a major part in the process by which women's behaviour became subject to economic rationality in the same way as men's behaviour (Fevre, 2000b). In fact the well-worn critiques of patriarchal capitalism suggest subtle parallels and contrasts with the moral entrepreneurship of the nineteenth century which included the idea of the family-wage for a male bread-winner. In effect, the nineteenth-century moral entrepreneurs were using moral arguments to get people *out* of work whereas the twentieth-century feminists used moral ones to get people *into* work!

The hegemony of economic rationality is only the most obvious expression of a more general cultural shift in which people have allowed their behaviour to be ruled more and more by 'common sense' (ibid.). This term is not used in the way it might be used in ordinary discourse where we are vague about the content of the term. In everyday speech common sense can encompass diffused religious beliefs and elements of scientific knowledge. Such a usage is not at all helpful to us here and, while retaining the useful emphasis on knowledge that is held in common, we must redefine common sense for our own purposes. We make progress to a redefinition if we say common sense means that we act towards others only on the basis of knowledge and never on the basis of belief, but we must then make sure we can distinguish common sense from science.

In the remainder of this book I use 'common sense' to refer to a way of making sense of the world which relies upon human experience, and in particular on the evidence of our senses. These are the characteristics that distinguish common sense from science. Science requires evidence derived from other sources and finds no reason to put human experience on a pedestal. By contrast, the form of knowledge that matters most to common sense is knowledge about human nature and the way in which interaction between people and with the environment can be shaped in accordance with that nature. Common sense claims to know the authentic human behaviour for any situation. This knowledge is derived from, and confirmed by, our senses and the spread of common sense brings with it the affirmation of sensations as the foundations of much human action.

Common sense is not reducible to economic rationality but economic rationality with its emphasis on self-interest and utilitarian calculation in pursuit of pleasure and the avoidance of pain often serves as its paradigm example (Gorz, 1989). Along with all other forms of common sense, economic rationality cannot take seriously the suggestion that human behaviour should be guided by, should have as its goals, prizes which can only be believed in. Codes which would have human behaviour guided in this way are dismissed as sentimental and indeed this way of thinking about the world can be described as 'sentiment' (Durkheim, 1893/1964, 1897/1952). Sentiment does not require that we be guided by our emotions (which can be aroused in the course of common-sense calculation and behaviour) but rather that we allow things that cannot be demonstrated and only believed in to become the ends of our actions as well as the means. This might easily be a description of religious behaviour so we have to insist that in sentiment the beliefs that guide our actions are not beliefs about the cosmos or a deity but beliefs about human beings, for example the belief in human goodness, in love, and variety of other ways of having faith in other people. What both religion and sentiment have in common is that they produce moralities. Common sense does not: it (ultimately) produces economics (Fevre, 2000b).[27]

Before the accession of large numbers of women into the labour market from the 1960s onwards, it was still the case that these two ways of making sense of the world were commonly accepted to be unevenly used by men and women. In Western society it was usually assumed that men were more likely to have recourse to common sense to guide their behaviour whereas women were more likely to

50

use sentiment. Neither of these assumptions were fundamentally undermined when women were temporarily drafted into the labour force during the two world wars in the twentieth century. Even if women were shown to be perfectly capable of undertaking 'men's work', the special wartime circumstances excluded any suggestion that they might be beginning to think like men. When women returned to the home, the gendered division of thinking between common sense and sentiment was restored and the gendered division of labour which it supported was reinstated.

In some senses this division was felicitous: women knew that what was important to them – what their duty was and where their identity and sense of self worth was derived – was in the care they gave to their families. While the exercise of this care required common sense, it also involved daily acts of faith and sacrifices which could not be inspired by utilitarian calculation. If mothers waited until they were rewarded for the care they gave, they would wait in vain. If it was nothing else, mothering was moral behaviour. Most women took up the role of mother when they returned to the home (for example, after the Second World War) but their re-entry into paid work from the 1960s coincided with the growth of doubts about the value of this role.

The growth of doubts about the value of mothering was part of a much larger trend – demoralization – which affected both men and women. In brief, sentiment was down-graded as a way of thinking which might guide human behaviour in a variety of different spheres. This was the latest, and perhaps final, ripple of the Enlightenment, reaching down into the most personal and intimate corners of human behaviour. Of course knowledge-based reason took other, more sophisticated forms like economic sociology but it was in the guise of common sense that it came to dominate human behaviour. In other words the driving force was much more fundamental than those mere labour-market changes which increased the proportion of jobs thought suitable for women or even the growth of feminism. Sentiment was replaced by common sense as part of the process by which Westerners applied this kind of reason to more and more of their behaviour. As the churches emptied, so common sense entered into the way people thought about family life. Mothering could no longer support all of women's aspirations and so they turned to the labour market in pursuit of their new common-sense priorities.

However gentle the re-entry of women into the labour market might have been (full-time before children, stopping paid work while they were young and then only working part-time and in undemanding jobs thereafter), it was necessary for women to have begun to jettison sentiment and replace it by common sense for the massive social

51

revolution to be possible. It was this conversion to a more utilitarian view, and not simply the increased demands of the labour market on women's time, that was to cause such problems in the division of labour between men and women. There was nothing about the cultural process in which common sense displaced sentiment which suggested that men could be converted to guide some of their behaviour according to sentiment; quite the reverse. Although a few men who had never accepted that sentiment was only for women might try to compensate where they saw sentiment leaching out of parenting, most were accepting that more and more of their behaviour should be guided by common sense (Fevre, 2000b).

The things that mothers had done were therefore not, on the whole, done by fathers, yet mothers had begun to think about mothering in much the same way as fathers had done. They were devaluing it and therefore devoted less and less time to it and cared less and less about how well it was done. All of this is pretty straightforward: we can see how men and women who are both pursuing common-sense goals (independence, possessions, time to themselves, fun, autonomy) will compete with each other to get out of the house. This will be particularly likely when men and women no longer believe in the value of the self-sacrifices they will have to make if they stay at home (and know that even asking for thanks for these sacrifices will earn them derision for their self-imposed martyrdom). As Hochschild pointed out (1997: 229 – see p. 45), many people deny that the needs that mothers satisfied ever existed. As part of the dominance of common-sense assumptions about human nature, the importance of the very existence of sentiments is denied.

The pursuit of common-sense goals might well lead people to spend less time with their families but surely it does not lead them to spend more and more time at work? Economic rationality would not, for example, lead people to spend so long at work that they had no time left to enjoy the possessions they had laboured to possess. We know that this sad and ironic outcome is a consequence of the operation of the moral pull of work but where in this account of the hegemony of common sense is there any place left for morality *of any kind* to take effect on people's behaviour?

From the point of view of morality that was once derived from sentiment, none of the three family strategies described by Hochschild (see pp. 44–45) are moral. Certainly her respondents *say* they have moral values, but they do not believe in these values enough to let them affect their behaviour: 'I am not putting my time where my values are' (Hochschild, 1997: 219). This is still having the morality but not believing strongly in it enough to allow it to affect your behaviour.[28] This is after all, why the whole cultural revolution can be understood as part of a process of demoralization: as women, in particular, gave up on sentiment they gave up on a way of thinking that could author a genuine morality. It follows, therefore, that the pull of work might ape morality but is not genuine at all and it is in making this argument that the next big step forward in the sociology of economic behaviour can be taken.

How have we got to the situation in which '[t]he worst thing I could possibly do is to acknowledge that my children have an impact on my life' (Hochschild, 1989: 96)? How on earth have we placed ourselves in the situation where it seems immoral to discharge our duty to our children? If parents feel this, their childfree co-workers feel it even more and have no hesitation in condemning employers' 'special treatment' of working parents. What sort of morality is it that makes them feel they can write off parenting as a lifestyle choice that everyone is free to make and must then bear the consequences? Even more to the point, what sort of morality is it that is making us override our own common sense? Crucially, the employees studied by Hochschild demonstrated a commitment to their employer that was well beyond anything merited by sober consideration of expectations of return. In other words, their behaviour was not guided by common sense, and it was particularly illogical according to economic rationality (for example, many 'Amerco' employees worked overtime without pay).

Work can only become a moral compulsion by a kind of sleight of hand. In effect, a trick is being performed which fools us into thinking we are applying the sense making that is employed in sentiment rather than common sense.[29] When this trick is accomplished, economic values come to occupy a superior position as meta-values standing above all other considerations. They do not earn this preeminence from the power of rationality to determine outcomes in a satisfactory way because the guidelines for behaviour which are grounded in economic rationality lack the necessary element of compulsion or 'deontology' (Etzioni, 1988). We can choose to use economic rationality but economic *morality* compels rather than facilitates choice, and it does so in an illegitimate way which makes us miserable and confused (Anthony, 1977; Lane, 2000).

As we know, a morality arises where belief is required (religion or sentiment) and not where we rely on knowledge (common sense and science). In the cases described by Hochschild and others, employers have persuaded us to understand our employment in the category of belief rather than knowledge (Anthony, 1977; Beder, 2000). The evidence for this lies in the level of commitment displayed by the individuals in these studies, a level and quality of commitment that normally only occur when people are making sense according to their beliefs.

53

Whereas the 'Amerco' workforce could no longer see the point in making sacrifices for their families, they were happy to do so for their bosses. They sacrificed their time, their marriages, and their relationships to their children and, in so doing, they sacrificed their own happiness to their work.[30] This kind of sacrifice only happens when we put the interests of others before our own well-being and it arises from a mistake that we make in the identification of the appropriate form of sense-making to use to guide our behaviour.

Of course we are systematically encouraged by employers (see Chapter 3) to make this mistake but it has to be voluntary: we have to be fully taken in so that we internalize a belief that we have to devote ourselves to our work. The essence of the process is that we must not be allowed to see things as they really are, even for a moment. We must always forget to make sense of our work in the terms of common sense:

> Because we fall prey to the compulsion of economic morality we fail to apply the useful cynicism of common sense: 'well, the boss would say that to me, it's in her interests to get me in work on a Saturday, but *I* don't have to see it *her* way'. Crucially, this failure to apply reason means that we do not fully calculate the costs (for example to our family and to our relationship with them) and benefits of our actions. Indeed, under the influence of economic morality there does not have to be a measurable, even demonstrable, benefit ... We take this on trust. (Fevre, 2000b: 214)

For employers the adherence of their workforce to an economic morality is part of a sensible economically-rational calculation, but for workers there is no sensible calculation at all. In Hochschild's studies the evidence that was needed to prove such calculation – proof that longer hours increased income or job security – was sparse but workers nevertheless put their *faith* in their employers. In Hochschild the payoff for all this effort was always in the future and never the present. This is highly suggestive: if economic morality never actually delivers the promised benefits, we are neither following self-interest nor calculating the consequences of our actions. Instead, we are following a rule: this is ethical behaviour for which the only motivation is the satisfaction we derive from following the rule.

The efforts that modern managers make to persuade their employees that work can be understood with human-belief logic are described in Chapter 3 but it will suffice to say that it is their aim to confuse us with a mixture of economic rationality and the spiritual (Casey, 1995). Hochschild was a little confused by this when thinking about the business case for family-friendly working. It is certainly clear that very long hours may not be associated with high productivity but there are benefits for employers from having the moral

54

commitment that these long hours connote and these outweigh any simplistic calculations of efficiency. It is usually thought far better to have employees who are willing to make sacrifices for you without any evidence of personal gain than have employees who are keen to be efficient at work so they can get home as quickly as possible and live their lives to the full. In the next chapter we will find out why employers have increasingly been pushed in this direction.

CONCLUSION

When Hochschild (1989) asserted that the revalorization of domestic work depended on men undertaking this work she had cause and effect the wrong way round. It is economic morality that keeps men and women at work and cultural change is needed to revalorize unpaid labour of all kinds (and not just childcare) before men will do it. We know that it has not ceased to be possible to motivate people by their beliefs from the success that 'Amerco' and all the other corporations have in making people commit to them. Thus the sociology of economic behaviour shows that we need a new sensibility to replace the sentiment that common sense undermined and displaced. For example, in this new sensibility parents might make decisions about the balance between work and family according to the effect these decisions might have on the love between them and their children. We will know when they are doing this because people will resent the intrusion of work into family life much more than they do at present.

As the Norwegian example of paternity leave discussed above (pp. 46–47) showed, it is possible for governments to legislate in a way that will give support to this sort of renascent sensibility but such non-economic considerations have not featured in policy-making in English-speaking countries. Indeed, policy has been rather more in tune with the economic morality being engineered by employers. In the United States and Britain, for example, governments have seen getting more and more people into full-time paid employment as the solution to a range of social problems. Far from helping parents to redress the work-family balance, governments conspired with employers to reduce the amount of time parents spent with each other and with their children.

Getting men to share domestic work will not revalorize it but a change in government policy might. A 'social wage' would make space for a revalorization of the time parents spend with their children but such a notion is entirely at odds with economic rationality and economic morality (Bowring, 2000; Gorz, 1989). In fact policy is continuing to move in the other direction, towards specifying that people must be in work before they qualify for full citizenship (Beder, 2000). For example, in the UK the New Labour Government (heavily influenced by US precedent) underpinned their new policy agenda with a new work ethic (Barry, 1998) and 'increasing participation in the labour market is at the heart of the current government's social policy' (Holden, 1999: 529). This brings to mind the way in which the Poor Law reforms of nineteenth-century Britain entailed the innocent victim of unemployment paying the price for unfettering the market (Polanyi, 1944/1957: 224–5).

Bowring (2000) explained the deeply conservative implications of the idea that social inclusion involves paid work and, indeed, of 'relative deprivation' measured by the values of consumerism. Sayer (2000b) pointed out that the individualistic route to social inclusion overlooked caring responsibilities and had a male bias. Sayer thought that the idea of self-sufficiency through the market was a zero-sum game which depended on unequal access to paid work and unequal sharing of caring responsibilities. As in the nineteenth century, the innocent 'failures' who could not achieve self-sufficiency were further damaged by the assumption that they must be of bad character.

The shared economic rationality of governments and economic sociologists in English-speaking countries meant they were in perfect agreement. Individuals were allowed to choose not to work at all, but economic rationality dictated that this only made sense to society as a long-term arrangement if these individuals were legitimately dependent or had the means of self-support. We can see how much economic sociology was in tune with this attitude from the way it dealt with the work-family balance issue. Again and again it concluded that it was up to governments to spend taxes on providing day-care and pass legislation which made corporations introduce creches and family-friendly hours. Yet these same economic sociologists would not countenance the idea that governments should arrange (with the help of redistributive taxation) that some parents should get a social wage for the years during which they had children under, say, ten years of age.

NOTES

1 Franklin was US ambassador in Paris until 1785.

2 I want to add a word of qualification here. When he writes about Merrie Old England and other pre-capitalist cultural forms Weber is apt to refer to the 'spontaneous' or 'impulsive' enjoyment of life. I cannot help thinking that he thinks that modern hedonism may be aimed at enjoyment but lacking in spontaneity. You might kick over the traces after work finished, but you would still finish your work.

3 See Stivers (1994) for more recent work on *techne* – the technical logic or way of understanding the world.

4 See Fevre et al. (1997) for another example of the frustrating way in which Weber puts down his pen at the most interesting point in his exegesis.

5 Tellingly, Parsons and Smelser dedicated *Economy and Society* to Weber and the economist Alfred Marshall.

6 For their own, very good reasons, Parsons and Smelser treat the personalities of individual actors as a third level but this further complication is superfluous here.

7 And an associated belief that this conviction showed that it was a serious and important science (like economics).

8 Polanyi had little time for this line of argument: '[t]o argue that social legislation, factory laws, unemployment insurance, and, above all, trade unions have not interfered with the mobility of labor and the flexibility of wages, as is sometimes done, is to imply that those institutions have entirely failed in their purpose' (Polanyi, 1944/1957: 177).

9 See pp. 39–40: Hochschild (1989) did not agree that it was because women were paid less that they worked the extra shift. This extra burden was not the consequence of discrimination in the labour market.

10 Hochschild (1997: 162) mentions a 'new emotional economy at home' but she is no longer nearly so keen to use concepts of exchange and economic rationality to explain people's relationships with one another.

11 The economic logic did not work in favour of women (it may have worked for men but we do not know whether the difference she observed was statistically significant).

12 Hochschild also observed that some married women were keeping up single women's orientations to work just in case they subsequently got divorced (1989: 141).

13 'Just as uninvolved fathers who praised their wives often said they wouldn't want to trade places with their wives, so wives often said they wouldn't want to trade places with their daycare worker' (1989: 233).

14 Women who chose not to observe the standards their mothers had attached to housework saw that old morality of housework as ridiculous in much the same way as they might have seen 'Victorian' sexual morality as ridiculous (1989: 248).

15 In the period immediately after Hochschild published her research Americans actually increased their hours of work. The International Labour Organisation working hours survey showed that between 1991 and 2001 the average number of hours worked per year had gone up from 1942 to 1978, an increase equivalent to one full working week This trend had not been followed in many other developed countries and Americans still worked harder than almost every other nation in the developed world. They worked 250 more hours per year than Britons and 500 hours more than Germans and the only workers who put in more hours were the Czechs and the South Koreans (ILO, 2001).

16 Very few of whom worked less than 40 hours a week (she quotes figures for parents with children under 12: only 4 per cent of men and 13 per cent of women worked less than 40 hours). Nor did working parents miss work much more than other employees, even if their children were home alone (1997: 27).

17 She also noted that national figures showed better-off women were no more likely to delay the return to work after having a baby than poorer women. Moreover, the culture of long hours was not related to fears about losing their jobs (1997: 28–9).

18 Hochschild also wonders whether the idea of 'quality time' is an innovation which is primarily designed to increase productivity (1997: 50).

19 Hochschild doubts whether a lot of the work that is done, for example the

work of senior managers, really needs to be done. She also understands that the only justification for this 'work' is as part of the reproduction of the ersatz morality of the workplace (see pp. 92–93).

20 Hochschild also noted the research on Xerox that was being directed by Bailyn. This work had shown that a Xerox project team kept missing their deadlines despite working very long hours. Their productivity was low because of all the interruptions which littered a normal working day and because they had so much time at work they had not learnt to be efficient at using it. Bailyn made the team introduce interruption-free quiet time in the middle of the day and cut down on the meetings and reports that were required. They met the deadlines without working all the extra hours. Perlow, a member of research team, reported on the subsequent failure of the quiet time innovations which might have temporarily increased the efficient use of time but did not persuade employees or managers of the case for shorter hours (Perlow, 1997). This experiment in the more efficient use of time was soon abandoned. The long-hours culture of Xerox was apparently sustained by more than the need to make up for interruptions.

21 Men in their position had no trouble admitting they left their children on their own and explained that it was all part of their plan to make their children self-sufficient (the lower paid employees preferred to get relatives and neighbours to help out) (1997: 224).

22 In an misplaced allusion to the rational choice literature, Crompton and Harris describe this as 'satisficing'.

23 Hochschild (1989) also noted that the division of labour was changing even where women were not in paid employment.

24 Her argument hinged on doubtful assumptions which were not supported by evidence: for example, she assumed that British men would rather look after their own children than pay for childcare because of the financial cost of doing so.

25 Windebank cites a source which suggested there were some signs that French women were beginning to opt for part-time work and perhaps their economic activity rates might be falling (this certainly happened for one group of mothers in the 1990s).

26 It his interesting to note that in his review of Marianne Weber, *Wife and Mother in Legal Development* (1904) Durkheim posited

> the anomic form of the family, an aberration in which men and women gain equality in 'public life' at the expense of an impoverished 'domestic life'... the dissolution of 'domestic life' because of divorce, egoism, the working status of both partners, and other factors ... dampens the progress of moral individualism, and lessens any real progress that has been made with regard to the subjugation of women. Rather than coldly equalize men and women vis-à-vis 'public life', Durkheim proposed that both men and women should be humanized vis-à-vis the home while keeping their respective individualisms in public as well as domestic life. (Mestrovic, 1991: 181)

27 The complex determination of behaviour which Etzioni (1988) tried to grasp with his 'I&We paradigm' is much better understood by common sense and sentiment. Etzioni was particularly misleading when he suggested people always tried to balance pleasure and moral commitment but this perhaps reflected his failure to recognize contemporary demoralization and his belief in the tenacity of morality. Common sense is a much better framework for discussing rationality than Etzioni offers (see, for example, 1988: 151–80 on *conflicting* rules of thumb

and so on; compare to Fevre, 2000b: 175–6). It also gives us a better explanation than Etzioni offers for the way in which those who are exposed to economic rationality (especially economists and economics students!) tend to be so inclined to free ride (for example).

28 'Everyone may know that they should spend more time with their kids, and that they will not look back over their lives and say they wish they had spent more time at work. They nevertheless feel irresistibly compelled to resist acting on this "knowledge" because it is no longer valid knowledge in a field of human behavior which has been staked out for common sense' (Fevre, 2000b: 209; see also Beder, 2000: 253).

29 Whereas for Weber the work ethic arose out of a confusion between economic rationality and religious morality. The way in which employers set about pulling off this new kind of trick is explored in Chapter 3 where the engineering of corporate culture is discussed.

30 Hochschild tells poignant tales of the way Amerco employees prepared for a happier life by buying things they never used. For example, they bought expensive camping equipment for trips with their families that they never took.

59

three
labour

Whereas Chapter 2 was concerned with the proportion of our lives which is spent in income-earning work, this chapter is about how hard we labour when we are at work or, to be both more general and precise, *how much of ourselves we put into our work*. You would not necessarily conclude this from reading economic sociology, but this issue is a profoundly moral one and the first task of this chapter is to illustrate this point with an example. It therefore begins by referring to one of the enduring preoccupations of the sociology of economic behaviour: the way people organize themselves into informal groups and then put limits on the amount of work they do. The most famous example of this preoccupation, the Hawthorne Studies, is a characteristic example of a wrong turning taken in the direction of economic sociology and away from classical critique when the researchers – chiefly Roethlisberger, Dickson and Mayo – only drew attention to the moral attitudes employees took to their work in order to manipulate them in pursuit of organizational goals.

In Chapter 1 it was noted that Mayo was a Durkheimian and this chapter will explore Mayo's view of anomie and demoralization. Mayo wanted social groups (led by managers and supervisors) between the firm and its employees in order to make the firm successful (Bendix, 1956). Among Mayo's many successors the question of morality was rarely explicit and, instead, all the talk was of the way managers must shape the 'culture' of their corporations. Yet the basic aim was the same: to make people feel compelled to produce more (or to a higher standard). Ordinary economic sociology has been pursuing a similar agenda for many years and, just as in the managerialism that it apes, its conclusions about the social organization that successful firms require are based on erroneous notions of the capabilities of social science.

For most of the latter half of the twentieth century the only alternatives to this economic sociology were critical studies of economic behaviour which remained inconclusive because morality was either endogenous to the theoretical framework in use, or more usually, entirely implicit to the argument. Sometimes this failure to deal properly with morality produced enthusiasm for theories (for example, about deskilling or insecure employment) which parted company with reliable empirical evidence. There may be a similar problem in critical studies which begin to incorporate some ideas of demoralization but conclude that this is largely a question of the way that, as the structure of work has changed, the morality which was once created in work has decayed.

As I have already pointed out in the previous chapter, the work of Arlie Hochschild exemplifies a clear break with economic sociology. Her work pointed in the direction of critique, and not simply criticism, because she was able to explore the conflict between economic rationality and morality directly. In her study of flight attendants (Hochschild, 1983), she explained that economic rationality would have us change the way we allowed our moral judgement to influence our behaviour (for example, our reactions to someone else's character, or the way in which we portray our feelings). Hochschild has inspired imitators and, at its best, this sociology convinces us that corporations wish to re-educate us in virtues – for example, limitless and effortless displays of human kindness including painstaking concern for the comfort of others and self-sacrifice – which they feel have been absent from their workplaces for far too long.

61

INFORMAL WORK GROUPS AND OUTPUT NORMS

The research project undertaken at the Hawthorne plant of the Western Electric Company between 1924 and 1932 is described in absorbing detail in Gillespie's marvellous history (Gillespie, 1991). The experiments established that workers regulated their output according to their idea of a fair day's work. While it was widely recognised, at the time, that workers would restrict output to prevent management raising the bogey - the level of output at which bonus payments began to be paid - the Hawthorne studies added a new element. They established that the idea of a fair day's work was not a result of individual decisions made by each worker but a collective goal which expressed common ideas and feelings. This solidarity had an overtly moral component and workers were consciously involved in self-sacrifice, for example restricting their earnings (even by failing to declare output they had actually achieved) to keep to the fair rate. This earned them the respect of other workers and underpinned their own sense of self-worth (Gillespie, 1991).

Gillespie explains that this behaviour also earned the

Hawthorne workers the respect of some of the researchers, especially Dickson, Moore and Warner. Dickson, for example, originally thought it was a rational way of providing some protection against management initiatives yet, when the full account of the experiments was written, his view had apparently changed. Roethlisberger and Dickson (1939) welcomed the social integration that flowed from the workers' sentiments and solidarity but denied they were capable of collective action. The effect of this denial was to declare the idea of a fair day's work useful in an instrumental way but not to be taken seriously as a goal.

The idea that workers might have been protecting themselves from management was now explained as a post-hoc rationalisation for behaviour which was based in emotions and the compulsive social impulse. Roethlisberger and Dickson suggested that workers were not capable of co-ordinated behaviour in pursuit of a logical goal (Gillespie, 1991). Moreover, there was no rational basis for any suspicion of management because the bogey would not have been raised if output had increased. In spite of what seemed to be common knowledge in American industry at the time, Roethlisberger and Dickson derived their certainty that management would not have raised the bogey from knowledge of how the company's piece rates reflected unit costs. They believed that output restriction which increased costs might actually lead to a lower piece rate whereas the workers would have simply earned more if they had worked harder (Roethlisberger and Dickson, 1939).

From this point onwards, the sentiments of workers became a means (to integration) not an end. Roethlisberger and Dickson concluded that management should pay more attention to the process by which social sentiments were shaped. The integration of the workers would lead them to identify with the company and its ends. In the simplest terms, since they could just as easily raise output as lower it, informal work groups, and the social relations employees had with each other, would then work to everyone's advantage, including the company's. Thus the Hawthorne experiments gave life to the idea of 'human relations' which became so influential in American management.

In other words, the key contribution of the Hawthorne experiments to Western management thought and practice depended on taking a wrong turning away from the idea that a fair day's work might be a moral goal. The influence of the human relations school on the subsequent development of management thinking, especially the enhanced role of personnel management, depended on decisively turning away from the idea of treating the idea of a fair day's work as an end as worthy of respect as any management goal. Instead it was now simply a means to ends which management defined (Gillespie, 1991). From the point of view advanced in this book, the Hawthorne researchers uncovered an economic morality and then attempted to transform it into a management tool.

The Hawthorne research did not discourage subsequent studies of informal social organization in the workplace from giving more credence to workers' economic rationality. In his study of 300 work groups in 30 manufacturing plants, Sayles (1958) extended the field of workers' behaviour to include a range of workplace conflicts and questioned whether this behaviour was really based on limited information, such as misunderstanding of the calculation of a bonus rate. He claimed that membership of the sort of groups originally observed in the Hawthorne plant occurred because collective action was a rational aim; and he explained variations in workers' rational action in terms of the 'structural conditions of work' and particularly technology.

In the language of rational choice theory, the occurrence of informal group membership and group norms in a variety of different workplaces derived from the need to solve a paradox of rationality (Olson, 1965). Members had to guard against free-riders who would take advantage (albeit temporarily) of the opportunity to bust the rate. That was the point of having an informal group in the first place: it could ensure that behaviour could be monitored and effective sanctions and rewards be put in place to discourage free-riding. As Hechter (1987) pointed out, it was much easier to beat this paradox of rationality in small groups with a high density of interaction where everybody could check up on everybody else without the need for special surveillance. Hechter also believed rewards were more effective than sanctions and the best rewards were not material ones but the intrinsic rewards like social approval that come with membership of such groups (Coleman, 1990, makes a similar point).

Assumptions about workers' pursuit of self-interest are explicit in the work of Marxists like Elster (1985) who developed a variant of rational choice theory, but less formal assumptions about the pervasive nature of economic rationality suffuse Marxist economic sociology (Shenhav, 1999). Writers in this tradition would agree with Sayles that this rationality underpinned workers' restrictions on output, and only take issue with the assumption that what was good for the company was good for the workers. It was their belief that capital never shared any benefits it acquired in this way and that the expenditure of extra workers' effort was only ever rewarded by speed-up and rate-lowering which ratcheted up the level of exploitation. If this was where you thought abandoning restrictions on output would lead, then it was clearly not rational to abandon such restrictions.

Because of its commitment to economic rationality, Marxist

63

economic sociology was open to its own version of the cosy view of an identity of interests between managers and workers. In state socialism (where exploitation has been simply legislated out of existence along with private property in the means of production), there could not be speed-up or rate-lowering and therefore restrictions on output were no longer sensible according to a higher economic rationality. This cosy view was, in turn, undermined by Haraszti (1977) who documented speed ups and rate cutting in factory production under state socialism.

Neither of these complacent views appear so attractive if we say that workers have moral reasons for controlling output in the way that they do. If we challenge the reductionist assumptions of economic rationality it becomes possible to construct a rather different world in which the Hawthorne workers (for example) were committed to behaving in ways that were neither selfish nor avaricious. Instead, they would believe that it was right that they should behave altruistically and that social solidarity was an end in itself and more important than material gain. The Hawthorne experiments exposed a strong and sophisticated system of beliefs about virtue and good character which had real effects on people's everyday behaviour. Shorn of economic rationality, we discover not atomized individualism but a system of collective values which had matured over time and told people not just how to be a Western Electric worker, or even how to be a worker, but how to be an American citizen, or perhaps even a human being. Yet the wisdom or legitimacy of seeking to mould or re-engineer this morality is far from obvious.

With the substitution of an economic morality for economic rationality the argument becomes much less clear-cut even where the (self) interests of capital and labour are assumed to be identical. Workers may make more money out of giving up group norms but they also lose something that cannot be weighed in the economic calculus (and what might be the unforeseen effects of its disappearance?). It is perfectly possible for economic sociology to admit that behaviour is determined by other considerations, including moral ones, and still be authentic economic sociology (Portes, 1995a), but economic sociology remains incapable of treating morality as anything more than a means to an end. The following section will illustrate this statement with the example of a fair day's work.

A FAIR DAY'S WORK

Further exploration of the significance of morality for wage-setting is reserved for Chapter 5, but here we need to understand exactly why economic sociology (whether of the Marxist brand or any other) cannot *assimilate* the idea of a fair day's work. Gorz made a similar point when he argued that the idea of 'enough' – as in 'enough money' – was alien to accountants (1989: 112). The problem is definitely not that economic sociology pretends that this idea of a reasonable day's work does not exist. It is quite clear that economic sociology can *accommodate* the idea, so what does it mean to say it cannot *assimilate* morality? Perhaps the easiest way to grasp this is to think of economic sociology treating morality exactly as Adam Smith (1976b) did, as a natural efflorescence which will definitely affect people's behaviour, and thus should figure in explanations, but has nothing whatsoever to do with theory building or choice of research topic.

Portes cites Burawoy (1983) as one of the authorities on a fair day's work. The problems that economic sociology has with this idea may become a little clearer if we recall the findings of Burawoy's classic ethnographic study. While undertaking participant observation in a workplace, Burawoy found himself asking why, in violation of all his preconceptions, he was voluntarily speeding up the pace of his own work (Burawoy, 1979). As a Marxist, Burawoy seems to have been more surprised than the Hawthorne researchers had been (fifty years earlier) when he discovered that workers produced more than the minima that would allow them to keep their jobs. He concluded that this was to be understood an act of self-exploitation made necessary by the need to survive the tedium of the capitalist labour process. The point is that Burawoy's avoidance of boredom could just as easily be accommodated in a utility function as the costs and benefits which were imagined to motivate the Hawthorne workers. Economic sociology can explain behaviour in terms of economic rationality, boredom avoidance or morality but it will continue to be economic sociology (Portes, 1995a), and this is a problem.

To try to understand why this is a problem we must recognize that economic sociology, of whatever hue, could not allow the Hawthorne workers' idea of a reasonable day's work to define its research programme. It is not the failure to accommodate morality as one of the causes of human behaviour, even economic behaviour, that is the problem here. The problem is that this is where the influence of that notion of a fair day's work ends. No economic sociologist would consider, for example, allowing it to influence their choice of research topic or how they designed a research project. The idea of a project to establish what a fair day's work might be, for instance, is simply preposterous. Economic sociology would never countenance this sort of intervention – this would be like asking anthropologists to interfere with the beliefs of pre-literate peoples (Shenhav, 1999). It is permissible to document the effect non-economically rational beliefs have on production but it would be totally inappropriate for the social scientist to play any part in constructing these beliefs. If the scientist happens to have some sympathy with a particular definition of a fair day's work, this is fine as long as they keep their beliefs out of their sociology.

The research programme of economic sociology is entirely defined by economic rationality. In a nutshell, its research priorities are defined by the need to investigate what it sees as aids or obstacles to the operation of economic rationality. If it is interested in social networks (see Chapter 5), for example, it is because they may help or hinder the more efficient use of scarce resources. The motivations for economic behaviour are neither good nor bad but a matter for empirical investigation. The only thing that is good or bad is the economic effect of this behaviour. If, for example, social capital permits a form of closure, then this leads to market inefficiency. If on the other hand, there is an effect on morality of the type Durkheim feared (see p. 4) this may be unfortunate, but it is no concern of economic sociology.

Outside economic sociology it has always been possible for the direction of research and scholarship to be influenced by moral considerations. There have been scholars who have thought of the idea of a fair day's work as a key component of working-class culture and morality (Scott, 1976; Thompson, 1971, 1974). This was not just a question of just desserts, rights and obligations, or a Rawlsian type of moral philosophy, because it also involved notions of human dignity (see Chapter 8). Moreover, these writers believed we should mourn the passing of this morality and that the world would be a much poorer place when it was gone. The fate of this morality has then defined the direction of their own work.

While Marx and Engels developed a critique of political economy that was steeped in their moral judgement of capitalism, economic sociology simply treats morality as one of the many factors that sometimes drive, and sometimes constrain, human behaviour. From this point of view, the sociologist is above morality and would not dream of letting it interfere with her/his choice of topic or explanation. The problem with this point of view is that another of the factors that drives and constrains human behaviour, economic rationality, is given a much more privileged role in theory building. Since, according to Portes, sociologists agree with economists 'that economic action refers to the acquisition and use of scarce means' (1995a: 3), economic sociology is forever, and everywhere, tied to economic rationality as the gold standard for economic behaviour. It is *from* economic rationality that this criterion of 'scarce means' is derived and, indeed, it is only *within* economic rationality that it makes any kind of sense. Once economic behaviour is defined in these terms, and these terms alone, there are no significant intellectual battles to be fought. It can readily be allowed that people have all sorts of motivations for their economic behaviour but this never changes the fundamental meaning of their action (which always remains 'the acquisition and use of scarce means'). Various people can choose to evaluate their economic action according to criteria derived from the I Ching, the Koran, the Upanishads, or the teachings of Ron Hubbard, but the social scientist can only ever legitimately evaluate it according to the criteria that make it characteristic (i.e. mark it out from other kinds of behaviour) and these are always the criteria of economic rationality.

We should not be content that economic sociology is in agreement with the economists who can accommodate in their theories any motivation we like to name but in doing so need make no adjustment to their theories. In the classical period sociologists did not share this approach, instead they defined economic action in a different way to economists. Whereas Adam Smith had written one book about morality and another about economy, Marx wrote about them both in one place (in the first volume of *Capital*, for instance). For Marx economic action was inescapably moral and it was, he thought, an ideological device to define it in scientific terms. His use of satire and irony to bring this out is underlined by Edmund Wilson: 'The meaning of the impersonal-looking formulas which Marx produces with so scientific an air is, he reminds us from time to time as if casually, pennies withheld from the worker's pocket, sweat squeezed out of his body, and natural enjoyments denied his soul' (in Wheen, 1999: 310). The bourgeoisie had a moral goal, their own partial moral goal, and they simply cloaked this partisan end in the seeming-scientific guise of a science of economics in order to better achieve it.

This recalls the theory of ideology developed by Marx in *The Eighteenth Brumaire of Louis Bonaparte*: 'upon the different forms of property, upon the social conditions of existence, rises an entire superstructure of distinct and peculiarly formed sentiments, illusions, modes of thought and views of life' (Marx, 1852/1934: 38–9). In this theory, classes thought the way that they did because of their economic position, and in their ideology they were thinking about their position (and their interests) although this might not always be obvious to us or even to them. Frequently classes became fond of ideas which were very convenient for them (landed aristocracies had 'honour', bourgeoisies had 'liberty'), and which also helped to cloak their interests, but this need not imply they were involved in a conspiracy:

> Only one must not form the narrow-minded notion that the petty bourgeoisie, on principle, wishes to enforce an egoistic class interest. Rather, it believes that the *special* conditions of its emancipation are the *general* conditions within the frame of which alone modern society can be saved and the class struggle avoided. (Marx, 1852/1934: 41–2)

We will return to Marx's theory of ideology in Chapter 6 but here we must not fail to note the sarcasm of that 'narrow-minded notion'. In Marx, satire, irony and sarcasm signalled *critique*. He was using them to show us how things really were, and how they really were in the case of economic behaviour was not to be understood in the abstract and general terms of economics (or political economy).

Compare this to the economic sociologist who is above morality and refuses to let it interfere with her choice of topic or explanation while giving a uniquely privileged role to the explanations of economic behaviour 'produced with so scientific an air'. The only way to escape from this is to put all the factors that drive and constrain human behaviour, economic and moral, on an equal footing and this means allowing morality into theory building. If economic sociology finds this anathema – and from all we know of its philosophy of social science (which can easily be discerned from its kinship with economics) we can be sure that it does – the solution is not to reform economic sociology but to abandon it. The remedy is to give up on economic sociology and go back to the classical sociology of economic behaviour which did allow a place for morality in its choice of topic and its theory-building.

What if Roethlisberger, Dickson and Mayo had treated the morality that they found amongst the workers at the Hawthorne plant as the end not the means to other ends defined by economic rationality? Then they might have asked how this morality could be enshrined within the basic ethos of the company. If the idea of a fair day's work could be a fundamental principle of an informal work group, why could it not be the fundamental working principle of a company? As soon as they asked this question, the Hawthorne researchers would have embarked on a voyage of real discovery. They would soon have begun to understand why a fair day's work could not presently be the company's *raison d'être* – economic rationality would not allow it – and from this point it is conceivable that they could have begun to mount a critique of economic rationality of the type begun by Marx. What the Hawthorne research produced instead of this was, of course, the writings of Elton Mayo (1973, 1932/1977) in which we encounter the first example of managerialism actually setting out to create a morality in the place of the one it has consciously destroyed.

ELTON MAYO

The Hawthorne researchers took their wrong turning under the influence of managerialism and they quickly made the managers' cause their own. Gillespie (1991) shows that it was under the influence of the Western Electric managers that the researchers denied the evidence of their own research. The managers could not believe that anything that went on in the workplace was beyond their control and therefore could give no credence to evidence of workers controlling output. Mayo found this view sympathetic with his own understanding of human behaviour and it was Mayo and his protégée, Roethlisberger, who reinterpreted evidence of output restriction (and workers' complaints about supervisors) as the non-logical behaviour of workers whose thought processes resembled those of children. This could not be collective behaviour and it certainly was not moral, indeed it was the product of demoralization (Gillespie, 1991).

According to Mayo, the workers 'pathological' behaviour showed what unhappy lives they led in the disintegrating society outside the factory gates. The social codes which they needed to guide them were no longer held in awe. They could rely only on their non-logical behaviour to cope with abusive and dysfunctional social, and especially family, relationships (Gillespie, 1991). Mayo (1932/1977) reported that the Hawthorne pant was situated in a particularly anomic community but the roots of this anomie could be found in the liberalism, individualism and materialism of American society. To be well-adjusted, workers needed the bonding and social certainty of informal social organization at work. Companies would be doing their employees a great service when they gave them the social interaction and support they craved but, in so doing, they could turn that interaction and support to good use. Workers would take a moral attitude to their work but it would be a morality that their employers approved (Bendix, 1956).

Progress towards this solution to demoralization depended on the social scientists who could train managers and others to recognise and treat psychopathology. Companies would provide counselling so workers could 'talk out' problems as well as manipulating the informal social organisation of the workplace which would be reconstituted under the control of the supervisors and managers (Gillespie, 1991). Managers were directed to do nothing which would threaten the workers' perception that this organisation remained their own in order to minimise the danger of the workforce perceiving group norms as the goals of management rather than as a corollary of their own morality (Bendix, 1956). This carefully manipulated social organisation would serve the same purpose as the entirely spontaneous kind, so far as the workforce was concerned, because Mayo defined that function in terms of humanity's emotional need for attachment and integration. A new morality would be put in place to counter societal demoralization with social scientists and managers serving as saviours of civilization. Here we find the first of several proofs that sociology has been implicated in the creation of substitutes for the morality which economic rationality first destroys and then latterly finds it still has a use for.

Bendix argues for the central importance to Mayo's doctrine of the idea that 'work should be done out of inner persuasion' rather than mere economic necessity (Bendix, 1956:319). Among Mayo's many successors these ideas were recast in new language which made less explicit reference to demoralization, particularly in ideas about the sort of corporate 'culture' which would persuade employees to produce more, or improve the quality of the goods they produced or the services they provided (Deal and Kennedy, 1982; Peters and Austin, 1985; Peters and Waterman, 1982). But the pursuit of the 'right' type of social organization for economic purposes has not been the sole preserve of management gurus like Mayo and his intellectual heirs. Mainstream economic sociology devoted much effort to telling managers how to get social organization right. For example, on the basis of evidence from the (recently nationalized) British coal-mining industry, Trist and Bamforth (1951) argued that models of technical and social organizations that appeared to represent the most efficient use of resources could deliver less than optimum results in practice. Better employee morale and higher productivity could be achieved where account was taken of coal-miners' desire for autonomy and variety and a degree of control over their work.

From the point at which the experiments at Western Electric began, economic sociology imagined that it was capable of conducting research which would give managers the information they needed to make their organizations more successful. Where sociologists have made some useful generalizations based on careful data collection, they may indeed have done this in a modest way on a few occasions. Nevertheless, on countless other occasions sociologists have pretended to have capabilities, and especially *predictive* capabilities, which allowed them to contribute to the solution of all of the most intractable problems faced by corporations. The proof that the corporations have rarely been impressed by this hubris is that they have routinely disregarded every word that economic sociologists have written. Trist and Bamforth are a case in point: neither the National Coal Board nor the miners' trade union showed any enthusiasm for the 'solutions' they proposed. Like the work of the Tavistock School – and, subsequently, the Quality of Working Life movement – which followed their lead, Trist and Bamforth's 'socio-technical systems approach' was simply ignored (Berg et al., 1979).

PROTO-CRITIQUE

There are hopeful signs in the pages of academic journals that the relationship between morality and economy that animated the critiques of classical sociology is being reinstated at the heart of a revitalized sociology of economic behaviour. We should be wary, however, of being over-optimistic about what can count as critique. Work which claims to show that it is an inevitable tendency of capitalist development to reduce the number of more skilled jobs (Braverman, 1974) or less skilled jobs (Jordan, 1982; Reich, 1991) does not amount to a critique. This sort of work does, however, tend to incite debate. The 'labour process debate' that was sparked by Braverman's work went on for many years. It was then followed by the 'flexibility debate' initiated by Atkinson (1984; see also Pollert, 1991; Fevre, 1991; Doogan, 2001). These debates provide useful opportunities for accumulating research funding and publications but they are unlikely to lead to the construction of a new critique of economic behaviour.

There were signs of critique in Braverman's writing but, paradoxically, they were least in evidence in the account of the degradation of work that stimulated the labour process debate (Nichols, 2001). In his chapter on 'The Universal Market' Braverman explained how, under capitalism, alternative social forms of getting by and getting on with each other were systematically destroyed and replaced by market substitutes. Markets did not simply take over the supply of food, clothing and shelter but every kind of human need as well: 'even the emotional patterns of life are channelled through the market' (Braverman, 1974: 276). Braverman argued that social and family life were fatally undermined by the universal market and in this way he began to construct a critique which attempted to break out of the integuments of economic rationality in order to create an alternative to it. By way of contrast, the labour process debate remained almost wholly within the confines of economic rationality: there was no alternative to deskilling because it made such good economic sense.

Around the same time as the ultimately pointless 'labour process debate' was raging, some scattered evidence began to appear that some sociologists had begun to worry about the decay of the sort of morality implied by the notion of a fair day's work and its replacement by a new commitment to economic rationality. This represented a movement, admittedly very small, towards critique. In effect, this work was talking about demoralization, in particular, the way that the morality that had existed in the workplace had decayed.

Goldthorpe (1978) put the blame for many of Britain's problems with high inflation and low growth in the 1970s on the conversion of the working class to economic rationality and their loss of earlier moral restraints. Writing about Britain in the same period, Nichols and Armstrong discussed sabotage as an indication of the 'negation' of workers' lives (1976: 83). The examples of sabotage they gave suggested demoralization rather than worker resistance and they warned against the temptation to romanticize sabotage as part of the workers' struggle for dignity (a warning not heeded by Hodson, 2001). In a companion study Nichols and Beynon (1977) tried to show the waste and sacrifice of workers' lives entailed in 'living with capitalism' (see also Chapter 6). In subsequent years Hochschild and Sennett again turned the question of 'how much labour is enough?' into the much more subversive one of 'how much can we afford to lose from work?'. These studies recalled the critique that Marx had developed in the mid-nineteenth century when he asked us to count the real cost paid by those who labour (the link to Marx was made explicit by Hochschild – see below – when she developed the idea of emotional labour).

In his study of demoralization at work, Sennett (1998) drew attention to the effects that economic rationality was having in the rest of our lives.[1] He analysed how we felt about our participation in the capitalist world of work, and how capitalism made us feel about ourselves, at a critical juncture marked by the ascendancy of a new kind of capitalism, a new kind of work, and a new relationship to the labour market. He thought that these changes – for example, changes in technology, flexibility and new ways of managing employees – were so radical that we could not think of ourselves in the same way as we used to do, and he summarized the effect by saying we were fast being deprived of the opportunity to form and transmit character.

By referring to character Sennett wanted us to see that neither material prosperity nor growing inequality told us everything that mattered about the new economy. Some of the people who most clearly exemplified the tendencies that worried him had fulfilled their parents' dreams of upward mobility into professional jobs yet in some ways they were worse off than their parents. Their work did not make them feel that they were worthwhile people and they were haunted by a fear of losing control. They might be paid a great deal more than their parents had ever earned in their blue-collar jobs but the decisions they made at work counted for less and they never felt they knew where they stood. In the new economy people were at a permanent disadvantage because they could never do well enough to know they had earned their employer's commitment. Under these conditions it is small wonder that there was little loyalty shown towards employers, in fact people now counselled, and celebrated, lack of commitment. The career of the average American was proof that people believed that to stay put was to be left out, yet if we had no meaningful narrative to our lives, how could character be formed? Outside a tiny minority of highly successful risk-takers, most of us were being set up to fail, not just failing to reach our highest ambitions but failing to make sense of our lives.

In these new circumstances it also became impossible for parents to set their children the examples that they would wish to. They might want to persuade their children of the value of resolution and commitment but could not do this when it was obvious that resolution and commitment were seen as value-less in the world that mattered, the world of work. Their children saw little evidence of commitment or self-discipline in the behaviour of anyone they knew. The only message that parents could transmit which was congruent with their children's real experience was that they should look after their own interests by avoiding commitment and eschewing pointless sacrifices. Instead of transmitting the building blocks needed for character formation, the workers of the new economy could not help but transmit all the components of rampant short-termism and individualism to their sons and daughters.

Because of the geographical mobility which was so common in America, Sennett was able to augment this argument at various points with allusions to the loss of community. The children of the workers of the new economy moved from state to state as their parents changed jobs, and learnt that it was not worth over-investing in friendship. Yet the most interesting parts of Sennett's account had less to do with simple nostalgia for *gemeinschaft* or even for workplace solidarity. Thus Sennett described some of the ersatz substitutes that the new economy put in place of the values it destroys. In particular he noted that the teamwork which modern corporations prized created superficial ties between individuals that were a grotesque caricature of real solidarity and friendship. The reality of teamwork was that everyone was completely indifferent to who the other team members were. Their character was irrelevant and all that mattered was how well they could act.

Sennett's argument that a recent increase in insecurity and the transient nature of work was implicated in the corrosion of character was persuasive (see, for example, Bauman, 2001) but evidence that the new economy bore some responsibility for the corrosion of character was thin. It is not difficult to find empirical evidence, for the period to which Sennett's book refers, of a move from 'collective value orientations based on solidarity and equality towards more individualistic value orientations based on self-interest and personal opportunities' (Madsen, 1997: 197). But in Madsen's Danish study, for example, individualization was most common among white-collar employees with plenty of autonomy in their jobs, wages determined by qualifications and job performance, and no strong attachment to their employer. Such workers were not particularly insecure and if work was transient in nature, this was probably the consequence of their decisions, not those of their employers. Indeed, it is very hard to see how insecurity could be a major cause of demoralization when its prevalence has been so grossly exaggerated (Doogan, 2001; Fevre, 1991; and Chapter 6). Sennett over-emphasized the culpability of the new economy because he put rather too much faith in research which had generalized the evidence of increased insecurity on the basis of trends in unrepresentative sectors. In fact, there was no need to identify the causes of the corrosion of character in any very recent phenomenon. After all, David Riesman (1950) had discussed character and its decline in some of the same terms as Sennett in the middle of the post-war Fordist boom which had occurred half a century earlier.

Sennett argued that change in the nature of work had taken away the moral-education function of employment – and the opportunity for acquiring character – but is it true that worklife ever spontaneously generated character? At the very least, economic behaviour could only begin to build character if people entered the workplace with some of their morality already in place. An alternative view to Sennett's – and that of several other writers (Casey, 1995) – is that morality, and character, have always been imported into the workplace and, once established there, have vied with economic rationality over the meaning of economic behaviour.[2] What Sennett was really commenting on was the way that the balance between these two ways of making sense of behaviour had changed. In workplaces of the end of the twentieth century, economic rationality destroyed character which was imported into the workplace just as it destroyed it everywhere.

Although flawed, *The Corrosion of Character* made a unique contribution to the development of a genuine critique of economic behaviour. This could be said of very few other works but one of them, Arlie Hochschild's *The Managed Heart* (1983), was perhaps even more important in contributing to the renaissance of the sociology of economic behaviour. Like Hochschild's later studies of the work-life balance, *The Managed Heart* shows economic rationality in direct conflict with morality and begins to open up all the possibilities of a new critique. This is not, however, really the way Hochschild understood her own study. In the next section I will recapitulate her arguments and reinterpret some of her evidence and analysis to draw out its full significance for the sociology of economic behaviour.

THE MORAL SIGNIFICANCE OF EMOTIONAL LABOUR

Hochschild began her book with an explicit reference to Marx's concern to mount a fundamental critique of labour under capitalism. As she understood it, this critique showed us the human cost of becoming an instrument of labour and she made explicit the link between exploitation and moral concern. But Hochschild also thought her book was a study of emotion: some kinds of work had always

involved our emotions but now, typified by the work of flight attendants, companies were saying that a standardized *'emotional style of
offering the service is part of the service itself'* (1983: 5, emphasis in
original). Demand for this service then went up and down in accord
with market conditions.[3]

For Hochschild the biggest problem with standardized emotional
labour lay in the psychological effects on those who had their emotions managed in this way. They learned to detach themselves from
their feelings and so had difficulty getting back in touch with their
emotions outside work. Of course there are many other circumstances
in which we detach ourselves from our feelings and show emotion we
do not feel. The problem for flight attendants was that they had to do
this to order and were required to turn their emotions into an instrument to be used in pursuit of someone else's ends.

In some ways this was the weakest part of the book (see 1983: 183,
on flight attendants' psychosexual problems, for example). Another
weakness was the emphasis on the effects of standardization. In some
ways this emphasis recalls both Braverman (1974) and Ritzer (1993).
Unlike these authors, Hochschild made no claims to have discovered,
on the basis of a study of a single sector, a deplorable, and probably
irresistible, increase in standardization which would degrade both
labour and the products of labour in all other sectors. Nevertheless,
her insistence on the standardization of emotional labour helped to
inspire other researchers to waste effort on arguments about the precise extent of this standardization when there was far more useful and
interesting work to be done.

Hochschild's seminal contribution to the sociology of economic
behaviour lay neither in her comments about the standardization of
emotional labour nor in drawing our attention to the psychosexual
effects of emotional labour, but in her exploration of what we should
really call a *moral economy*:[4]

> In the absence of an English-language name for feelings-as-contribu-
> tion-to-the-group (which the more group-centered Hopi culture called
> *arofa*), I shall offer the concept of gift exchange. Muted anger, conjured
> gratitude and, and suppressed envy are offerings back and forth from
> parent to child, wife to husband, friend to friend, and lover to lover ...
> Acts of emotion management are not simply private acts; they are used
> in exchanges under the guidance of feeling rules. Feeling rules are stan-
> dards used in emotional conversation to determine what is rightly
> owed and owing in the currency of feeling. Through them, we tell what
> is 'due' in each relation, each role. We pay tribute to each other in the
> currency of the managing act. In interaction we pay, overpay, under-
> pay, play with paying, acknowledge our dues, pretend to pay, or
> acknowledge what is emotionally due to another person. In these ways
> ... we make our try at sincere civility. (1983: 18)

There are echoes here of Mauss (1954), Goffman (1959, 1961) and Blau (1964) but Hochschild introduced more of the language of morality into her sociology than any of these writers. With the idea of what is 'due to another person' and 'feeling rules' Hochschild brought in standards derived from a morality. Hochschild might not agree, but the feelings that are displayed or hidden by people were only a small, and perhaps superficial, part of the theory-building to which she was contributing. A moral economy is not limited to setting rates of exchange between feelings but determines how people behave: what they *do* because they think it is right to do so. Suppressed anger and 'conjured gratitude' are only small parts of this moral economy: civility consists in much more than the display of feelings that are due.

Hochschild understood the relationship between feelings and moral behaviour in this way: '[s]ince feeling is a form of pre-action, a script or a moral stance toward it is one of culture's most powerful tools for directing action' (1983: 56). These scripts were the feeling rules to which Hochschild referred. One of the important things that she told us, but she failed to spell out properly, was that rules supplied by the airline companies were being used to guide emotion *instead of moral rules*. This explains why, of all of the human emotions that Hochschild might have discussed, it is the feelings that can linked, in a simple way, to beliefs about right and wrong that figured most prominently in her study. In effect, she made a theoretical sample of emotions and we learnt a great deal less about less obviously moral feelings of fear,[5] excitement or boredom, for example.

In fact, Hochschild's text was littered with signs that she did know her book was a study of the manipulation of moral behaviour. Spontaneous feeling was treated 'as if it were scarce and precious; we raise it up as a virtue' (ibid.: 22). She showed us how common managing feeling really was (for example, it is intrinsic to jobs as actors, physicians and day-care workers) and yet she knew something different was happening in the case of flight attendants and that this difference was related to morality. We see this in her discussion of the way that '[i]n the context of the theater, this use of feeling is considered exciting and *honorable*. But what happens when deep and surface acting become part of a day's work, part of what we sell to an employer for a day's wage?' (ibid.: 54, emphasis added).

Hochschild also pointed out the way flight attendants monitored themselves and each other to see if the mask that their employer required them to wear was slipping: '[t]alk about phoniness was serious because it was usually seen not merely as an instance of poor acting but as evidence of a personal moral flaw, almost a stigma' (ibid.: 134).

In her brief excursion into the technique of debt collectors, Hochschild explained that they withheld empathy so debtors 'pay not only in cash but in moral standing' (ibid.: 145). Then there was the 'niceness' in which the flight attendants excelled, and which enhanced the well-being and status[6] of others and served as 'a necessary and important lubricant to any civil exchange' (ibid.: 167). For Hochschild this vital quality was multi-faceted but included: 'the moral or spiritual sense of being seriously nice, in which we embrace the needs of another person as more important than our own.' (1983: 168). This was almost the language of Arendt or Bauman (1991, 1993) and it was so suggestive that it excited the best of the researchers who followed in Hochschild's footsteps to look for further examples of self-sacrifice amongst employees.[7] I think I am fully justified in claiming that, by bringing out the question of morality in Hochschild's work, I am simply drawing out an important strand of her thinking which is usually overlooked rather than inserting meanings of my own.

Hochschild saw the airline companies taking over the job of making 'feeling rules' and standardizing them, thereby condemning their employees to the same exchanges of feeling – exchanges they felt were good for business – over and over again. She called this a 'transmutation' in which feelings were taken into a different realm and used for a different purpose. If we consider the implications of this for the wider picture in which we focus on morality as well as feelings, we understand that these companies were taking over morality, or reinventing it for their own purposes. They were attempting to take over the responsibility for making the moral guidelines about what behaviour is right and what is wrong. The idea of transmutation is useful but perhaps it does not quite grasp the audacity of the experiment these companies were engaged in.

Hochschild drew our attention to the way profit is insinuated into the gift exchanges: '[a] profit motive is *slipped in* under acts of emotion management, under the rules that govern them, under the gift exchange' (1983: 119 emphasis added). In order to make this possible, trainee flight attendants were encouraged to work the same deception on themselves:

> Trainees were asked to think of a passenger *as if* he were a "personal guest in your living room." The workers' emotional memories of offering personal hospitality were called up and put to use. (ibid.: 105, emphasis in original)
> Impersonal relations are to be seen *as if* they were personal. Relations based on getting and giving money are to be seen *as if* they were relations free of money. (ibid.: 106, emphasis in original)

Hochschild remarked on the standardization, the ritual and the inescapable quality of the exchanges in a way that reminds us of the elements of a well-practised confidence trick. In a moral economy, feelings were exchanged fairly but it is a sort of confidence trick to pretend this can happen when those feelings are commodified: '[w]e have carried our ancient capacity for gift exchange over a great commercial divide where the gifts are becoming commodities and the exchange rates set by corporations' (ibid.: 194). Moreover, the airline companies appeared to be quite aware that they were engaged in a confidence trick since they knew that when we interpret 'a smile, we try to take out what social engineering put in, pocketing only what seems meant just for us' (ibid.: 34). The possibility that customers might see through the confidence trick was a fundamental assumption under-pinning flight attendants' training and this showed that the companies were well aware that what they were trying to achieve could be understood as deception. Indeed, this did not bother them unduly since it was not necessary that airline customers should be utterly deceived, just fooled enough to make them buy more airline tickets.

The insinuation of the profit motive into gift exchange seems to me to be a perfect example of morality being put at the service of economic rationality but it is also a good example of what I have referred to elsewhere (Fevre, 2000b) as a 'category error' in which people are encouraged to mistake a commercial transaction for one in which different rules of behaviour apply and so be more easily parted from their money. In cases such as the one Hochschild describes, and others,[8]

> sentiment is represented, through the extension of hospitality, as one category, perhaps the most important category, in which people should make sense of the exchanges that take place. In other words, people are actively persuaded that sentiment is appropriate in order to get them to open their purses. (Fevre, 2000b: 165)

The same could be said of other marketing techniques and advertising is usually meant deceive us about the sorts of sense making we should be applying to information about products or services.

If this is correct, why should we now find ourselves so commonly invited to make these category errors? Hochschild argued persuasively that airlines began to manage flight attendants' emotional labour at a certain point in recent history and that nothing like this had been present in any of the previous incarnations of the flight attendant's role in the history of air travel. Why should the training of flight attendants in emotional labour only become necessary in the last quarter of the twentieth century? It would certainly be possible to answer this question in terms of the 'postemotional society' discussed by Mestrovic (1997) but it can also be seen as the direct result of the creation of new business opportunities as one of the side-effects of demoralization. If, by the 1970s, airline customers were no longer sure that they could expect civility in public life, or even when they were paying for a

78

service (Bell, 1979; Lasch; 1979; Mestrovic, 1991), and if civility and 'niceness' could be synthesized, or counterfeited, in an airline cabin, then this offered (at least temporarily) the opportunity to create comparative advantage.[9]

In this view, the flight attendant's smile made money because, in our demoralized world, people long for the resurgence of ways of thinking, and behaving, which do not derive from the cold calculation of economic rationality or the broader category of 'common sense' (Fevre, 2000b). So desperate are we for such a revival that we lay ourselves open to manipulation by airline companies or, indeed by advertising:

> The more we find that sentiment is degraded, and the more difficult we find it to believe in our feelings, or the feelings of the people around us, the more gullible we seem to become to the exploitatative sentiment of advertising which has been designed simply to make us pull out our credit cards. (ibid.: 167)

Hochschild did not make this connection, but it is in pursuit of the business opportunity created by demoralization that the airline companies recruited the nice, middle-class women whom they wanted to train to become flight attendants. These women were, in effect, judged to be the members of society who were probably least likely to have suffered demoralization (Fevre, 2000b). Indeed candidates were required to demonstrate that this judgement was correct as part of their recruitment interview. This was made clear to them in pre-interview pamphlets and indeed Delta explicitly asked for applicants with a 'friendly personality and high moral character' (Hochschild, 1983: 97).

Explicit reference to demoralization also helps to get over some of the difficulties Hochschild got into, for example when she tried to differentiate what flight attendants did from the emotional labour of social workers, day-care providers and doctors. For Hochschild the point was that these other emotional labourers supervise their own labour (ibid.: 153) but I suggest that social workers, day-care providers and doctors remain in occupations into which it is still possible to import morality rather than manufacture a morality-substitute. Similarly, Hochschild tried to differentiate what flight attendants did from the way in which, throughout history, people had always used their feelings like a kind of capital in all sorts of competition with others. For Hochschild the crucial difference was that, in the case of flight attendants, companies were responsible for manipulating feelings rather than individuals, but demoralization makes the difference clearer. Even before Shakespeare gave us Goneril and Reagan, there were individuals who represented their own emotions, and manipulated the feelings of others, to their own advantage. Demoralization simply means that there are places in our societies where sentiment has no other life than that given to it by people who pretend to have feelings they cannot really possess.

Of course demoralization did not begin in the 1980s and commercial solutions to the problems and opportunities it presented had been observed by sociologists a generation earlier, including C. Wright Mills:

> In many strata of white collar employment, such traits as courtesy, helpfulness, and kindness, once intimate, are now part of the impersonal means of livelihood ... [W]hite-collar people ... sell by the week or month their smiles and their kindly gestures, and they must practice the prompt repression of resentment and aggression ... Here are the new little Machiavellians, practicing their personable crafts for hire and for the profits of others, according to rules laid down by those above them. (Mills, 1951: xvii)

Just as *The Managed Heart* did not mark the onset of demoralization, so it did not mark its high-water mark. Long after it was first published, airlines had to learn to become accustomed to dealing with 'air rage' and varieties of sexual exhibitionism from passengers. All the same, Hochschild's flight attendants could tell her how the incivility and selfishness of passengers had to be routinely ignored and minimized. Moreover, they recounted more exotic in-flight experiences which included sexual assault, being spat at, having tea thrown at them, and having to condone petty theft. The working environment of the flight attendants was already a thoroughly demoralized one which made their work all the more onerous. Indeed this environment made it increasingly unlikely that any customer would ever forget how manufactured the flight attendants' morality was. Hochschild's book (and the subsequent research she inspired – see below) are full of examples of flight attendants having to suspend part of authentic moral judgement, in fact fully half of it – the half that says certain behaviour is wrong. They were continually being asked to condone, and even reward, behaviour which morality would condemn as wrong. Hochschild showed in finely perceived detail how the flight attendants' training and supervision changed the way they exercised moral judgement about how they might react to someone else's character (about, therefore, how they portrayed their own character). Twenty years later it is, perhaps, not always so easy for companies to control the reactions of their employees.

Taylor and Tyler (2000) studied tele-sales staff and flight attendants in a British airline. They found that selection panels were much more likely to select women for tele-sales because they thought they could endure incivility from customers. In addition, they were trained to put the commercial interests of the company before any other judgement.

Many female tele-sales staff reported that they had to put up with sex-ualized encounters and among cabin crew there were also explicitly sexualized elements in emotional labour. But the thrust of Taylor and Tyler's article was that staff only met what they saw to be the more extreme demands for emotional labour when they knew they were being monitored.

When there was no monitoring, tele-sales staff disconnected calls and limited the information given to callers they found offensive. Cabin crew developed other ways to keep their emotional labour at a distance and appeared to take it a little less seriously than Hochschild's flight attendants had done. Taylor and Tyler even came close to sug-gesting their respondents were engaged in a knowing, post-modern parody of emotional labour ('Of course I still smile, I just don't go out of my way to ... hide the fact that it's a pretend smile', 2000: 90). Taylor and Tyler concluded 'our own findings demonstrate how a *sur-face* commitment or act can conceal "deep" or "genuine" resentment and cynicism of quality improvement programmes in the service sec-tor' (ibid.: 93).

Even in Hochschild's study it was clear that the effort to manage feelings in demoralized conditions becomes morally ambiguous and fraught. Hochschild might not agree that her work supports this con-clusion but she wrote a great deal about the way airline companies insisted that the flight attendants were being asked to endure treat-ment that they would not normally have to put up with for the sake of the company. She also remarked that 'workers have weaker rights to courtesy than customers do' (1983: 89): 'a customer assumes a right to vent unmanaged hostility against a flight attendant who has no cor-responding right – because she is paid, in part, to relinquish it' (ibid.: 186).

If there were no demoralization there would not be such estrange-ment from feelings, and nor would there be the emotional, or rather moral, dissonance Hochschild found so common.[10] The extreme example of this was the sexualized commercial encounter. The flight attendant 'must try to feel and act as if flirting and propositioning are "a sign of my attractiveness and your sexiness," and she must work to suppress her feelings that such behavior is intrusive or demeaning' (ibid.: 94, see also ibid.: 28) – what could be better proof of demoral-ization?

In subsequent years, sociologists sought similar evidence of demor-alization and discovered (verbal, violent and sexual) harassment in a variety of hospitality work in the service sector (Adkins, 1995; Folgero and Fjeldstad, 1995; Giuffre and Williams, 1994; Hall, 1993; Leidner, 1993; Scott, 1998; Sosteric, 1996). Of these, Hall (1993), like Hochschild, found a sexual element had become a part of the job.

Elsewhere it was reported that some restaurant chains trained waiters of both sexes to flirt with customers in order to get them to spend more and visit the restaurant again (Gilbert et al., 1994).

More recently, Guerrier and Adib (2000) conducted a study of hotel workers in Britain, the USA, Europe and South East Asia. They found hotel staff of both sexes being sexually harassed by guests who seemed to think that, if they paid a bit more, the sexual services – of the hotel receptionist perhaps – would be included as part of the trans-action. Guerrier and Adib saw this as a part of both the feminization of these jobs and the expectation of a particular kind of emotional labour (also see the discussion of the work of Jones et al., 1997 below). Senior managers believed, as many customers might, that a hotel was 'a rational, safe and desexualised working environment' (Guerrier and Adib, 2000: 701) but

> Management rhetoric suggests that the customer is sovereign and the service employee is there to do everything to satisfy his or her needs. Hotels function most of the time on the basis of an assumed rational-ity in which both customers and service staff work within the same social norms about what is or is not acceptable behaviour ... The inci-dents described in this paper ... represent a breakdown in the process of reciprocal exchange; a breakdown of the hosts and guests' mutual sense of obligation that normally places some limits on their behaviour. (ibid.: 701)

These references to reciprocity and acceptable behaviour clearly recall the moral economy which Hochschild described, but the most inter-esting insight we can derive from her work is of broader relevance. Although this rarely features in the subsequent literature inspired by her work, the most penetrating insight we can derive from *The Managed Heart* is Hochschild's observation that we would all be a lot more familiar with the characteristics of our demoralized world if it were not for the efforts of the flight attendants and all the others who perform emotional labour for us. Of course, Hochschild did not refer directly to demoralization but it is not difficult to infer that the emo-tional labour of others insulates us from many of its disturbing effects:

> Taken as a whole, these emotional laborers make possible a public life in which millions of people daily have fairly trusting and pleasant transactions with total or nearly total strangers. Were our good will strictly confined to persons we know in private life, were our offerings of civility or empathy not so widely spread out and our feelings not professionalized, surely public life would be profoundly different. (1983: 153)
>
> Massive people-processing – and the advanced engineering of emotional labor that makes it possible – is a remarkable achievement. It is also an important one, for a good part of modern life involves exchange between total strangers, who, in the absence of countermeasures and in

the pursuit of short-term self-interest, might much of the time act out suspicion and anger rather than trust and good will. The occasional lapses from the standard of civility that we take for granted remind us of the crucial steadying effect of emotional labor. (ibid.: 186–7)

These remarks were precisely aimed in the direction the sociology of economic behaviour must develop but, thus far, there has been little progress, perhaps because they suggested no obvious research agenda (in contrast to comparative studies of more flight attendants or other kinds of hospitality workers).

Where subsequent research deserves more praise is in respect of the work which has been done to document the attempts companies have made to regain (temporary) comparative advantage by trying get their employees to perform their emotional labour in a way which customers do not suspect is scripted. Hochschild cited the work of Trilling on the way the value of sincerity rises in an era of common insincerity, and argued that authentic emotion was valued when the commercialization of feelings have become commonplace. Hochschild saw this cultural shift as creating yet another marketing opportunity and so did some of her successors (Bowen and Basch 1992; Leidner 1993). Jones, Taylor and Nickson reported that hotel companies 'believe that providing high quality, "authentic" ... social interactions between employee and guest is the key to gaining competitive advantage' (1997: 541). Their study of an international hotel chain in Britain, Austria, Poland and the USA showed that 'authentic' meant non-routinized, individualized and more intense. This study discovered a variety of examples of this 'authentic' interactions, including some which were used in company advertising:

> These ranged from a waiter on night duty driving round town to find a favourite bedtime drink, to a porter retracing a guest's journey on a city's trams to retrieve a lost wallet. (Jones et al., 1997: 544)
> All forms of behaviour could apparently be appropriated for corporate consumption; for example, one manager recounted how two of his employees chased a robber, not because this was a normal if somewhat foolhardy reaction, but because 'they felt empowered to do it'. The manager felt that the company could not 'dictate' such responses: 'it comes from within'. (ibid.: 547)

More and more hospitality service providers have decided that there is competitive advantage to be won from reworking the strategy originally pioneered by the airlines Hochschild studied.[11] They clearly think there is money to be made by up-dating niceness for a demoralized world.

Whereas Sennett felt work no longer generated character, I propose that *The Managed Heart* documented the creation of an *ersatz* morality

83

which could serve in the place of the morality that economic rationality had helped to destroy. It was this ersatz morality that kept public life bearable (as Hochschild rightly observed). It was ersatz precisely because its existence depended on a category error. In Hochschild's terms, it had crossed the commercial divide and been transmuted and it was no surprise that she was able to find that such an ersatz, manufactured morality had adverse effects on the people who were meant to internalize it.

WORKPLACE CULTURE

In fact, emotional labour is only a special case of a more general trend in which employers manufacture ersatz moralities to guide *all* employee behaviour, and not simply employees' behaviour towards customers. A renascent sociology of economic behaviour is beginning to show that a succession of managerialist initiatives have been enacted in order to fill the gaps created by demoralization in the workplace. Initiatives like 'employee empowerment' are intended, in effect, to train people to behave as if they were not in thrall to economic rationality. Instead of airline customers paying for civility and 'niceness' which were increasingly rare in the rest of public life, companies wanted their workers to behave morally to each other, their bosses, and the company as a whole, as well as to customers. As with the airline business, there was money to be made from getting people to behave as if they did not take their cue from the cold calculation of economic rationality or the broader category of 'common sense' (Fevre, 2000b).

The implications of this will be explored in the final chapter but, for present purposes, it is enough to observe that Fordism was closely associated with the spread of common sense and, particularly, economic rationality throughout the manufacturing workforce (Gorz, 1989). Not only did Fordism promote economic rationality (through its payment systems for example) but it also instituted forms of work organization and technology that could cope (to an extent) with its effects. But Fordism did not provide complete protection against the effects of demoralization: demoralized workers might engage in demarcation disputes and unofficial strikes and use extreme, perhaps criminal, methods to try to win industrial disputes. Workers in large Fordist enterprises also had a tendency to engage in more individualist guerrilla actions against their employers (Haraszti, 1977). There was often a continuous battle over the control of labour time and even raw materials (which employees often sought to appropriate for their own uses). Almost all of the ends to which workers wished to devote their time and their employers' resources were economically rational, indeed they were quite likely to want to use them to make some money on the side (Fevre, 1989).[12] It is as if, with the spread of economic rationality, large enterprises like this became the focus for economic behaviour of every kind, not simply that part of it that was mediated by the employment relationship (Nichols and Armstrong, 1976; Nichols and Beynon, 1977). Indeed, there had always been difficulties in applying Fordism outside manufacturing (and even to some manufacturing sectors).

A growing proportion of employment was not governed by Fordist arrangements but, of course, this did not mean that this kind of work was immune to demoralization. In more skilled jobs, those with more autonomy, and certainly among the professions, it was necessary for people to exhibit the characteristics of empowered employees. Yet it was not just blue-collar workers who Riesman (1950) thought were becoming other-directed and there was a limit to what could be done to ameliorate the effects of demoralization with work organization and technology.[13] The alternative was to remake the morality that had been lost and to create what could no longer be created by society at large within the workplace.

Long before the language of employee empowerment was common, Anthony (1977: 308) drew attention to a new kind of managerialism which used 'all the resources of the psychologist and sociologist' to make sure workers brought their 'unhindered energy' to work. Later, Du Gay and Salaman (1992) warned that 'new' management was concerned to bind people to a new, ersatz morality: Quoting Foucault alongside Peters and Waterman, they observed that

> These firms get the most out of their employees by harnessing 'the psychological strivings of individuals for autonomy and creativity' and channelling them into the search for 'total customer responsiveness', 'excellence' and success. Enterprising companies 'make meaning for people' by encouraging them to believe that they have control over their own lives; that no matter what position they may hold within an organisation their contribution is vital, not only to the success of the company but to the enterprise of their own lives. (Du Gay and Salaman, 1992: 625)

Although customer relations were explicitly mentioned here, Du Gay and Salaman were clear that much more was involved. The ambitious (and long-term) aim of Peters and Waterman (1982) was to persuade managers not to sacrifice quality and service for costs and efficiency. The way they shaped the culture of their organizations would allow them to achieve these seemingly incompatible ends.

We have already noted that Elton Mayo's ideas were later recast in theories about the sort of corporate 'culture' which would make people work harder, better or smarter. It was quite explicit in Tom Peters' writing – for example, see Peters (1987) on the enterprise's driving 'aesthetic and moral vision' – that 'culture' meant morality (Maclagan, 1998; Pattison, 1997). With the help of Foucault (1988a), Du Gay and Salaman argued that in the new culture of the workplace the good employee was a substitute for a person of good character:[14] '[t]he discourse of enterprise brooks no opposition between the mode of self-presentation required of managers and employees, and the ethics of the personal self. Becoming a better worker is represented as the same thing as becoming a more virtuous person, a better self' (1992: 626). This of course recalled Hochschild's 'transmutation' across the commercial divide and Du Gay and Salaman quoted Miller and Rose approvingly: '[w]ork is an essential element in the path to self-realization. There is no longer any barrier between the economic, the psychological and the social. The government of work now passes through the psychological strivings of each and every individual for fulfilment' (Miller and Rose, cited by Du Gay and Salaman, 1992: 627).

Du Gay and Salaman cited Rose for the observation that this omnivorous managerialism thought good government of the firm would be achieved because its employees were governing themselves to behave as good people. Du Gay and Salaman also understood that the intention was to turn morality into a means to an end: '[t]hrough "capitalizing" the meaning of life, enterprise allows different "spheres of existence" to be brought into alignment and achieve translatability' (ibid.). This did not simply imply transmutation but also the (deliberate) category mistakes discussed above (p. 78) in which companies set out to combat the effects of demoralization by trying to ensure that employees, as well as customers, substituted sentiment, and seemingly moral behaviour, for what might usually be understood in rational terms, and particularly the terms of economic rationality.

Du Gay and Salaman did not, in fact, think that it was really possible to capitalize the meaning of life or translate morality into the workplace. For one thing, they were fully aware that those who were meant to have their behaviour guided by this translated morality were not really deceived into thinking that this was the authentic morality that guided, or used to guide, their behaviour outside the workplace. Employees knew in their hearts that a category mistake was being made and they recognized that the engineered morality was an ersatz one. Nevertheless, Du Gay and Salaman observed that, even though everyone involved knew the morality was *ersatz*, they would still be prepared to let it govern their behaviour. 'Recruitment auditions', assessment centres and personality profiling played a key role in conveying to employees the necessity that cynicism should be covert and appearances should be marked by enthusiastic co-operation.

Much subsequent research effort was spent trying to gauge how deep either cynicism or enthusiasm went.

WORKPLACE CULTURE AND DEMORALIZATION

Kunda (1992) described an attempt to put workplace culture – meaning a particular combination of values nurtured in the minds of employees – at the heart of managerial strategy. The company he studied ('Tech') described itself as existing to pursue moral aims to which all of its employees were expected to subscribe. Sometimes Tech was portrayed as a beacon of moral behaviour in a demoralized world. The metaphors and imagery used to convey this often involved comparing Tech to the hard-pressed, moral institutions of religion and family. Tech's status as a moral institution was (at least until some time after Kunda's study) exemplified by its no lay-offs policy. Just as a family would never make some its members redundant, so Tech would never repay the loyalty of its family by letting them go.

Yet Tech's moral aims – commitment, honesty and responsibility and so on – were not presented as deontological goals so much as ethics which were justified by their outcomes (see Weber on Franklin – p. 000). Honesty was the best policy for customer relations, responsibility led to production and quality, trust and ethical behaviour meant more teamwork, communication and innovation. It was not at all difficult for anyone to see through the idea that these were moral aims, after all 'profit' always figured prominently in the supposedly moral corporate philosophy.

When it came to the delivery of the Tech culture below the level of senior management the moralistic emphasis which Kunda sometimes refered to as 'ideology' was played down and sometimes omitted altogether. Kunda's choice of language to describe this process was important. At the level at which the culture was actually transmitted there was an acknowledgement of the 'ideological façade' but the ideology was tempered with 'common sense' (1992: 77). As you would expect from common sense and economic rationality, motivation at this level was usually reliant on self-interest (which would be perfectly happy with no lay-offs, of course).

The trainers and culture managers at Tech presented the culture in a very skilful way, playing with ambivalence and self-parody. Ordinary employees were also given the opportunity to undermine the culture's pretensions with common sense in a controlled manner which limited the damage inflicted on the ideological façade. As Du Gay and Salaman would have predicted, they did not internalize culture but went along with it. Kunda concluded that they were being driven by 'normative control' (after Etzioni, 1961) rather than simply economic rationality. There is no difficulty if this meant employees were 'driven by internal commitment, strong identification with company goals, intrinsic satisfaction from work' but Kunda also considered it involved 'a moral orientation to the organisation' (1992: 11) yet norms are not synonymous with morals.

Kunda certainly did not think that the Tech employees became more moral as a result of their workplace culture. Whatever else you might say about them, the last thing they were capable of was the moral evaluation of their company's actions: 'analysis of the role, use, and social consequences of the company's technology was conspicuous by its absence' (ibid.: 226). Indeed, their capacity for any sort of moral action may well have been undermined by their exposure to a conscious attempt to step up normative control. The fact that they had to go along with this while quietly despising it, caused collateral damage in their everyday lives:

> The engineers of culture see the ideal member as driven by strong beliefs and intense emotions, authentic experiences of loyalty, commitment, and the pleasure of work. Yet they seem to produce members who have internalised ambiguity, who have made the metaphor of drama a centrepiece of their sense of self, who question the authenticity of all beliefs and emotions, and who find irony in its various forms the dominant mode of everyday existence. (ibid.: 216)

Catherine Casey's research uncovered a rather similar workplace culture in a company she called 'Hephaestus' but in her work the idea that an ersatz morality was being constructed to make up for demoralization was a little closer to the surface. Since older employees remembered it as being more moral than it now was, demoralization seemed to have affected the company directly. In particular, employees took the idea of the company much more seriously than Kunda's respondents appeared to. They talked with emotion and gratitude about the way the company was a parent to them when they were younger. Yet belief in the company as parent, the company as family and the virtuous company more generally was waning among the over-45s. Casey thought this decline helped persuade Hephaestus to take management consultants' advice that they instigate the kind of cultural revolution recommended by Deal and Kennedy (1982), Ouchi (1981) and Peters and Waterman (1982). The popular proponents of this cultural revolution argued that rational controls exacerbated the problems of demoralization and might thereby lead to declining productivity (Barley and Kunda, 1992).

Hephaestus determined to have less employees but every one of them would be a new kind of employee. Casey could find evidence to suggest that the new culture had affected the character of employees. There was increased civility and people would tell her they were proud of the sacrifices they made for the company and that it was a matter of regret when they felt they fell short, risking an adverse effect on their colleagues' opinion of their character. The point of the 'desired Hephaestus character' was that people should shape their behaviour according to the moral pull that the company exerted. They were learning the difference between right and wrong, accepting and acknowledging their need for correction. Casey thought it worthy of remark that this new culture seemed to be more attractive to older employees. For her the explanation lay in the familiarity of the attitudes they were being asked to assume: '[t]he new culture is an effort to revive an old Protestant bourgeois self with a strong superego that will once again goad employees into hard work, devotion and productive service, and away from self-indulgence, rebelliousness and cynicism' (Casey, 1995: 161).

Rather like Sennett, Casey explained the need for an ersatz morality as the result of structural change rather than the broader social change implied by demoralization. She referenced Bellah and Lasch and mentioned cultural narcissism and ambivalence. She described a more general crisis in the social that was not just to do with the loss of the old communities and occupations but was brought on by a postmodern loss of faith in the promises of modernity. Nevertheless, when she argued that '[t]he new team-family displaces and compensates for the loss of these older forms of identification and solidarity ... employees find that there is nowhere to go [at work] except to the team's simulated sociality and relative psychic comfort' (Casey, 1995: 123–4), she identified technological and organizational change as the root cause of 'the loss of older industrial and occupational belongingness and identifications' (ibid.: 131).

Instead of finding a moral crisis, Casey interpreted the need for a new workplace culture as a consequence of a 'crisis in the *social*' (ibid.: 132, emphasis in original). Industrial production made problems for the social (alienation and anomie) but these were solved by the growth of occupational and class communities and solidarity. Post-industrial society destroyed these communities and created the need for synthetic substitutes because sociality (simulated or otherwise) was a necessary condition of production. Put simply, companies had to make their workers feel solidarity with each other (and not alienated or exploited) to keep production going. This was really not so far from welfare capitalism, or even Elton Mayo, but I doubt it fully represents the interviewees who told Casey 'Hephaestus is like a very moralistic, righteous parent. It's the kind of parent everyone should be lucky enough to have ... It's a very moral company. It does the right thing' (Casey, 1995: 104).

In respect of the familiar speculation about the extent to which workplace culture is internalized or merely tolerated, Casey argued

89

there might be effects on behaviour outside work which were not of the type Hephaestus might wish for. Some employees appeared to have grown ever more cynical and Casey was told by some respondents that they were *less* likely to socialize with colleagues after hours because there was enforced sociality at work. Casey suggested that one common reaction to the new culture was a strategic decision to 'capitulate' which allowed Hephaestus employees to remain cynical and narcissistic, shunning the public sphere and civil society and remaining privatized, individualistic consumers. To sweeten the pill these employees could take pleasure in the narcissistic, and perhaps sexual, gratifications on offer at work. Their part of the bargain involved them becoming 'dependent, over-agreeable, compulsive in dedication and diligence, passionate about the product and the company' (ibid.: 191).

The fact that simulated sociality did not bring the same rewards as genuine sociality but merely masked insecurity and a war of all against all[15] made it all the more obvious that employers were relying on their employees' acts of faith. Managers tried to persuade their employees that work could be understood with human-belief logic. Casey showed that, not surprisingly, this belief sometimes wavered but she also showed how the success of these efforts depended on peoples desire to put their faith in something (see also Pattison, 1997). Casey understood that at its heart the new culture depended upon, perhaps consisted of, a new way of believing and in her final pages she discussed the 'secular revival of early modern religious forms in corporate culture' which involved the 'reinvocation of religious rites to provide not only structure and meaning, but legitimation for corporate changes that irreligious or disbelieving employees would find unacceptable' (Casey, 1995: 192).

More recently Casey turned her attention to a spiritual revival which could be understood as evidence of emerging resistance to demoralization in the wider culture (Fevre 2000b; Maclagan, 1998; Pattison, 1997). Spiritual revival, particularly among highly-paid and highly-valued employees, might be threatening to corporations which fear people discovering a new set of priorities and finding something else to focus on than work. Yet Casey found that management gurus and consultants were taking part in the spiritual revival themselves: '[t]he programmes currently extolled by organization culturalists and management motivators now overtly encompass the utilization of religio-affective, desecularized, impulses and non-economically rational values emerging among even the mainstream professional middle class' (Casey, 2002: 209). Casey considered that, in spite of appearances, this kind of culture would only be welcomed by the corporations if it was thought to be of help to profit and production. The gurus might be sincere in their beliefs but organizations were only interested in turning their employees' interests in spirituality to their own ends. In any event, to Casey this suggested that managers were running out of motivational ideas.

Casey suggested that Hephaestus largely failed to blur the distinction between work and non-work. In her study, manual workers were particularly resistant to such attempts and a British study by Collinson (1994) suggested that manual workers were not as easily persuaded to swap cynicism for what they saw as American attempts to co-opt workers into the managerial cause. These workers were adamant that they would keep work separate from the rest of their lives, and continue to wage the daily war of stealing time (including the time they needed to work on their own account) and goods from their employers. They thought managers were paid to manage and that this meant them joining battle with the workforce to pursue the company's aims. It was pointless (and perhaps morally dubious) to try to persuade workers to manage themselves as part of their jobs. They saw any attempt to persuade them that their interests were identical with the interests of their managers as an American import which would not take root in the British workplace.

Of course some of this resistance to change in organizational culture was overcome in time, especially where incoming employers established new workplaces in green-field sites (Garrahan and Stewart, 1992), but as British workers increasingly gave the appearance of co-operation with, if not enthusiasm for, the new workplace culture, researchers also found that they might turn the new, ersatz morality against the managers who introduced it. In a study of a British supermarket chain, Rosenthal et al. (1997) showed how service sector workers took on board the language of service excellence through training, but used this new morality to evaluate the way they were treated by management. If it was correct for managers to judge the behaviour of workers towards customers according to such criteria, then why should the behaviour of managers not be judged in this way? Other studies confirmed similar attempts to turn the morality against managers in small but significant ways.

Korczynski et al. (2000) studied the role of the customer service representative (CSR) at call centres in the USA, Australia and Japan:

> Management, driven by efficiency requirements, wanted CSRs to relate to a disembodied concept of the customer. CSRs, for whom a central satisfying aspect of the job involved helping specific customers, preferred to identify with embodied customers. This contradiction was also carried through in the considerable resistance to the management attempts to introduce elements of sales into the predominantly service jobs of the CSRs. (ibid.: 684)

In a British study of call-centre management Lankshear et al. (2001) found that staff took on board attitudes to customer care that fitted with their managers' expectations but added that this had a lot to do with the employees' own notions of moral behaviour:

> it is too simple to see this simply as an internalised form of self-discipline. Evidence that matters were more complex is provided by the difficulties ... management had in persuading agents to increase revenue by being more sales orientated, particularly by persuading agents to take more expensive packages ... as one manager put it: 'We've tried time and again to get them to sell and they won't do it. They do everything else we ask them to do, but *they will not sell*.' (Lankshear et al., 2001: 603, emphasis in original)

The agents confirmed this: they didn't want to 'sound too pushy', tried to treat everyone the same no matter how big the booking, and thought it was *right* to let the customer decide what they could afford (ibid.: 604).

Martin Parker found evidence of a diverse but powerful upsurge of opposition to managerial power and legitimacy which might turn ersatz moralities against managers as a tactic: 'mission statements are intended to serve particular interests, but they *also* might be used to subvert the probable intentions of ... managers' (Parker, 2002: 59–60, italics in original). Parker also thought it hopeful that identity and morality were taking root in work rather than in private life (where morality might once have been on surer ground). If your work gave you a solid identity as a member of a community, you would 'act "generously", give enormous time, effort and care to matters that, from a selfish utility-maximizing point of view, make little calculative sense' (ibid.: 77). Of course we have seen in the previous chapter how such an identity can have unwelcome effects for partners and children who are left outside the community.

When Hochschild (1997) returned to the subject of the work-family balance with her study of 'Amerco' (see Chapter 2) she confirmed the observations of others such as Casey about the way the relationship between work and the rest of people's lives was being affected by their managers' attempts to manipulate culture. In essence Hochschild's later work synthesized the concerns of her two earlier books: it was the moral entrepreneurship of managers that led their employees to work longer and longer hours. Hochschild's respondents were generally neither hostile, or ambivalent towards the culture associated with Total Quality Management (TQM), indeed, empowerment and all the positive aspects of this morality actually made people feel good about turning up at the office: '[i]n many ways the workplace appeared to be a site of benign social engineering where workers came to feel appreciated, honored, and liked' (1997: 43).

When Amerco's managers spoke about TQM, they talked about 'engineering culture' and 'managing values' and employees, especially those higher up, deliberated all this and took it seriously. Amerco employees did not wear their wedding rings but they did wear their company pins and tee shirts – this was a minority activity for enthusiasts in Hephaestus – and they turned up to the 'company sponsored ritual gatherings' in droves (ibid.). Like Casey, Hochschild understood that 'the company borrowed culture from family and community ... explored ways to make friendship work for the benefit of the company' (ibid.: 19). In consequence, 'Amerco employees spoke warmly, happily and seriously of "belonging to the Amerco family" and everywhere there were visible symbols of this belonging' (ibid.: 44).

In Hochschild's analysis the moral element of cultural engineering was always close to surface: 'a message such as "valuing the individual" or "honoring diversity" seemed moral, unifying, and agreeable' (ibid.: 19). Company surveys 'provided a way for workers to cast a moral vote on company matters' (ibid.: 21); workers operated under 'the moral mantle of Total Quality' (ibid.: 209). There were official and unofficial 'recognition ceremonies', reciprocity and altruism were encouraged and

> By officially espousing 'values', Amerco had established itself as something other than a cold, economic machine ... Amerco now said to its workers, in effect 'You don't have to check your values at the door. We have them here. Morally speaking, you are protected, safe, as if you were at home.' (ibid.: 20)

93

In Hochschild's view, many employees made the implied category mistake and took the ersatz morality for a real one:

> While Amerco's goal was production and profit, with its mission statements and surveys it wasn't simply trying to seem like a moral world; it was trying to be a moral world. It's not surprising, then, that employees would get upset if they thought a colleague or superior wasn't 'walking the talk' on one or another of Amerco's missions. (ibid.: 21)

Hochschild noted the way in which the success of the engineered culture depended on faith ('Under Total Quality at Amerco, the worker is not a machine; he's a believer', ibid.: 206) Like Casey, she was struck by the religious strain in the ersatz morality and the similarities with revivalism (see also Barley and Kunda, 1992; Pattison, 1997). She described a 'Large Group Change Event' for manual workers at a failing plant that was 'like a revival meeting ... Its purpose was to convince each worker to renew his commitment not to his spouse or church but to his workplace' (ibid.: 206). The event was successful to the extent that the employees 'vowed to "cast out the devil" of taking petty revenge on the company for the tediousness of their jobs' (ibid.: 208). The purpose of the meeting was to get 'these blue-collar workers to take on a managerial viewpoint in which people skills matter more than brawn, in which you and the company both should care about what type of personality you have and how it best suits the workplace' (ibid.: 208).

Amerco seems to have taken even more care than Hephaestus to 'put thought and effort into blurring the distinction between work and play ... "dress down" days ... company picnics, holiday parties ... free cokes ... Amerco has also made a calculated attempt to take on the role of helpful relative in relation to employee problems at work and at home' (ibid.: 205). Amerco provided free courses to be taken in company time which helped their employees to cope with themselves and their relationships with others. The company was helping them to improve their character and become more effective human beings at the same time:

> As a result, many Amerco managers and professionals earnestly confessed to me that the company had helped them grow as human beings in ways that improved their ability to cope with problems at home ... One Amerco handbook for its managers lists a series of 'qualities for excellence at work' that would be useful at home – an employee would be judged on whether he or she 'seeks feedback on personal behaviours', senses changes in attention level and mood', or 'adapts personality to the situation and people involved'. (ibid.: 205–6)

But was it always so easy for companies to abolish the familiar distinction between work and everything else? Given the resistance to American management innovations among British workers – as described by Collinson and others (see p. 91) – it is well worth investigating the fate of such managerial initiatives in a British setting.

Grugulis et al. (2000) were particularly interested in the ways in which managers systematically set about using new culture management practices to obliterate the distinction between work and non-work:

> reminiscent as this may be of earlier attempts to influence and control the moral character of employees, new culture management practices are highly distinctive. While traditionally social life and participation in appropriate community activities were considered just as important as diligence within the workplace, modern character formation emphasises workplace participation to the exclusion of all else. The work provided is often interesting and responsible, a degree of autonomy may be granted; but the price paid for doing interesting work is that the employee has little opportunity to do anything but work. 'Free' time is captured and colonised by the employer. (ibid.: 99)

Grugulis et al. supported this view with a case study of what, on the face of it, might have been an extreme example. Nevertheless, their study of a successful UK software consultancy served as an example of what a revitalized sociology of economic behaviour could achieve and it is worth discussing their findings at some length.

The company that Grugulis et al. studied had started life as the group of friends of a charismatic owner-manager and had since grown rapidly to employ 150 people. The leading item on the company culture statement issued to employees told them to 'Have Fun and Enjoy Work' and this culture was promoted by a culture manager who organized leisure time so that staff and their families were immersed in, and constantly engaged in reproducing, this culture outside working hours. The culture that prevailed *at work* was doggedly fun-filled (also see Hendricks and Ludeman, 1997). According to Grugulis et al., internal training sessions were indistinguishable from company social events. They were dedicated to the same purpose (the renewal of company culture) and used very much the same methods (employees were expected to wear fancy dress and there was much playing of games). Families were even encouraged to attend these training events in a further blurring of the distinction between work and non-work.

The company founder, together with the specially appointed culture manager, made sure that the non-working hours of employees were occupied by a large number of company social events in which they were expected 'to *want* to participate and to actively enjoy themselves' (Grugulis et al., 2000: 103). The company therefore took care to judge the fit between new recruits and the desired culture during selection and recruitment. Interviews were always timed to coincide with a national charity fund-raising event which staff, including the interviewers, marked by wearing costumes and playing japes. The way that candidates reacted to all of this was evaluated as part of the selection process.

Once hired, many staff 'were vividly aware of the purposive nature of social events and approved of them wholeheartedly' (ibid.: 112). The selection process was not foolproof and some workers who could not abide the culture were hired and these employees subsequently resigned from the company in spectacular circumstances or were dismissed (for example, because they did not attend enough social events).[16] No matter whether there was a degree of self-selection of employees who could live in this culture, Grugulis et al. found that they were disturbed by this form of 'normative control': '[w]e also found this form of control *morally* problematic. The mechanics of conversation, social events and shared jokes that fuelled its success are also the stuff of which more innocent, social relationships are made and we felt uncomfortable with their commodification' (ibid.: 112, emphasis added).

The researchers felt the culture had 'the potential to offer certain freedoms and contains distinct totalitarian tendencies' (ibid.: 113). Combined with their feeling that this form of control was 'morally problematic', these insights amounted to the rudiments of an authentic critique of economic behaviour within which the sociology of economic behaviour could lay bare some of the hidden costs of working in the company they studied. Once more the researchers raised the question of whether *pretending* to go along with the company's demands might be enough. The answer to the question about how much of themselves employees must put into their work might just be 'everything' (Bowring, 2002; Gorz, 1999).

CONCLUSION

The Hawthorne studies should be remembered as a stark example of the kind of wrong turning which set economic sociology on the road to perfidy. Early economic sociology set about undermining the morality of workers' ideas of how much they should be asked be to put into their work where it might have used these lay ideas as a resource to help society evaluate industrial work. With such evaluation sociology would have been able to inform people about the kind of world that was being made around them and help them to think about whether this was the sort of world they really wanted.

As it grew more mature, economic sociology showed no inclination to import lay values to evaluate the world of work on behalf of society but it did take an increasingly positive view of the persistence of non-economic values in the workplace. In common with some managers, economic sociologists could even see how such values could be turned to economic ends. From this point onwards both managers and sociologists began to believe that business could interfere with people's morality and make them more productive. Hochschild problematized the effect of such interference on employees but she also showed how morality was being domesticated, and even synthesized, for business use in a world where morality really was an increasingly rare *commodity*.

It became increasingly common for companies to try to persuade their customers and even their staff into making a category error in which an ersatz morality was created in the place of the morality that economic rationality had undermined as part of the process of demoralization. The second half of the chapter summarized studies of attempts to create such an ersatz morality using the vehicle of employee empowerment. Kunda, Casey and Hochschild (once more) monitored the success of such attempts to create ersatz morality. Research seemed to suggest that the success rate was rising over time but there was some suggestion that these ersatz moralities might one day be used to judge the companies that brought them to life (Parker, 2002).

One of the key indicators of the strength of an ersatz morality was the extent to which it blurred boundaries between work and non-work. In a post-modern world management gurus and consultants were telling managers what sort of people they needed to be 'in order to be happy and morally conscious citizens with fulfilling lives' (ten Bos, 2000: 24). According to ten Bos, these gurus and consultants insisted on the same blurring of work and non-work, the public and private in managers' lives. Just as workers might one day turn an ersatz morality to better use, so ten Bos thought the kind of management fashion being promoted by the gurus was a kind of step forward too. It could not help but be an improvement on managers' devotion to rationality and pursuit of managerial utopias. The next chapter will discuss management's utopian tendencies in some detail.

NOTES

1 The following passage draws upon my review of Sennett's book for *Work, Employment and Society*.

2 Compare to E.P. Thompson (1971, 1974) who shows – as we might hope a historian would – that morality was brought to capitalism, not created there. We might also compare Sennett and others who have thought morality was once created at work to Robert Tressell whose fictional study of the painters and decorators of Hastings presents a view much closer to Thompson's.

3 Demand for emotional labour is lower when airlines are trying to cut costs: in such conditions flight attendants avoid eye contact with passengers in order to minimize their requests for service.

4 Cf. Sayer (2000a, 2000b) who employs the term in its traditional usage (Scott, 1976; Thompson, 1971): '"Moral economy" can indicate both the ways in which economic actions are influenced by moral sentiments and norms, and a standpoint form which we can *evaluate* economic arrangements, including those which have everything to do with power and interest' (Sayer, 2000b). I can quite understand why Sayer wants to use it that way but if we use other terms like political economy, or even the sociology of economic behaviour, we can reserve 'moral economy' for this more specific usage.

5 Fear is mentioned (see, for example, Hochschild, 1983: 107) but gets much less attention than we might expect in a study of flight attendants but perhaps these expectations have been altered by the events of 11 September 2001.

6 As in the theories of Goffman (1959) and Blau (1964), the airline passengers in receipt of the flight attendants' smiles and ministrations find their moral standing confirmed and even enhanced.

7 Indeed, it sometimes seemed as if the companies they studied were demanding ever more extreme examples of just this sort of behaviour (see p. 83).

8 For example, the 'party selling' in people's homes which is an even more blatant example of the way profit is insinuated into a gift exchange Davis (1972, 1973) – Hochschild also makes the link to party selling.

9 An advantage that was soon lost because it was incorporated as an industry standard and simply taken for granted until it conflicted with later cost-cutting initiatives.

10 It was not simply causal incivility that distinguished the working environment but some passengers' determination not to join in the illusion: they would apparently have preferred to be served by robots (1983: 108).

11 These include the makers of the movie *Toy Story II* which satirizes the flight attendants' ever-present smile and determinedly sunny disposition to great effect while simultaneously giving generous product placement to Barbie.

12 Gorz reports a study in which undeclared economic activity increased at the same time as legitimate work (1989: 118).

13 There has been comparatively little research on those attempts that were made in the service sector to respond to demoralization by changing work and technology. Call centres (see below) seem to offer increased technological determination and surveillance of customer-employee interaction and would figure as one of the most popular examples of such a response.

14 Gillespie (1991) reports on the management ideology of the 1920s in which workers were to be made to feel part of the corporation, and prized by management, and therefore able to live more wholesome lives and be contented citizens. Gillespie quotes the Hawthorne works manager addressing senior supervisors, in 1929, on the 'social and moral role of industry'. In this address he explained that the workers were going to be saved from the moral effects of their own misguided actions. Workers would be helped to stop wasting time at work and this would restore their self-respect (Gillespie, 1991: 145).

15 The fact that project teams have a limited life makes it possible to square this circle.

16 In 2001 a compensation claim was brought by a Jewish employee of a London financial firm who had been required to dress up in a Nazi uniform as part of the fun-filled atmosphere of his place of employment.

four
management

So far, much of our attention has been focused on the omission of the moral element that, I have suggested, is an essential component in the renaissance of the sociology of economic behaviour. It is necessary for us to rediscover this element if we are to breathe life into the sociology of economic behaviour, but this is not enough to guarantee that economic sociology has been superseded. In addition to rediscovering a moral purpose, we must take steps to disarm the opposition. One of its most potent weapons has been the claim for efficacy made by economic rationality. The sociology of economic behaviour will always be disadvantaged unless this claim can be challenged.

MANAGERIAL EFFICIENCY

Zygmunt Bauman explored a similar difficulty in respect of claims made for the efficacy of science and technology (see, for example, Bauman, 1993). The operation of efficiency-rationalities within the corporations and governments that had responsibility for the development and disposition of modern technology led to the subordination of other goals and the courting of ecological disaster. The idea that bureaucratic management could produce hell on earth by concentrating on providing the means to any given end was already a familiar theme in Bauman's work. Mannheim (1935)[1] had explored the way bureaucratic rationality could produce results – world wars, the Depression – which would have been deplored by those who put the bureaucracy in motion. In Bauman's work the tension between formal and substantive rationality was given a specifically moral twist. The spell of efficiency-rationality led to the complete displacement of morality: it was always too late to undo the effects of bureaucracy by the time moral questions were raised (see also Stivers, 1994, 1999).

Bauman's best-known example of the displacement of morality by efficiency-rationality is the Holocaust (Bauman, 1989). Bauman argued that a genocide of anything like this scale could not have happened without bureaucratic management and means-ends rationality. The Nazis could never have accomplished it and, indeed, they would never even have settled on the Final Solution to the Jewish Problem without it. Why then did we continue to privilege efficiency – the rationality that made bureaucratic management the be-all and end-all for Weber (see below) – when this privileged sort of rationality got millions killed? It squeezed out all morality, all feeling for fellow human beings, and how could we say it is the best of all rationalities when it led to such inhuman results? But it was in Bauman's subsequent work that he developed the line of thinking that will be followed in this chapter.

In Bauman (1993), for example, he explained that technological rationality could never deliver on its grandiose claims. It only appeared to be able to deliver on its promise of efficacy by 'close focusing' on one aspect of problem-solving and judiciously ignoring all the problems that had either not been solved or, indeed, had been newly-created as part of the technological fix. In this chapter I will not be trying to suggest that economic rationality produces morally undesirable ends but rather that it does not work. The idea that economic rationality works in the sense that it delivers measurable goods is fundamental to both economic sociology and managerialism. If we can show that managerialism cannot help but promise more than it can ever deliver, we will undermine the present basis for managerial legitimacy and thereby open up the possibility of subjecting management to moral critique. At the same time we will also undermine the claims to efficacy that economic sociology depends on for its pre-eminence (Etzioni, 1988). While managerialism is able to hide behind its claims to efficiency, it seems to be above criticism, but if these claims can be shown to be ideological, and without a sound evidential base, then the playing field might be levelled and we would be able to measure managerialist priorities against moral ones (Shenhav, 1999).

To give a concrete example from the previous chapter, the research by Casey, Hochschild, Kunda, Du Gay and Salaman showed that managers manipulated the moral urges of employees for their own ends. The idea that managers have to manufacture an ersatz morality to make up for societal demoralization is an important one, but it does not do much to disarm the claims to efficacy for economic rationality which underpin managerial authority. In fact, that claim is bolstered: we cannot help but admire the way corporations resorted, with apparent success, to cultural engineering to keep on accumulating capital and, creating large numbers of attractive and rewarding jobs which brought prosperity for all. Thus the behaviour of corporations has not been made a proper subject for critique and the reason for this failing lies in our acceptance that cultural engineering has brought results, for example, higher profits.

In essence, this remains the view summarized by Michael Rose when he described the way in which employee sentiments could be shaped by employers as part of the 'fifth dimension of control' (Rose, 1988). Allowing for some change in terminology, evidence that employers have pursued economic ends with normative means, and especially with normative control, dates back at least as far as Robert Owen. Rose thought that making people feel they *wanted* to do things rather than just telling them what to do was an essential, and intriguing, component of industrial behaviour. With the help of sociologists like Bendix (1956) he described the inculcation of attachment to the workplace, the need for positive consent to capitalism among the workforce, and of the value to employers of self-discipline and the right sort of positive employee attitude. To the extent that Rose explained that capitalism was manipulating the workers' hearts and minds, this sounds like a critique but it misses the point by making morality entirely instrumental. Economic sociology is able to encompass the idea that economic rationality enlists morality in a subaltern role without even the faintest suggestion of a challenge to economic rationality because economic rationality's claims (as enshrined in management practices) to omniscience, omnipotence and *effectiveness* remain beyond criticism (Gorz, 1989). In fact, these claims have been reinforced and validated (Shenhav, 1999; ten Bos, 2000). If managers are shaping sentiments in the cause of effectiveness, this simply proves how clever and resourceful they are!

The most hopeful signs in the work of people like Rose were suggestions that sociology should now attend to the way management ideology played an active, and perhaps decisive, role in constructing the things managers had to do and their right to do them. Although this insight could be assimilated along with the revalidated supremacy of economic rationality, we at least began to entertain the possibility that, at some stage in the future, the fact that management required an ideology might one day be turned against it. In this chapter I hope to show that this has now happened.

101

MANAGERIAL LEGITIMACY AND MANAGERIAL RATIONALITY

Gillespie's account of the Hawthorne experiments (see chapter 3) shows that much of what the researchers saw as their contribution to social science was already in the minds of the managers who began the experiments. Indeed, many of the 'results' of the Hawthorne experiments which have subsequently been seen as new and exciting were already counted as received wisdom in the wider business community. Even before the experiments were planned, at the very height of

America's efficiency craze, American management had been concerned about demoralization and anxious to explore the possibilities of 'human engineering' (Gillespie, 1991:32). There had already been some research in pursuit of 'grand plans for a nationally selected and socially engineered workforce' (ibid., 35) but the Hawthorne experiments were American industry's big research investment in this project (most of the investment came from Western Electric itself although Mayo also had wider sources of corporate funding).

In fact the Hawthorne results were as confusing and puzzling as those produced by earlier, smaller-scale studies. The really significant feature of the whole episode was the way that the researchers interpreted their confusing evidence in a way that bolstered the position of personnel managers. They gave personnel managers their 'professional ideology' (ibid., 238) which included a social scientific seal of approval on their monopoly of knowledge and power. In order to achieve this, the Hawthorne researchers had to impose the appearance of scientific certainty on confused and contradictory data. Gillespie (1991) shows that, even in the final stages of the experiments, the researchers, and particularly the Western Electric managers, were not at all sure what most of the data meant. None of this uncertainty and confusion appeared in the publications of Mayo, Roethlisberger and Dickson which were, instead, vindications of the managers' aspiration to 'grand plans' (Gillespie, 1991). The researchers told managers what they wanted to hear and in the process they were able to put social science on the same elevated plane as management. The claims of both social science and management to power and knowledge were built on the same very shaky foundations.

This chapter will show that economic sociology has been based on a false premise, a premise that it shares with managerial theory and managerial practice. The premise is that managers have, or can be capable of, an impossible kind of expertise and competence, a kind of technical omnipotence in fact (ten Bos, 2000). This is a false claim but, because it is usually left unexamined, it allows managers to exercise legitimate authority over other employees (Gillespie, 1991; Shenhav, 1999). Put simply, their authority lies in widespread social beliefs about the efficacy of reason in the direction of human affairs which obscure or make secondary (for example, they become unfortunate side-effects) the moral character and consequences of managerial behaviour (Gorz, 1989).

In practice, the effectiveness of management is very much a hit-and-miss affair (Pattison, 1997). It is always hard to know where to look for the evidence of this effectiveness, hard to measure its effects (especially versus other possible causes), and hard to know what would might have happened anyway without management intervention (might things have even been better?). No doubt there are good and bad managers and good and bad approaches to management (although these might be a lot less generalizable than people often imagine) but it is frequently not easy, or even possible, to tell the good from the bad except in extreme situations or over a very long period of time. These hard-to-win, but still qualified, judgements have little to do with the sort of knowledge that apparently underpins the managerial legitimacy which we have become accustomed to taking for granted (Gillespie, 1991).

The recognition that management is a hit-and-miss affair is not what gives managers the right to tell others what to do, to (sometimes) strongly influence the course of their lives, or the right to receive high salaries and fancy fringe benefits. Managerial legitimacy is derived from other sources including the institutions of managerialism. Telling good from bad management may be a very imprecise science but this is not the way management is written up in the pitches of management consultancies, the brochures of MBA courses and the how-to-manage titles that fill the bookstores. There is nothing here about management being a hit-and-miss affair, about there always being some doubt about whether it has worked, or in which direction. In the managerial(ist) institutions the ubiquitous assumption is made that good and bad management can be specified in the abstract and in advance. Indeed, it is a fundamental tenet that the principles of good management can be codified, taught, certificated, and sold as a service (Shenhav, 1999).

103

As Alasdair MacIntyre pointed out, the content of these codes, lessons and services changes completely from one decade to another and this is a potentially dangerous thing for managerial legitimacy (MacIntyre, 1985). If the fundamental principles of management can change so thoroughly and so often, we might begin to wonder whether it makes sense to think of management in this way at all. Should people begin to wonder whether management really is much more like a hit-and-miss activity in which reliable judgements about efficacy are hard to make, two popular arguments can be deployed to show that management is indeed a superior and highly efficient activity. First, it can be argued that the fundamental principles of management change only because the circumstances change and that their mutability is therefore highly rational. For example, what might be good management for one decade would become bad management for another because there was a technological revolution which required a radically different approach to work organization and the management of people. The second possibility is that the specification of the principles in one period or the other was wrong and could stand correction. This solution tends to be favoured by management gurus who use it as the major selling point of their latest book. Tom Peters, for example, became famous for getting into the best-seller lists with books which showed where his previous advice had been flawed.

There is a third explanation of the way in which the fundamental principles of management change so thoroughly and so often. This explanation suggests that the principles are never right – in the sense that the institutions of managerialism claim them to be – and that it is not possible to achieve the aims that anyone would apparently have in mind when specifying the principles of best management practice. This is not to deny that when people are educated in these principles they change their behaviour. Nor is it to deny that, when they are implemented, management programmes have real effects on people. All this explanation suggests is that MBA-qualified managers and 'world-class' companies (that 'pursued excellence') all have the same hit-and-miss experience of the efficacy of management. Productivity might increase, but it will never be clear whether this is due to the latest management programme, or the pay-off from the MBA training, or from some other cause such as greater capital investment. Beyond these considerations there may be hidden costs associated with the increased productivity (more sickness and accidents perhaps) and nobody will ever really know how things would have worked out without management intervention. Finally, and crucially, nobody will ever be confident that this same intervention will produce the same result elsewhere.

104   The practitioners of omnipotent management would take issue with this[2] but there is little evidence to support their defence. In the previous chapter we noted how the latest generation of managers were engineering culture to make their companies profitable but what proof did we really have that TQM or HRM were actually profitable (Barley and Kunda, 1992)? In fact the usual defence is not to produce evidence but to argue that managers would not go in for such things – or, at least, they would not *keep* doing them – if they were not good for business. Etzioni pointed out that most of the commentaries which claimed to be able to identify the secrets of business success were 'highly deductive: "Firms must have arisen because ..." Empirical evidence is scant. The very fact that rather inefficient firms exist next to quite efficient ones, in the same industry, for long periods of time, casts grave doubt on this approach' (1988: 178).

I have already tried to argue at several points in previous chapters that the 'business case' for various common managerial actions is neither obvious nor uncontested (remember the business case for family-friendly policies, for example). We can now develop this initial insight into a deeper critique that will take us beyond the weaknesses and limitations of economic sociology. The reason why the 'business case' is always so hard to pin down is that reason – economic rationality, bureaucratic rationality, and managerial rationality as propagated by McKinsey and on a thousand MBAs – is not as efficacious as it is claimed to be. The basic problem with all of these different incarnations of rationality is that they are claiming to be able to do the impossible: to shape human behaviour in complex environments in a reliable way (MacIntyre, 1985). Of course the crucial point is what is meant by 'reliable' since it is the *degree* of effectiveness that is really at issue here. I am not suggesting that managers cannot make crude predictions about the effect of managerial decisions that will often be borne out. What I am suggesting is that they do not have the power to shape behaviour that they lay claim to when they ask us to grant them great power and an unequal share of available resources (Gillespie, 1991; Shenhav, 1999).

This argument should not be confused with the suggestion that there are practical (and, indeed, economic) limitations on the extent to which managers can engage in rational behaviour (March and Simon, 1958). I am not arguing that the limits are put on the efficacy and, indeed, the goals of management, as a consequence of the difficulties of getting hold of enough information. This may be true but here we are discussing more fundamental questions, indeed we are putting in question the basic nature of the whole management enterprise.[3] I do not think that managers would have anything more than very imperfect rationality even if they had perfect information. Perfect information would not help because the managerial enterprise is inflated to promise far more than it can deliver, and much of this inflation follows from management's ambition to control the behaviour of human beings (Gillespie, 1991). Management speaks as if it only had to deal with widgets – for example, we now hear of management's abilities to 'engineer' people and of the sophisticated 'metrics' that inform and confirm its judgments[4] – and widgets, like the subjects of natural science, are predictable in a way that human beings are not.[5]

Shenhav's (1999) account of the role of engineers in the construction of management in the USA explained exactly why management learnt to speak of people as things. The role of engineers was written out of history by the managerialists who succeeded them but, using contemporary records and publications, Shenav documented the political campaign that engineers began in the nineteenth century and won in the early decades of the twentieth century. The ultimate aim of this campaign was to proselytize a kind of social theory which saw the kind of *technique* analysed by Stivers (1994) as the solution to every problem. When applied to management, this theory decreed people should be treated like the mechanical parts in an engineering problem. Shenav saw this as a category error (see Chapter 3) in which a type of sense-making was applied in an inappropriate place. This category error also entailed the colonization of the moral sphere and Shenav supplied examples of the social institutions that were responsible for this colonization. The more interesting of these were not the expected institutions of managerialism but, rather, the 'efficiency societies' which were immensely influential immediately prior to the First World War in both the domestic and industrial spheres.

The goal of these institutions was the diffusion of a more refined and rigorous common sense in the sense this term was defined in Chapter 2. Shenhav showed how engineers constructed management as a superior form of common sense.[6] The goals and methods of management arise with those refinements of cognition that have the same basic uses and limitations as common sense (Fevre, 2000b). We know that common sense can be self-contradictory and misleading and that mere possession of common sense is not considered a good basis for the legitimate monopolization of power over others. Maybe the refinements that are built into managerial common sense justify giving it some limited authority, but the case made by the institutions of managerialism for managerial authority knows no limits (Gillespie, 1991). The general case for managerial authority is not based on the effectiveness of individual managers but on the technical efficacy of management *in principle* (Pattison, 1997; Shenhav, 1999).

No management theorist – and, indeed, no manager – would claim that every theory is a good one and that every manager is doing their job perfectly. It would be recognized that some managers are better at management than others, and that some management theories are better than others, *but* there would be nothing accidental, unpredictable or mysterious about this observed variation. It is fundamental to managerial legitimacy that we all accept that the reason why some managers (and theories) are better than others is that someone has not properly understood what is required. Problems are always caused by the failings of the individuals concerned, never the limitations of the enterprise they are engaged in.

Of course, given what was said earlier about the scarcity of clear evidence for the efficacy of 'good' management, it is rarely necessary for managers and management theories to be judged by any proof of their success. The usual test is simply how persuasive other people find their logic and their methods. If, over time, evidence that this type of management is ineffective becomes impossible to ignore, this can be written off as an isolated mistake rather than as the unavoidable consequence of putting too much faith in management's capabilities. If pressed further, most of the believers in managerialism would adopt an evolutionary perspective: management is getting closer and closer to the ideal all the time, mistakes are still made but these are rooted out by natural selection in short order, and to prove it, just look at the wealth and power of modern corporations. But what if this wealth and power had different sources and the real function of the notion of management potency was only to justify managers' monopoly of the wealth and power they did very little to create (Gillespie, 1991)?

In sum, the orthodoxy (and not just among managers) is that managers manage in order to make profits: they do this job very well and the efficacy of management justifies managerial authority. Yet real managers do not always care to make profits (Etzioni, 1988; Ohmae, 1983) and Berg and his colleagues (1979) found managers who were only interested in initiatives like the Quality of Working Life programme to the extent that this gave them an opportunity to boost their prestige (see also Burns and Stalker, 1961). Nor do managers always agree on what constitutes profit or know how to make one (Johnson, 1992). Generalized goals such as maximizing profits, minimizing costs, maximizing output, or increasing productivity can be surprisingly hard to operationalize and, in any case, frequently contradict each other (Etzioni, 1988). More difficulties arise if we ask exactly how managers might work towards these aims. There is never one obvious way to achieve economically rational goals. As Stephen Pattison showed, using a range of examples drawn from public sector management, 'much of modern management practice depends on unproven and unprovable faith assumptions about reality' (1997: 28). What managers should do and what they are for are not self-evident at all and there are no obvious answers to questions about the management role and what informs and even constitutes management practices (Grint, 1995; Maclagan, 1998). In the public sector the identification of the goals of economic rationality may be even more difficult: '[t]here is some evidence that VFM audits tend to prioritize that which can be measured and audited in economic terms – efficiency and economy – over that which is perhaps more ambiguous from this point of view – effectiveness or performance' (Power, 1997: 13). I am also going to suggest that managers are not as effective as they claim to be even when they have worked out what they think their goals should be.

In Chapter 5 I discuss the impossibility of making hiring and firing decisions in the way that is claimed to justify managerial authority (see also Fevre, 1984, 1992) in order to show just how far removed from the ideal of calculable, rational action employers' behaviour is. Knights and McCabe thought 'TQM's benefits are largely intangible' (1998: 451) and found TQM much less effective in controlling employees than its advocates or critics might think. They also explained why managers had a vested interest in portraying their behaviour as rational and effective: '[a]lthough management tend to conceal failure through deploying post hoc rationalisations ... TQM strategies may frequently fall short of "planned" intentions. Managers at all levels are inclined to rationalise behaviour and events in ways that secure their career and identity as competent managers' (Knights and McCabe, 1998: 450). In the bank Knights and McCabe studied, failure would jeopardize careers and/or necessitate more investment that would reflect badly on managers who were meant to concentrate on short-term cost savings and profits. Failure was not acknowledged and TQM (and indeed quality) was overridden by the need to concentrate on the short term and initiatives which could be clearly translated into costs savings.

Drawing conclusions from a British study mentioned in the previous chapter, Lankshear et al. (2001) explained 'that there are dangers in assuming that what participants say they do is necessarily what occurs' (ibid.: 604). Their study had brought into question managers' claims about the way job performance was measured because there was 'a genuine uncertainty among agents, supervisors and managers, about what counted as good performance (ibid.: 601). Harley (1999) reported an Australian study which showed 'empowering' initiatives had little effect, certainly not the widespread empowerment of employees, indeed, '[such] measures do not lead even to the *perception* of enhanced autonomy on the part of workers ... like many fads that have preceded it, empowerment does not appear to have the consequences that it is claimed to have' (ibid.: 59, emphasis in original). Scepticism about the efficacy of all such managerial initiatives was shared by others including Parker: '[t]here is simply no compelling evidence here that organizational culture – whatever it might be – is related to profitability, efficiency, job satisfaction and so on' (2000: 17).

My final justification for scepticism about management's more grandiose claims to efficacy is less empirical than philosophical but before I make this point it is worth remembering that one of the main purposes of this book is to show how economic sociology represents a diversion from the path on which classical sociology embarked, and perhaps even constitutes a betrayal of the founding fathers' vision. In support of this charge I will show how economic sociology has uncritically accepted the view that management has taken of itself.

We begin with the wrong turning taken by two 'Marxists', Marglin and Braverman. I will then explore examples of economic sociology – including several which were not thought to have anything in common with the Marxist approach – to show how they made the same mistake as Braverman and Marglin. Their common error not only involves seeing management's job as self-evident and eminently achievable, it also increasingly requires that the sociologist join forces with the manager. Throughout economic sociology it is axiomatic that managers manage to make profits and know how to do it (very well). Explicitly or implicitly, economic sociology confirms that their authority is grounded in their technical expertise, their mastery of rationality but, as we move away from the Marxist approach, we find economic sociology (along with other social science disciplines including psychology) actually joining in the construction of that technical expertise (Anthony, 1977; Gillespie, 1991; Shenhav, 1999). It is particularly galling that some of this work – for example, the classic study by Burns and Stalker – made clever use of empirical material that opened up the opportunities for a proper sociology of economic behaviour and then, irritatingly, marched off in the other direction.

WHAT DO BOSSES DO?

For Sidney Pollard, the economic historian, the overseer's lash was not a form of management but an alternative to it. He described the antecedents of modern management as physical force, varieties of legal compulsion including indentures, and sub-contracting (Pollard, 1965). Craft apprentices, prisoners, paupers and orphans did not have managers when they laboured in the first, experimental factories, nor did workers in the 'putting-out system' in textiles and other forms of gang work in textiles and coal mining. According to Pollard, subcontracting did not necessitate management because it was an alternative to *employment* (defined by the presence of a contract of some kind between an employer and an employee). Management came into being when employment did and that was why it was born with industrial capitalism. In pre-industrial society free labourers only laboured to the point at which their needs were satisfied (hence the 'backward-sloping supply curve of labour' characteristic of these societies). While this might be satisfactory when those labourers were working on their own account, or as part of a family, this would be highly unsatisfactory within an employment relationship. When it first appeared, management was rather like an exercise in domestication, breaking people in to this relationship.[7] Further development of the factory system entailed the institutionalization of the need for managers and, eventually, the creation of a distinct managerial role. Pollard made much of the increase in both the size – not simply of the workforce[8] – and complexity of enterprises as part of this development. From the 1830s in Britain, it began to make sense to speak of *managers* in the plural, and distrust of delegated servants was gradually replaced by acceptance of management as a separate function (see also Child, 1969).

Pollard's work provided the necessary context for Stephen Marglin's blissfully simple question, what do bosses do? Marglin's answer that bosses sought and exercised power over employees would have been approved by the great majority of economic sociologists[9] but he reached it by reasoning which might just as easily have been developed into an authentic critique of economic behaviour. According to Marglin (1974), management was not introduced as a technical solution to problems of increased scale and complexity. He disputed the idea that early capitalism displaced household production because specialization, the division of labour, and technology increased productivity. These

109

innovations did not increase productivity at all and the division of labour and centralized organization that made managers necessary were in fact introduced in order to redistribute income from the workers to entrepreneurs.

Without discipline and supervision the working class tended to cash in productivity gains in the form of increased leisure (the 'backward-sloping supply curve of labour' again). Management's discipline and supervision were needed to increase production (and reduce embezzlement) in the way that was needed if profits were to be produced and capital accumulated through reinvestment. Marglin thought the factory system had succeeded because it achieved more production at a given cost rather than because it increased workers' productivity once they were in the factories. Anyone who thought otherwise was using the deductive logic criticized by Etzioni (see p. 104). Just because the factory system had survived did not mean it was necessarily more efficient.

The fact that productivity did subsequently grow within the factory system only served to obscure the naked class interest that explained its genesis and this subsequent growth in productivity was not the consequence of hierarchical organization. It was still the case that specialization was needed to 'sustain the illusion that hierarchy is necessary for integrating the efforts of many into a marketable product' (Marglin, 1974: 78). This was not to deny that technological change could increase productivity but we should remember that this was the product rather than the cause of industrial capitalism and that factories were no more efficient than subcontracting 'until technological change was channelled exclusively into this mould' (ibid.: 95). Marglin's criticism of the notion that managers were needed because these managers' increased efficiency is invaluable. On this foundation he could begin to mount a critique which argued that it would be *better* if workers were not dominated in this way (Marglin cites Polanyi at this point in his argument).

The idea that innovation does not happen because it is more efficient but rather that this is just an excuse for economically and politically powerful classes to use innovation to change the distribution of income in their favour is an immensely powerful one (to which we will return in later chapters). The problem with Marglin's argument lay not in what he thought managers could not do (increase efficiency) but in what he was confident that they could do, namely, increase output and profits. Marglin steered his argument in entirely the wrong direction when he conceded that the better alternative (more leisure, personal and cultural integrity) might well be bought at the cost of lower output and wages. He was conceding without a fight the idea that managers increase production and in doing this he was conforming to the orthodox view in economic sociology that managerial power is effective.

The insertion of managers was a marvellous way of bringing about redistribution in favour of capitalists and getting managers involved in this way allowed capitalists to set the agenda for production (defining aims and so on). We need to be more wary of the implication that managers would have no difficulty in following this agenda. When Marglin argued that managers were inserted into production so that they could seize resources he was right. When he said they were inserted in production so that they could increase output and exploitation, he was wrong. Supervision and discipline did not give managers the reliable power to control production that Marglin thought they did.[10] Nor did supervision and discipline allow them to control the rate of exploitation by, for example, reducing the returns to labour for a given output. It has frequently been suggested in this book that the sort of management Marglin had in mind was very unreliable at meeting these aims and that many alternatives, including alternatives to hierarchical control, have been tried. Of course none of these alternatives have proved any more reliable: the difficulty here is the impossible aim, not the inadequate means employed to achieve it. In sum, we should conclude that the insertion of managers into production was legitimated by more than one misleading claim: that this would increase productivity *and* that this would increase profits and exploitation.

In economic sociology nothing about control is ever thought of as problematic. For capitalists control is never an ambiguous or obscure matter: they know that they want it, they know how to get it, and they know what to do with it when they have it – simply exploit! And exploitation is never an ambiguous matter either. It is always assumed to be self-evident how this is to be done, the only problem is that other capitalists know how to do it too and so there is always pressure to exploit more (and therefore to control more). This is all based on a gross misunderstanding of what bosses do and on some totally unrealistic assumptions about the possibilities of understanding and predicting human behaviour that underpin the general assumption about the efficacy of control.

'Marxist' economic sociology never corrected the misunderstanding or abandoned the unrealistic assumptions. The best it did was to admit that workers might resist managers' attempts to exercise control over them, and try to retain some control over their own actions. There will be more discussion of worker resistance later in the chapter, but for the present, it should be emphasized that 'Marxist' economic sociology departs from the classical sociology of economic behaviour. One proof of this is the way in which Marx's description of the increase in the 'detail division of labour' as one way of increasing capitalist exploitation was used by Braverman (1974) and in the subsequent labour process debate (Thompson, 1983; Wood, 1982).

According to Braverman, capitalist development necessarily entailed the 'degradation of work' because competition and the drive to accumulate impelled managers to increase control, especially through the separation of conception and execution typified in scientific management.[11] Control was not to be thought of simply as something imposed on the workers, it was rather that control over what went on in production was wrested from the workers by their managers: 'new methods and new machinery are incorporated within a management effort to dissolve the labor process[12] as a process conducted by the worker and reconstitute it as a process conducted by management' (Braverman, 1974: 170). Braverman noted that this might even entail the wholesale replacement of one group of workers by another; in any event the degradation of work involved 'a step-by-step creation of a "labour force" in place of self-directed human labor ... knowledge of the machine becomes a specialised and segregated trait, while among the mass of the working population there grows only ignorance, incapacity, and thus a fitness for machine servitude' (ibid.: 194). But the idea that people were gripped by, and which was debated endlessly within economic sociology (especially in Britain), was the role of new machines in this process. What really captured the imagination was the idea that capitalists wrested control from the workforce by way of technological change. This idea could be summed up in one word: deskilling. The new technology – and Braverman had in mind the introduction of numerical control technology in the machine tool industry – did away with the need for workers to exercise their skills and thus shifted control over production to the managers.

Thus began the deskilling debate that was hinged on interminable empirical studies designed to find empirical evidence to test this simple thesis. After more than a decade of 'Bravermania' it was clear to all but the most obdurate that there was no pre-determined relation between new technology and deskilling. There was evidence for up-skilling as well as deskilling and there was no predictable, linear process in which work was degraded. This was all very well, but the 'debate' failed to problematize any of the underlying assumptions that economic sociology, including its *soi-disant* Marxist variant, made about managers' apparently limitless ability to control workers and their labour and use that control to increase exploitation. For example, the fact that deskilling was not as ubiquitous as Braverman had claimed did not, on the whole, cause economic sociologists to suggest that those capitalists who did go in for deskilling might have made a mistake. The reason why they did not reach this conclusion seems to have been that it would not occur to economic sociologists that capitalists could make mistakes, at least not such *systematic* mistakes. Thus economic sociologists did not seem prone to question whether it really was self-evident how to increase profits and to wonder if managers simply had a good guess at what might work, or copied what others were doing, and were therefore quite likely to come up with the wrong answer (Grint, 1995). As I have already pointed out, the only correction to this was the suggestion that workers might sometimes be able to 'resist' and hang on to control for themselves (Edwards, 1979; Friedman, 1978).

Earlier in this chapter it was suggested that managerial legitimacy could be defended against the implications of its changeable principles by making reference to the changing circumstances in which management is practised. Thus, good management for one decade becomes bad management for another because there is a technological revolution that requires a different approach. Richard Edwards offered a version of this argument. He described different conceptions of the management role, and different things for managers to do, in different sorts of work and organizations with different sorts of workers.

In the secondary sector, with its low-level technology and its low-waged unskilled or semi-skilled work, there was 'simple control' in which orders were followed at the pain of sanction. This kind of control would be counter-productive in the primary sector with its more sophisticated and productive technology base, its higher skills and well-paid workers who benefited from internal labour markets (ILMs).[13] Where workers had ILMs, there was 'technical control' but again this would not work in the elite sections of the primary labour market where careers were made (or ruined) by changing from one company to another rather than making progress through an ILM. 'Bureaucratic control' was reserved for this elite minority. Although some organizations (for example, low technology, low-value-added secondary sector firms) would make predominant use of only one kind of control, other organizations would have a mixture of all three types. Variations in the components of this mixture between companies were largely explained by variations in technology. Moreover, each of the three types of control made its first appearance at a different point in history. Simple control was the first to appear but, as technology changed, it became necessary to turn to the other two forms of control. Bureaucratic control, with its emphasis on the internalization of rules and identification with the company, was the most recent form (Edwards, 1979).

Edwards offered a view of the role of management in capitalist development that was meant to be more sophisticated than the 'Marxist' versions provided by Marglin or Braverman. There was not one thing for managers to do but several things, depending on the circumstances, but all of these things were still labelled 'control' and in Edwards' theory it still sounded as if management knew exactly what it was about. Management might have to employ more varied methods

113

to achieve the same end product but we never get the feeling that management is in less than total command. In the work of another 'Marxist' writing at the same time as Edwards, this was no longer so obvious. In the work of Burawoy (1979) – introduced in the previous chapter – management needed *consent* from the workforce as well as the will to control. Here at least managers were not omnipotent even if they retained their supernatural knowledge of the best methods to exploit workers. But at this point we need to leave 'Marxist' economic sociology in order to widen our approach.

CONTINGENCY THEORY

Outside the 'Marxist' strand in economic sociology, consent had already received some attention (Hodson, 2001). Writing at a time when functionalist economic sociology was the orthodoxy, Bendix (1956) pointed out that there was no more effective way to commit sabotage than by complying with orders but refusing to use your own judgement, i.e. management depended on the good faith of the employees (see also Hodson, 2001, on passive resistance and 'social' and 'procedure sabotage'). Bendix was keen to point out that most British and American management was able to rely on a degree of good faith but this was not true, for example, in Russia (and subsequently in the USSR) where managers were forced to rely on political controls in tandem with executive controls all the way down the chain of command.

The notion that the task of management might vary according to the situation within which it was attempted was also present in the work of Joan Woodward (1958, 1965). Woodward identified work organization itself, or rather work organization as included in *technology*, as a contingency that would affect the kind of management that was appropriate. In her research in the UK, in the 1950s, she found that there were many variations in what managers did, even how many of them there were, but these variations did not appear to be related to the organizational goals like growth, profits or industrial relations. In effect, Woodward thought that different answers were needed to the question about what bosses did according to the technology involved. As technological complexity increased (from unit and small batch through large batch and mass production to process production), chains of command lengthened, the proportions of managers and clerical workers increased, and the span of control for CEOs narrowed. Woodward thought the point was to get the right kind of management for the technology and work organization in use.

An alternative and more radical thought might have been that no firm was using the right kind of management, that the differences were contingent only in the sense that they were historical accidents, and that the reasoning that Woodward carefully uncovered for the differences was a fine example of how social scientists could join in the work of supporting general managerial legitimacy even where managers appeared to be doing very different things (recalling the Hawthorne experiments explored by Gillespie, 1991). Woodward used technology as the escape clause that preserved managerial legitimacy in the face of observed variations in managerial practice. In the years that followed, her thinking was elaborated into 'contingency theory' which progressively added a list of other factors to the ones that might account for the observed variations in what bosses did. In most of this work there was also a significant departure from Woodward that was deeply unhelpful to the cause of making management a more problematic activity than economic sociology allowed it to be.

Woodward considered the type of management to be the independent variable. The challenge companies had to rise to was to choose the right type for the technology in use. Other researchers turned management into a dependent variable. In the 1970s contingency theorists Pugh and Hickson (1976) identified lists of dependent variables including the division of labour, the level of bureaucratization, the extent of formalization of communications, centralization and the shape of the power structure. The independent variables which explained variations in the dependent variables included the pattern of ownership and control, size, goals, technology, resources and level of interdependence with other organizations. This framework produced highly complex, multi-factor explanations of variations in management between companies. Here, much more than in the work of Woodward, was an incarnation of economic sociology that was dedicated to telling managers how to do their jobs. This kind of social science had joined forces with technological rationality and claimed to be able to identify the appropriate kind of management needed in particular circumstances. This perhaps makes it all the more surprising that contingency theory quickly fell out of favour. The only version of this theory that survives in the inspirational management handbooks of the 1980s and 1990s was an earlier version – developed at about the same time Woodward was writing – which made it clear that the most important contingency was change itself.

Burns and Stalker (1961) moved further than anyone else in economic sociology away from the idea of management being about control and, through recognizing that managers can make *systematic* mistakes, they opened up the possibility that there was no right way to manage. Earlier in this chapter it was pointed out that managerial legitimacy required that we accept that the reason why some managers are better than others is that someone has not properly understood what is required. Problems were meant to be the result of the failings of the individuals concerned, and never the consequence of the pursuit of a

115

fundamentally deluded enterprise. In Burns and Stalker's work, managers could understand exactly what was required, and act in the most rational way, and still manage their companies into crisis.

Of course Burns and Stalker then took a wrong turning in the direction of contingency theory when they concluded that there was a right way to manage change (and a perfectly good way of managing in stable conditions would be disastrous when those conditions were changing). The idea of the right way to manage was reinstated, salvaged once more by the idea that what this right way could be would depend on the prevailing circumstances. But at least Burns and Stalker had managers who were making systematic mistakes. The managers who managed in the way that was functional for stasis when everything about them was changing were not trying to be bad managers: they still thought they were doing the right thing but they clearly were not. It was, then, not always so blindingly obvious to managers how to manage in the right way.

Burns and Stalker sought connections between rapid industrial change, commercial success, organizational effectiveness and individual anxiety. From Durkheim they took the distinction between mechanical and organic solidarity and applied it in the form of two ideal types of management system that they thought helped them to make sense of empirical data from their own research on British companies. The mechanical management system was organized around tight job descriptions and an organization chart. People concentrated on 'the technical improvement of means, rather than the accomplishment of the ends of the concern' (Burns and Stalker, 1961: 120). They worked in a hierarchy reinforced by concentration of knowledge at the top. Loyalty to the company and obedience to superiors mattered above all (certainly more than selling things). The organic management system had, by contrast, ill-defined functions and much more flexibility and it was better suited for a firm responding to change in markets and technology.

According to Burns and Stalker, the organic system succeeded for two reasons. First, in this system the market was perceived as a source and not a sink and sales were the goal of all employees. All functions – sales, design and production – were integrated and fully orientated towards this ultimate goal. The organic system was much more responsive to changing market conditions. Second, in contrast to the autocratic, fixed roles of the mechanical system (as determined by the organization chart), the organic system demanded flexibility, role-swapping and interaction. Individuals were continually re-orientated to new tasks and new teams were created to take on new projects and dissolved when the projects were completed. Interaction, and particularly *horizontal* communication, ensured reiteration of common purpose and consensus. Anyone who has read Rosabeth Moss Kanter, James Champy, Charles Handy or Tom Peters will recognize at least some of the secrets of successful management that they disclose in this description of the organic management system developed in the 1950s.[14] There are also many pointers towards the principles of modern human resource management (Storey, 1992, 1995) and employee-empowerment programmes (see Chapter 3), for example:

> The adjustment and continual redefinition of individual tasks through interaction with others ... The spread of commitment to the concern beyond any technical definition ... A network structure of control, authority and communication. The sanctions which apply to the individual's conduct in his working role derive more from presumed community of interest with the rest of the working organisation in the survival and growth of the firm, and less from a contractual relationship between himself and a nonpersonal corporation, represented for him by an immediate superior ... Commitment to the concern's tasks and to the 'technological ethos' of material progress and expansion is more highly valued than loyalty and obedience. (Burns and Stalker, 1961: 121–2)

In Burns and Stalker's scheme, companies did not make the switch from mechanical to organic management as some sort of automatic response to changing conditions. Many companies did not make the switch when they should have because individuals were too mindful of office politics and anxious about their status. Thus Burns and Stalker thought there were managers who chose to act against their own economic interests as defined by the success of their firm. On the other hand, general anxiety about the consequence of changing management style and function was justified because the organic system was tough on managers. Work became much more central to their lives and the effects of organic management on managers included increased anxiety and insecurity. In Burns and Stalker's sociology there was a real conflict between organizational efficiency and what might be good for the individual. (We will return to the effects of managerialism on the managers when we return to MacIntyre, see p. 123).

Like later contingency theorists, Burns and Stalker saw management style as the dependent variable: a company needed organic management to cope successfully with change in technology and markets but whether the organic solution was put in place depended on other independent variables like the commitment of individuals to political and status-gaining ends, and the quality of leadership. In Burns and Stalker's view, CEOs bore the key responsibility for changing to an organic management system. The way in which Burns and Stalker describe some CEOs' reluctance to make the necessary change serves as a simple but powerful explanation of companies' use of the services of management consultants on such occasions. CEOs shift the burden of

117

suggesting the painful changes that are necessary onto consultants while boards of directors and major shareholders use consultants to shift, and sometimes remove, recalcitrant CEOs.

Burns and Stalker were adamant that a mechanical system would serve a company well enough in stable conditions. In this they part company with later management gurus who recommend constant change (and associated insecurity and anxiety) as the key to organizational effectiveness and corporate success. But of course change in markets and technology became the dominant characteristic of sector after sector during the post-war period in which Burns and Stalker conducted their research. For all practical purposes, it was imperative that companies recognized the need for constant change and innovation. Since stability was not an option, the alternative of the mechanical management system was simply academic. Unfortunately, many of Burns and Stalker's admirers seemed to forget the theoretical possibility of a successful company run with a mechanical management system. In their minds, Burns and Stalker became an eerily prescient sociological study which confirmed all the best contemporary ideas about how to manage well (Marshall, 1990).

This reworking of Burns and Stalker loses almost everything that is of value to sociology in their work. Their predecessors, and many of their successors, had been heavily influenced by the Weberian idea of the successful bureaucratic organization. Whatever else it was (exploitative, controlling or responding to contingencies), management was bureaucratic. It obeyed all the principles of bureaucracy (following an abstract, legal code of conduct, and so on) and was concerned with operating rational procedures on the principles of expert knowledge and calculability. Burns and Stalker now said this bureaucratic solution would not be successful where change was needed. Their list of the mechanical system's key characteristics (many of which have been described above) matches much of Weber's characterization of bureaucracy. Yet Burns and Stalker found these characteristics were handicaps to any organization that wanted to innovate.

Up to this point the study of management and its development had proceeded on the foundations established by Weber: the progressive application of rationality, bureaucracy, choice of the means necessary to achieve identified ends, and so on. Burns and Stalker could have taken the next step beyond Weber. They could have looked at the evidence they had now produced of a de-bureaucratized wave of the future and decided Weber had made a fatal error and that bureaucratic rationality was simply a story told to legitimate (and construct) managerial power. They might have argued that bureaucratic rationality had not been attractive because, as Weber claimed, it was simply more efficient, but rather because it served as a political ploy and an ideology. If

they had made this leap, Burns and Stalker might have thought differently about the new management style. Instead of thinking that the
organic management system was the most efficient way to deal with
change, they might have seen it as another story that served the same
ideological and political purpose in the 'organic' enterprise.

Burns and Stalker went closer than any sociologists had to mounting a critique of management's economic rationality. They simply chose
the wrong option when they concluded there was a right kind of management for change and another for stability. Instead, they might have
taken the evidence of de-bureaucratization that they so brilliantly gath-
ered and analysed as the basis for further development that might have
subverted economic sociology. There was a real opportunity here to
turn economic rationality into a means rather than an end. We can see
a very dim glimmer of this idea in Edwards (1979). Here the way management was constructed depended on the particular type of economic
rationality in use. The problem with this theory was the deterministic
way in which these different rationalities succeeded each other with
changes in technologies, products and markets. Burns and Stalker
nearly made a significant advance on this theory[15] and we do not have
to take their theories very far to reach the point at which changes in
technology and markets become simply the occasions or contexts (or
even pretexts) for changes in management ideology.

119

KEITH GRINT'S SOCIOLOGY OF MANAGEMENT

If we now start to think about the whole of the history of management
in terms of a succession of different ways of using rationality to justify
the management role and management prerogative, we can make some
progress in the deconstruction of economic rationality. Of course economic sociology after contingency theory steadfastly ignored this possibility. Readers will remember the second argument used to defend the
myth of managerial super-efficiency in the face of evidence of constant
revision of management's basic principles: management was changing
because it was getting better and better at being effective and efficient.
The fact that it was changing was not proof that it was impossible to
achieve super-efficient management. It was, rather, only what you
would expect if management was evolving towards this goal. This is the
category into which much economic sociology that looks at comparative evidence on management in different countries falls. Grint's (1995)
study of the sociology of management provided a very good example.
He attempted to synthesize the existing sociology of management,
rather than reporting on an empirical study like Burns and Stalker, but
his work had something of the same promise although, once again, he
failed to take the right option after doing valuable preparatory work.

Grint was writing at a point in British history when it was widely accepted that British management bore a major share of the responsibility for the relative decline of the UK economy (Coates, 1994).[16] Grint's basic idea was that managers in other countries had learnt rather more quickly how to manage well and that British managers were less evolved than their Japanese or, particularly, American counterparts. Grint pointed to all the research that showed American industry and culture had taken the need for managers seriously at a much earlier stage in history, and had recognized that management was a super-rational activity and that to be good at it you would have to be well trained. In Britain, by way of contrast, 'those who engaged in business tended to be self-taught or apprenticed individuals whose skill was measured by the degree to which they could replicate what their forebears had been able to do' (Grint, 1995: 58). The Americans had professional managers and MBAs decades before the Britons – was it any wonder that British industry suffered as a result?

Since a strong recovery of British industry became evident at about the same time that Grint's book came out, one might argue that this thesis can be safely ignored. On the other hand, perhaps this reversal of fortunes showed how well British industry had done when it finally learned to copy the management techniques employed by the Americans and Japanese? Certainly there was ample evidence of the import of foreign management practices to the UK along with foreign direct investment (see Collinson, 1994, in Chapter 3, for instance). If British industry still had some way to go, perhaps this was because short-termism remained a problem and this was not necessarily the fault of managers? Short-termism could also be a consequence of the financial structure of British industry and the importance still attached to short-term fluctuations in share values by those who defined managers' room for manoeuvre. This sounds plausible but I want to argue instead that Grint's insight into the failings of British management represents another missed opportunity. Instead of arguing that British managers made mistakes because they had not yet evolved to the level of American managers he could have used this insight to problematize the activities of all managers. This is not a far-fetched suggestion because for much of the book this seemed to be exactly what Grint intended to do.

Grint showed how the nature of the management role was not self-evident at all. He showed, as a sociologist of economic behaviour might, how the management role had to be socially constructed and he showed how this role was constructed in a different way in different cultures. Thus he tried to paint a picture of the British approach to management in terms of a contrast between Napoleon (strategic, populist, theoretical) and Wellington (reactive, aristocratic, practical).

British management got its character from the story that was told when national character first became important (during the Napoleonic Wars). The essence of this character was trusting in experience rather than theory; pragmatism not planning; muddling through; seeing no need for change for change's sake. British management was typified as reactive and forever fire-fighting instead of planning. It was also to be seen as incapable of invention: always copying what (apparently) worked in the past.

Grint inserted this characterization of British management into his story of its tardy evolution and responsibility for relative economic decline, but it was still a remarkable step away from economic sociology when put beside the usual managerialist claims to omnipotence and omniscience. Grint applied much the same technique to the contemporary management fad of Business Process Re-engineering (BPR) but, before we discuss this, we should briefly note a further contribution Grint made which recalled the work of Burawoy. For Grint, the outcomes of management behaviour were really dependent on the workers who granted management legitimacy by offering various forms of consent and co-operation. Grint produced a typology of these forms within categories of fatalism that could be contrasted with the free will exercised by someone who did not grant management the right to influence and even determine their future.

According to Grint, slavery was synonymous with wholly fatalistic workers who typically saw death as the only release from having others determine how their days passed. Much less extreme forms of fatalism fitted two familiar ideal types of management. Fordism would have been impossible without the 'situational fatalism' within which workers recognized that they had free will but would certainly pay dearly for it if they exercised it in the workplace. In contrast, the 'Boethian fatalism' of workers in post-Fordist organizations suggested that they might exercise their free will and know that this would produce the ends management also desired. In each case workers not only accepted their fates but granted authority to managers to determine them in a particular way (for example, with scientific management or the techniques of 'soft HRM', see Storey, 1995). This was a marked improvement on economic sociology's orthodoxy in which omnipotent and omniscient managers needed no assistance from the objects of their will to power.

Grint also undermined such claims to omnipotence and omniscience when he analysed the components of what was, at the time, a fairly new management fad, Business Process Re-engineering (BPR). In analysing each of the ten components of BPR Grint did not have much difficulty in finding out that BPR had no clothes. Decreasing fragmentation and moving from functions to processes were judged by Grint to be nothing new, although the vigour with which these were pursued was novel.

The shift from simple to multi-dimensional tasks, integration, team-work, less supervision and multi-skilling rather than deskilling was not new either. Grint pointed out that it would all sound very familiar to the enthusiasts of the Quality of Working Life Movement but Burns and Stalker would also have recognized their early work. To continue, the notion of empowerment in BPR was only reinterpreting the exist-ing arrangement and the emphasis on training and education – hiring people who already knew how to learn – might be new to Britain[17] but there were educated generalists elsewhere. The insistence in BPR on a reward system that paid for results rather than attendance was, again, hardly new (especially in Japan) and could lead to inefficiency. The idea that performance and advancement were looser than conventional career progression was not innovative either, and so on with the final BPR components: the customer is not always the bottom line (think of product development); the idea of coaches instead of supervisors recalls the Human Relations School and (particularly) Elton Mayo. In respect of flattened hierarchies, surely teams had been around for two hundred years? Finally, the scope for scorekeepers to become leaders was some-times pretty limited.

Grint concluded that BPR did not find enthusiastic followers because it was a super-rational solution to all management's problems. There could never be such a solution because the problems were too complex and events were too unpredictable. The success of BPR came from putting ten ideas *together*, from the value of the basic principle – which again recalls Burns and Stalker – that boundaries equal obstacles (for example, people and technology should change together) and from getting people to re-think systems and processes at one go rather than undertaking incremental changes. Grint concluded that BPR really only worked because it was change personified and change was always what would be required. Capitalism required a permanent revolution because organizations would ossify without it. Grint's discussion then followed similar lines to Burns and Stalker's account of the way office politics got in the way of the necessary changes.

Grint displayed admirable scepticism about the idea of a linear pro-gression to ever-greater rationality with BPR as its most rational stage so far. We now need to go one step further and consider the possibility that BPR and all the other re-inventions of the secret of super-rational, super-efficient management were *solely* fads or fashions. That man-agers are particularly prone to following such fads should return us to Grint's insistence that management is a construction and not a discov-ery (ten Bos, 2000). Management does not change because it is evolv-ing in an ever more rational way, but changes simply because, as long as we persist in wanting or tolerating management, it has to be recon-structed in each generation that passes (Pattison, 1997). For one thing, management had better be reinvented for each new generation if the preceding generation keeps deciding that what it knew as management has been discredited as ineffective or proven to be positively harmful to social well-being! At this point it would be wise to introduce the opinions of MacIntyre, the phiolosopher, on the other profession that shares this characteristic, the profession of therapy. We will then be in a position to discuss the mistaken assumptions of power and efficacy that the professions of therapist and manager share.

ALASDAIR MACINTYRE

MacIntyre (1985) had something to say which was much more interesting, and had wider significance, than the suggestion that there was nothing at the heart of the enterprise of management except what we construct (according to whatever rationality we happen to hold to). He wished to discover why, given this vacuum, we continue to put up with (and pay dearly for) the pretence that management has the substance its supporters claim for it. He was not interested in this problem for the sake of the sociology of management (or even for sociology) but used it as an illustration of something that he felt had gone wrong in Western thought (a deep crisis brought on by a wrong turn in Western philosophy after Aristotle).

123

MacIntyre argued that Weber had given one sort of rationality a privileged place over all the others. Perhaps reluctantly, and certainly unhappily, Weber had conceded that the *efficiency* of bureaucratic rationality, and thus of the bureaucratic manager, was really unassailable. It was this claim to *efficiency* that prevented Weber from taking the argument beyond the iron cage. MacIntyre was entirely unconvinced by the special rationality of efficiency. This was not a natural legitimation of managerial *authority* so much as another excuse which allowed some people to exercise *power* over others. This must be the case since the efficiency claims were a fantasy (also see Gillespie, 1991).

As part of his account of the social construction of management, Grint (1995) argued that the idea of a management role, rather than any particular thing that any manager might do, was what managers had in common and was, in fact, the only thing that set them apart. For MacIntyre this idea of the modern manager was the best representative of a whole modern way of thinking that was something of a sham yet immensely influential. This way of thinking had effects at the macro-level – it underpinned the distribution of power and resources – and at the level of the individual. MacIntyre thought that 'manager' was more than a role that could be slipped in and out of at will. The skin got stuck on and the role invaded the personality of the individual. You never really escaped being the manager because you came to believe it, you believed in what it stood for – what MacIntyre called a cultural and moral ideal.

The Manager was not the only 'mask worn by a moral philosophy'. There were others, like the Therapist. Both managers and therapists manipulated others while telling them there was no alternative and that they were only trying, in the most efficient way they could, to achieve ends that they have been given. The job of manager and therapist is simply to find the most efficient means. The great thing about the comparison with therapists was that therapists were even more subject to fads and fashions than managers were. Compare MacIntyre's comments on therapy to the succession of different kinds of management thought:

> each school of therapists is all too anxious to make clear the theoretical defects of each rival school. Thus the problem is not why the claims of psychoanalytic or behavioural therapies are not exposed as ill-founded; it is rather why, since they have been so adequately under-mined, the practices of therapy continue for the most part as though nothing had happened. (MacIntyre, 1985: 73–4)

Why, according to MacIntyre, is the managerial role everywhere and always a sham? Why can it never accomplish what it promises and can only amount to the cloaking of power in the authority or naturalness or necessity?

> The claim that the manager makes to effectiveness rests of course on the further claim to possess a stock of knowledge by means of which organisations and social structures can be moulded. Such knowledge would have to include a set of factual law-like generalisations which would enable the manager to predict that, if an event or state of affairs of a certain type were to occur or to be brought about, some other event or state of affairs of some specific kind would result. For only such law-like generalisations could yield those particular causal explanations and predictions by means of which the manager could, mould, influence and control the social environment. (ibid.: 77)

Here MacIntyre exposed the management role as a sham using an argument within the philosophy of social science. He suggested that the foundation of a manager's claim to be able to manage was found in the suggestion that s/he had (miraculously) discovered what sociologists and other social 'scientists' had been searching for – and had so dismally failed to find – a science of human behaviour. By 'science' MacIntyre meant 'factual law-like generalizations' for predicting the outcome of particular actions. These factual law-like generalizations had not been discovered, and would remain elusive, because the subject matter of our enquiries was the behaviour of people – rather than the natural world – and people were unpredictable.[18]

124

MacIntyre cited Andreski (1972) and Winch (1990) on social science's limited powers of prediction. He reminded us that, while physicists could accurately predict a range of non-human behaviour, they could only guess at how other physicists will behave (even in the medium term). The best any of us could do in such cases was to generalize in the full knowledge that there would always be many exceptions to our generalizations and that we will not be able to predict where most of the exceptions will turn up. In practice, managers could not rely on a science of human behaviour but must rely instead on all-too-flawed generalizations, usually taking the form of common-sense observations. Once the sham glamour of effectiveness was removed, it would be plain to see that such common sense could never justify all the power and manipulation associated with the managerial role.

Where does this leave the idea that management is only making mistakes because it is progressively evolving into a higher and more rational form? It might be reasonable to expect managers (and therapists, come to that) to change their ideas from time to time if they were learning how to do things more effectively. But if we accept MacIntyre's intervention we can no longer believe that this learning process is so different from the way ordinary citizens improve their effectiveness, for example, as parents. We must also be aware that many choices between different management approaches will be more or less arbitrary. Since the legitimacy of academic argument (just as much managerial authority) remains stubbornly rooted in the belief in the efficacy of economic rationality, we would also expect people to continue to argue that each of their arbitrary choices is the essence of economic rationality. This casts new light on a range of recent debates but particularly those about the modernization of British management and about industrial democracy, worker-shareholders, profit sharing and other forms of partnership and corporate governance more generally (Hutton, 1996). More recently, some academics have begun to argue in similar terms about the merit of supposedly feminine management approaches which are explicitly contrasted with the bad old (masculine) rationality they are meant to replace (Wajcman, 1998).[19]

There is nothing at the heart of the enterprise of management except that which we construct in order to fill up the vacuum. Managers are just like academics in that they have to construct the managerial role, and managing, and management. This is why they are so prone to fads and fashions. This is not a question of shopping around, trying on the wrong things until you get the right one, since there is no such thing as the right one (ten Bos, 2000). Management styles are a question of taste – each one can be acceptable depending on whether one can find the right yardstick for it, the right *rationality* according to which it can be favourably judged. Economic sociology has spent its time joining in the

125

production of these various rationalities. By taking part in the construction of a variety of different economic rationalities for managers, economic sociologists have helped to construct that which they sometimes thought they were criticizing. In fact, social science as a whole is deeply implicated in the construction of the management role and management practices (Anthony, 1977; Shenhav, 1999).

CONCLUSION

The claims for accurate prediction and the facility to determine behaviour which economic sociology shares with managerialism are impossible to support. The effectiveness of management is very much a hit-and-miss affair but management would be deprived of most of its legitimacy if this were widely recognized. Economic sociology made every effort to make sure this truth was kept hidden. For example, while all economic sociologists failed to problematize managerial control of exploitation, Burns and Stalker provided a salutary example of a wrong turning when they concluded that there was a right kind of management for change and another for stability. Burns and Stalker might have used de-bureaucratization to subvert economic sociology by turning economic rationality into a means rather than an end. Instead economic sociology continued to play a loyal supporting role to managerialism as both gained ground as part of the spread of economic rationality and demoralization.

Once the explanations that economic sociology or managerial institutions might offer for the existence of management are found wanting, it begins to look as if the persistence of management's will to power can best be explained in baldly political terms. Deetz reached this conclusion with the help of Critical Theory and Foucault rather than Bauman or MacIntyre, but he raised similar questions:

> Why does management control rather than co-ordinate and how is that secured? Why isn't the co-ordination function seen as largely clerical and facilitative? To understand modern domination, we must take the routine, the commonsensical and the self-evident and subject them to reconsideration. The more distant dominations by the church and kings were not simply forced on subjects but were routine and ritualized, reproduced in innumerable practices; they were consented to but not chosen. Reproblematizing the obvious requires identifying conflicts which do not happen. (Deetz, 1992: 43)

It is no coincidence that we still talk about the managerial *revolution* when we are describing the increased legitimacy of managerial expertise and the concomitant increase in the numbers and powers of managers. The managerial revolutionaries' overblown, and indeed fantastical, claims for managerial competence are really no different to the middle-class revolutionaries' cries of liberty for all (Barley and Kunda, 1992; Shenhav, 1999). In Chapters 5 and 6 we will pursue the idea of a political strand within the sociology of economic behaviour in relation to the behaviour of classes.

Recently a number of studies have been carried out on more specific examples of the politics of managerial power and expertise. Thus Kirkpatrick and Martinez-Lucio (1995) considered which groups were favoured by the economic rationality of 'Quality' in the public sector, and Power (1997) discovered evidence of the way (auditing) rationalities were marshalled by the groups they favoured and refered to 'ritualized practices of verification whose technical efficacy is less significant than their role in the production of organizational legitimacy' (Power, 1997: 14). At the micro-level it also becomes clear that managers are not always the undisputed winners of such political behaviour. From a study of European corporations that claimed to have introduced empowerment programme, Hales (2000) concluded the lack of evidence of empowered employees did not mean that the programme had failed. Instead, empowerment carried with it 'the inescapable implication that the role of and, hence, the need for, junior line managers/supervisors has diminished ... junior managers are obliged to try and defend their role in the language of empowerment' (ibid.: 516).[20]

The principles of management may change in line with shifts in political conflicts over access to jobs and legitimate authority, but why do the various expressions of the fundamental principles of management take the form they do? The previous chapter suggested that cultural shifts in wider society might shed some light on this question. In this chapter we learnt that the management system that Burns and Stalker labelled 'organic' became popular at the same time as 'other-directedness' (Riesman, 1950).[21] Perhaps other-directed managers needed inumerable meetings and projects and the constant reiteration and reinforcement of the company's purpose because this was how they knew what they were meant to do?

This is a glimpse of the proper subject matter of the sociology of economic behaviour in those areas where politics, culture and structure overlap and where real critiques of existing social and economic orthodoxies can be developed. The key to the development of these critiques is to problematize power and culture and economic behaviour (what people actually spend their days doing) together. This is the strategy pursued in the next two chapters.

NOTES

1 See also Michels (1911/1962).

2 Like Casey's respondent who thought their culture was good for an eight-year advantage before it could be reproduced elsewhere, when, like any

other *technology*, it would deliver the same goods (Casey, 1995).

3 Note how bounded rationality does not challenge the notion of management omniscience and omnipotence but is designed to keep that very idea alive (Shenhav, 1999). Bounded rationality is a key defensive move because it heads off the critique of the over-estimation of managers' knowledge, skills and ability to influence events by using chosen means to achieve defined ends.

4 Daniel Bell was an early enthusiast: 'Ideology, to this extent, becomes irrelevant and is replaced by "economics" in the guise of production functions, capital output ratios, marginal efficiency of capital, linear programming and the like' (1976: 76).

5 Theo Nichols (personal communication) points out that 'human *resource* management', which is meant to represent capitalism in a softer light, is similarly objectionable in that it reduces men and women to the same status as land and capital (see also Polanyi, 1944/1957). By way of contrast, André Gorz thought it was implicit in HRM that labour was a 'not a resource like any other' (1989: 60).

6 In Fevre (2000b) I show how, until the last decades of the twentieth century, common sense/cognition (rather than science) were entirely responsible for technology and technological change. Shenhav would surely insist that engineers were central to this application of this kind of sense-making.

7 The etymology of 'management' takes us back to an Italian term for breaking in horses.

8 And of course these are big and complex in every sense, not just in relation to employees. It cannot really be true that management is all about dealing with the people in the enterprise rather than the money, the raw materials, the buildings, the machinery, the suppliers, the customers, and all forms of government.

9 See, for example, Rose (1988). I am very grateful to Finn Bowring (personal communication) for pointing out just how close Marglin's argument gets to becoming a genuine critique. It would also be more accurate to say it is social economics that Marglin nearly escapes.

10 Marglin discussed the way other forms of power than the power wielded by managers had been used to redistribute resources from one class to another. For example, various legal arrangements were quite good at it too. The problem is that he seemed to assume that hierarchical organization could redistribute resources in an unproblematic way rather than that he presented hierarchy as a uniquely successful means of achieving this end.

11 Rose (1988) thought Braverman was more of a romantic than a Marxist. Braverman venerated craft skill in the way Proudhon had – seeing it as a source of absolute value and therefore seeing its loss as by definition equivalent to the degradation of work. In this view Braverman is making very similar arguments to those advanced some time before by Georges Friedmann (1955).

12 Note that by 'labour process' Marx meant a form of 'production process' in which labour is the 'governing unity' rather than machinery (in full automation).

13 The original work on the significance of ILMs and 'dual labour markets' comprised of a primary and secondary sector was done by Edwards's colleagues, Doeringer and Piore (Doeringer and Piore, 1971; Doeringer, 1986). Other contributions to their self-styled 'radical economics' were made by Gordon (see, for example, Gordon, 1972) and Reich (Edwards, Reich and Gordon, 1975).

14 Burns and Stalker's description of the shortcomings of the mechanical system is equally remarkable although perhaps not so unique as some later readers might think. In 1951 Ealing Studios released a movie – *The Man in the White Suit* (directed by Alexander Mackendrick, starring Alec Guinness and Joan Greenwood) – that explored many of the same themes. While the movie was a story of resistance to technological innovation in a textile factory, the original inspiration for

Tom Burns's idea of a mechanical management system had been his research in a rayon mill.

15 Is the reason why they failed to do so tied up with their commitment to seeing management as the dependent variable?

16 The early British start to industrialization now gave the appearance of a special problem of British decline.

17 Although surely this has long been accepted practice in the British civil service?

18 MacIntyre even refers to Burns and Stalker to prove the point about our inescapable unpredictability. He thinks that what makes 'organic management' work it is that it copes better with that inherent unpredictability.

19 Wajcman (1998) offered a good example of a doomed attempt to escape economic rationality which simply made a rhetorical case for the authors' own preferences. The example was provided by Mumby and Putnam (1992) who argued that organizations should rely as much on emotion as on (bounded) rationality. They wanted more nurturing and supportive organizations, for instance.

20 In this, junior managers were apparently helped by ambiguities in the concept of empowerment.

21 Given the way Burns and Stalker relied for inspiration on the Durkheimian theory in which the replacement of mechanical by organic organization necessarily entailed the risk of anomie, it is no surprise that their sociology can be so easily linked to ideas of demoralization.

129

five

classes and labour markets

If managers do not behave in the way that managerialist ideology and economic sociology imagine, then how do they behave? The sociology of economic behaviour seeks to understand managers' behaviour in the same way that it understands other economic behaviour. All of this behaviour is influenced by a range of values that include, but are not reducible to, economic values. These values can legitimate action as well as motivate it and we cannot understand the division of labour or the wider allocation of resources in society if we ignore the role these values play in economic behaviour. This chapter will suggest that, when deployed successfully, some values legitimate a form of economic advantage that establishes a moral claim to particular resources. In other cases, different kinds of values (usually, but not always, economic values) allow individuals and groups to establish a claim that takes precedence over competing moral claims on these resources. As capitalism has developed, and economic rationality has become hegemonic, the legitimation of privilege and advantage has increasingly derived from these alternative kinds of values (Jewson and Mason, 1986).

We can see how this advantage is gained if we consider the behaviour of groups engaged in labour market competition. By looking closely at the limitations of economic sociology in this field we can begin to understand how the persuasive power of economic rationality provides some social groups with a trump card which vanquishes other potential competitors for jobs. Economic sociology concerned with the study of social stratification and, particularly, social mobility, fails to reduce economic rationality to the level of other values when explaining the division of labour (Gorz, 1989). We will consider an example of work in this field which approaches a break-through by beginning to deconstruct the idea of 'merit'. With the help of moral philosophy, this sociology begins to expose its own shortcomings, for example, the assumptions it shares with those who believe that natural differences underpin the division of labour. At this point, however, the immanent critique is abandoned in favour of a return to the orthodox belief of economic sociology that labour markets operate in order to allocate resources efficiently.

When economic sociologists attempt to explain how labour markets operate to allocate resources efficiently but also to reproduce privilege and advantage, they frequently take recourse to the concepts of economics. This work, and particularly economic sociology which deploys the notion of various kinds of capital (human, social and cultural), introduces values into explanations of economic behaviour but non-economic values nevertheless only appear as a means to economic ends. Other work offers a more realistic picture of the way labour markets operate and increases our understanding of the range of values involved in economic behaviour and the place of economic rationality among these values (Jewson and Mason, 1986). The sociology of labour markets can show that labour market behaviour is motivated and legitimated by an array of different values in such a way that some groups withdraw from competition for particular jobs while other groups claim a right to them (Fevre, 1992).

Economic sociology has paid remarkably little attention to the way labour markets function. Where labour markets have figured in theory and research, economic sociology has, as usual, introduced morality into its analysis only in an instrumental role in which it was clearly subordinate to economic ends. This is certainly true of the most frequently cited economic sociology in this field, the work of Mark Granovetter. In Granovetter (1985) 'embedded networks' were presented as the quintessential concepts of an economic sociology for the labour market. Attention to these networks was a corrective to the theories of atomized actors common to the over-socialized (mainstream sociology) and under-socialized (mainstream economics) approaches to economic behaviour.

If this was a simply an initial step in which the field of labour markets was delineated for sociological attention, there would be little problem with Granovetter's approach. According to Granovetter, both under-socialized and over-socialized accounts ignore the fact that actors' behaviour is embedded in social relations. If such behaviour is not embedded, then labour markets cannot function. Networks allow us to re-establish the embedded nature of action. By focusing on networks we move away from the conception of individuals as slavish followers of society's norms that is just as reliant on atomized actors as is the theory of 'economic man', but bear in mind that this analysis is intended to show us how labour markets get people into jobs. Granovetter shows us that people use social networks to get into jobs and, on the basis of empirical research, he demonstrates that, contrary to what might be expected, weak ties are more effective for getting people into work. This finding has had an extraordinary impact, indeed for many years a very large amount of economic sociology concerned with markets (of all kinds) was actually secondary work on, first, weak ties (see the second edition of *Getting a Job* for a select bibliography), and latterly, the embedded nature of action (Burt, 1992; Powell and DiMaggio, 1991; Powell and Smith-Doerr, 1994).

The 'debates' to which all this research effort was devoted were usually about the way that social networks made markets work. When this approach was applied to the study of business networks, for example, it was argued that networks could reduce transaction costs. Economic rationality dictated that exchange would be more efficient if its costs could be reduced. One of the big costs of exchange transactions was the provision of information (about what exchange possibilities were available, for instance). Numerous articles were written to demonstrate that business networks reduced the costs of providing information to their members and therefore made them more competitive.

In economic sociology after Granovetter and Burt, moral phenomena – friendship, obligations, reciprocity and trust, for instance – were entirely devoted to the service of economic rationality, namely to getting labour markets to function and getting people into jobs. What could sociology have done instead, for example if Granovetter had been inclined towards a critique of economic rationality? As we know, the idea of embeddedness is simply another way of saying economic behaviour has a social component, it only gets us to the point at which the field is designated as of interest to sociology. The wrong turning comes with networks and weak ties. A proper sociology of economic behaviour would be interested in friendship, obligation and trust for their own sake (Beder, 2000; Gorz, 1989) and would wonder what the effect on these elements of the glue of society might be if they were used as a means to an economic end? For example, we might begin by asking whether the use of networks to facilitate labour markets reinforced those networks but we could then move on to more interesting questions. For instance, what is the moral effect of creating a hybrid social form in which friendship and acquaintance are put to an economic end? Is it possible, for instance, that weak ties prove more effective because people feel more confident that the moral effects of using weak ties to facilitate exchange can be minimized? By neglecting such issues, economic sociology has found it quite easy to avoid seriously engaging with any moral issues of weight, including the issues of inequality and social injustice that seem so germane to labour markets. But at the margins of economic sociology, in the sociology of social stratification, we do find sociologists who are not prepared to relegate all morality to an instrumental role.

132

MERITOCRACY: ECONOMIC RATIONALITY AND SOCIAL JUSTICE?

In their efforts to understand the way in which different societies allocate resources, sociologists have often made a distinction between
ascription and *achievement*. By ascription, sociologists mean that
resources (including status and prestige) are distributed according to
the sort of personal characteristics which the bearers of these qualities
took no part in making and can do little or nothing to change.
Typically, such characteristics include one's 'race', one's gender, and the
place in society already accorded to the family one happens to be born
into. When sociologists refer to achievement as a basis for the allocation of resources, they mean to refer to characteristics that cannot
simply be ascribed by other people but require us to demonstrate or
construct them.[1] Science and modern surgical techniques have been
able to blur the distinction between ascribed and achieved characteristics for some of us but in general it remains the case that ascribed characteristics are qualities which we can do little or nothing to change
whereas achieved characteristics are those which we have played an
active, and often conscious and intentional, role in changing or constructing.

That part of economic sociology that deals with social mobility has
tended to assume that the allocation of resources on the basis of
achieved characteristics (which individuals play an active part in shaping) is fairer than the allocation of resources according to given,
ascribed characteristics. Much of the empirical work in the field has
been intended to measure the degree of progress made towards the substitution of achievement for ascription (Blau and Duncan, 1967; Halsey
et al., 1980). Until recently there was widespread agreement amongst
the sociologists who have conducted this work that patterns of social
fluidity were similar between countries and remarkably stable over time
(Erickson and Goldthorpe, 1992; Featherman et al., 1975; Marshall et
al., 1997).[2] Almost all of them agreed that education had played an
increasingly important role in mediating the relationship between
people's origins (their socio-economic background as indicated by
parental occupation) and their destinations (their own occupations).
This change was held to signify the steady replacement of ascription by
achievement as an appropriate and legitimate basis for the division of
labour and, of course, it was held to be a good thing.

Since Weber founded the sub-discipline, it has been assumed within
economic sociology that rationalized society, with its care for the choice
of the most efficient ends to achieve specified goals, and a commitment
to universal principles, would make achievement rather than ascription
the basis of its labour markets. Apart from Weber, the sociologist who
we are most likely to think of here is Parsons (in fact, he cites Ralph

133

Linton as the originator of the distinction between ascription and achievement 'in the sociological literature'). Parsons made his own preferences crystal clear in his introduction to his translation of a part of Weber's *Economy and Society*, published as *The Theory of Social and Economic Organisation*:

> the valuation and its expression in recognition and status, of ability and achievement by such universalistic standards as technical competence has, particularly in the occupational field, a far wider scope in modern Western society than in most others. No other large-scale society has come so near universalizing 'equality of opportunity'. An important consequence of the universalistic pattern in these two fields is the very high degree of social mobility, of potentiality for each individual to 'find his own level' on the basis of his own abilities and achievements, or, within certain limits, of his own personal wishes rather than a compulsory traditional status. (Parsons, 1947/1964: 82)

From a vantage point outside economic sociology, there is a lot that is (inexplicably) glossed over in this quotation, especially the ways in which ability and achievement will be reliably identified and measured in order to reward them. Subsequent research on social mobility has barely given a moment's thought to such difficulties. Instead, it has relied on blind faith in meritocracy's mechanisms (neither specified or understood) to ensure that ability is recognized and rewarded and that the right people get into the right jobs.

As the role of education became more important, researchers within the sociology of education documented the way access to educational resources was structured. They frequently used the notion of a meritocracy to criticize the way in which prevailing structures, for example, those which ensured the allocation of educational resources on market principles, were unlikely to ensure that merit was properly rewarded. Those who already had material resources could use them to secure unfair advantage for their children (see, for example, Halsey et al., 1997; Brown and Lauder, 2001). Educational sociologists might go on to argue that there could be no real meritocracy unless the state intervened to make sure the less advantaged had equal access to educational resources. Without this intervention the recognition of achievement (giving better jobs to people with better qualifications) could not be synonymous with meritocracy.

Within economic sociology there has been considerably less scepticism about the way in which meritocracy operates in practice. The sort of rationality that is meant to underpin labour market behaviour, for example, the hiring and firing decisions made by managers, is assumed to achieve quite naturally some sort of perfection in the distribution of resources to higher uses. Only if there are imperfections (discrimination and so on) can this rationality be subverted. As we saw in the previous chapter, this sort of reasoning is closely allied to the mistaken notion of the capabilities of social science and also to managerialist notions of omnicompetence. Where managers are seen as applying perfect rationality to the direction of human resources, economic sociology assumes meritocracy will somehow automatically ensure that the recognition of ability and achievement is achieved in an unproblematic way when people get qualifications and jobs. Some social mobility researchers (for example, Marshall et al., 1997) recognized that difficulties were faced by managers trying to select for unproven ability or competence that was *uncertified* even by a record of achievement, but the sociology of economic behaviour needs to do more. For example, it needs to be prepared to critique the magical status assumed by certificates within meritocracy. In meritocracy certificates magically transform the mundane allocation of labour into the fully sanctified recognition of merit (or legitimation through demonstrable competence).

The assumption, on the basis of no evidence whatsoever, that meritocracy will automatically achieve the impossible things claimed on its behalf, also recalls the assumption that there is a business case for employers' family-friendly policies (see Chapter 2) and that equal opportunities are good for profits. The equal opportunities literature takes it as axiomatic that equal opportunities are economically rational and, indeed, promotes equal opportunities as an aid to profitability and competitiveness. It is assumed (usually in the absence of evidence) that the economic rationality of equal opportunities follows naturally from the economizing logic that links rationality and efficiency to universalism. Thus researchers assumed that equal opportunities and organizational effectiveness could be pursued together by rigorously following the precepts of bureaucratic rationality. Jenkins (1984, 1986), and Collinson et al. (1990) traced any shortcomings of bureaucracies in this regard to procedures which were not fully or properly (economically) rational, for example, Collinson et al. pinpointed failures in the training of personnel managers. In all of these cases, the assumption that patronage and discrimination could be equated with economic irrationality could be traced back to Weber.

In *The General Economic History* Weber analysed the origins of capitalism by comparing the East with the West. Weber thought that the reason the East had not taken to capitalism could be found in the irrationality that prevailed there: its irrational law and its magic and superstition (see also Chapter 7). The prime irrationality of the East in respect of markets was the way restrictions were placed on who was allowed to trade goods or labour with whom. Discrimination and patronage were less favoured in Western cities where citizens were meant to have a rational attitude and treat each other equally. In the East there was still a special sort of difference between your group (the tribe, the brotherhood, the community, the religious community) and others which justified this particularism and, indeed, underpinned ascription. The West benefited from Christianity which favoured universalism and pushed aside the 'magical barriers between class, tribes, and peoples, which were still known in the ancient *polis* to a considerable degree' (Weber, 1981: 322–3).

As far as the 'rational organization of labour' was concerned, in the Indian caste system:

> workmen who dare not accept a vessel filled with water from each other's hands, cannot be employed together in the same factory room. Not until the present time, after the possession of the country by the English for almost a century, could this obstacle be overcome. Obviously, capitalism could not develop in an economic group thus bound hand and foot by magical beliefs. (ibid.: 361)

Whenever economic sociology dismisses evidence which does not suit its assumptions, or does without evidence altogether, this passage can be cited as a precedent. In particular, this passage explains why economic sociology is so accustomed to treating alternative value systems as collections of irrational beliefs (possibly based on false or outdated information), and why the working classes' rejection of education is so frequently seen as an atavistic departure from the behaviour needed in a meritocracy.

Like the middle classes everywhere, economic sociology assumes that meritocracy creates incentives to identify and develop aptitudes and capacities that will make society more productive. Murphy (1990) pointed out how the evidence of widespread resistance to the extension of education (among those who stood to benefit from it the most) was dismissed by sociologists. The happy alliance of a more rational allocation with social progress would be undermined by the recognition that huge numbers of working-class men, women and children had refused to co-operate in the way that was necessary if educational achievement was to translate ability into access to appropriate jobs. Yet this was just what British twentieth-century history showed: the working class had been consistently opposed to the raising of the leaving age for compulsory schooling. Economic sociology's unalloyed enthusiasm for ability signalled by educational achievement as the rational and fair successor to ascription was maintained at the cost of ignoring this information.

According to the economic sociology of social mobility, allocating jobs according to merit was both economically rational and socially just. Meritocracy made possible the (more) rational use of human resources because it claimed to be able to move resources – like aptitude and intelligence – to more productive uses. In the process, it served

136

social justice by allocating jobs to those who deserved them because they were competent to do them. Meritocracy took over the language of just desserts in which people might be held to deserve particular jobs because they possessed particular ascribed characteristics (which made them particularly well suited to performing these jobs) and turned just desserts into the necessary outcomes of efficient resource allocation.

Economic sociology was therefore interested in finding out how far meritocracy had advanced, where the remaining obstacles to its advance remained and how these could be addressed. In other words, economic sociology made its mission the extension of meritocracy, a fact reflected in its jargon of 'status attainment', 'common social fluidity', 'increasing merit selection', and so on. All of these central sociological concepts lay within the world as defined by the middle class and, to the extent that economic sociology was driven by the need to advance meritocracy, it did very little else but proselytize a middle-class attempt to put merit at the heart of the division of labour (Collins, 1979).

The clearest expression of this was to be found in the work of Saunders (1990, 1995, 1997) who unblinkingly followed the logic of economic sociology through to the conclusion so many of his colleagues found unpalatable. Since meritocracy distributed according to merit, and since Britain was now a meritocracy, then, Saunders concluded, those who did not fare so well plainly had less merit. In Saunders's case the uneven distribution of merit was a logical consequences of natural differences in intelligence. Marshall et al. (1997) did not think British society quite as meritocratic as Saunders did. Their research gave them cause to wonder how labour markets might actually work, for example, did some people get jobs on merit where that merit had not been certified by educational achievement? They also expressed some fundamental doubts about the operation of a meritocracy even with free compulsory education.

137

MISGIVINGS ABOUT MERIT

Marshall et al. began to question the cherished idea that employers attempted (hampered by the failings of the educational system of course) to sort people into jobs according to merit. They found that the extent to which stubbornly persisting inequalities in access to paid employment could be understood as the outcome of meritocratic processes was confused and inconclusive because the meaning of 'merit' was so hard to pin down. But they did not stray very far from the orthodoxy (and, indeed, seemed to readmit merit by the back door) since they simply suggested that employers could be using additional personal qualities other than intelligence to decide if people 'merited' particular jobs.

Selecting for unproven ability or *uncertified* competence complicated the picture, moreover, as Murphy (1990) had argued, not everyone wanted to join in the competition to achieve and demonstrate merit. Marshall et al. could not fault the meritocratic argument which justified the way working-class people got working-class jobs because they failed to achieve sufficiently well in the education system. Yet they were very uncomfortable with the implications of this argument: how could it be just, they asked, to condemn children who happened to be born into working-class families (which would not teach them the value of education) to lose out in this predictable way? Here Marshall et al. turned the meritocratic argument against itself because meritocracy found the allocation of jobs according to the accident of birth unjust. Moreover, Marshall et al. argued that children, as opposed to adults, could not have developed freedom of choice when they were 'choosing' to do badly at school. The denial of equality of opportunity and freedom of choice implied by the fate of working-class children was therefore anti-meritocratic.

Marshall et al. only began to make real progress towards a critique of the idea of meritocracy when they wondered whether, when pushed to these extremes, the relationship between the morality of meritocracy and its economic rationality came under pressure. We are left uncertain as to whether they would satisfy some portion of economic rationality in order to extend the notion of just desserts to these working-class children who seemed to be excluded from meritocratic processes. At this point, however, Marshall et al. took a decisive, and backward, turn in the direction of economic sociology when they introduced, with the idea of just desserts, the notion that people who were the most valuable to society – value being in large part a function of scarcity – would be the best rewarded.

In the end, Marshall et al. returned to the orthodox economic sociology in which the labour market is seen as economic rationality incarnate.

> We do not challenge the explanation of inequality that sees it, in very broad terms, as the result of processes whereby labour markets reward people differently, depending on the supply of, and demand for the competences they have, and for the jobs that those competences enable them to do. This may indeed be the right way to explain the inequalities that we have found but does it also then allow us to regard those inequalities as manifestations of social justice? (Marshall et al., 1997: 160)

Raising doubts about the happy coincidence of economic rationality and social justice was all to the good, but Marshall et al. passed up the opportunity to develop a properly founded critique of economic behaviour because they chose not to question the notion that market conditions decided whether people and jobs were valuable or important. As is customary in economic sociology, a reckless series of unsupported non sequiturs was stacked on top of the belief that the importance of a job is always a function of its supply and demand. If the market was the measure, the argument went, then the most valuable characteristics must be hard to acquire and/or naturally scarce because the demand for them exceeded their supply and that was why they must be differentially rewarded (ibid.).

It is hard to imagine a better example of economic sociology accepting economic rationality at face value. One obvious problem lies in the equation of value and scarcity. Arguably it is the more common services that humans perform for each other – the services that almost all of us are capable of providing – that we could least afford to do without. This does not necessarily mean the less essential services of the arbitrageur, the CEO and the film star should be less well rewarded than those of the daycare worker, the undertaker and the short-order cook but it might make us wonder why the former are paid so much more (see pp. 159–61). The other problem with the reasoning employed here is that any response to a demand for evidence to support what is said about the *characteristics* of people or jobs relies upon tautology.

Were you to ask Marshall et al. what the more valuable characteristics are, you would be told they are those that the better-rewarded people display. The only way we know a Harvard MBA is harder to acquire than the characteristics of an inspirational teacher in the public school system (see p. 39) is because the MBA pays ten or twenty times as much. Where the argument is generalized, as it logically must be, to uncertified abilities, things get even sillier. By definition, we are told, it must be the charm and charisma of the TV anchorwoman that earn her an enormous salary. Any resemblance between her charms and those of her sister on the shopping channel must be fanciful because the market has spoken! It is hard to understand how naturally sceptical social scientists are so taken in by this without beginning to wonder whether their natural scepticism has to be suspended because economic sociology takes the moral basis of market capitalism as its unexamined starting assumption. Economic sociologists may disagree about all sorts of things but they all agree that the fair and free operation of labour markets is a good thing. In this way they ratify the idea that all moral criticism of markets is thenceforth disarmed since there is no better way of allocating resources.

139

CAPITAL AND COMPETITION IN THE LABOUR MARKET

Social mobility researchers have drawn our attention to the persistence of structured inequality within meritocracies. For 60 years or more, economic sociology has sought explanations of some individuals' failure to take advantage of meritocratic opportunities (Davis and Moore, 1945; Sorokin, 1959). If such failure was not to be explained by natural differences in ability, then the usual solution was to bring cultural differences into the explanation. Such cultural differences might explain, for example, the outright rejection of the educational route to advantage by the working class (Murphy, 1990). Thus Marshall et al. suggested that working-class children lost out because of the decisions their parents made (on their behalf) to opt out of education.

At this point in the argument, economic sociologists were increasingly likely to turn to the economics for inspiration. As a result they imported some key economic concepts into sociology in order to help in the work of explanation. It was Coleman (1990) who first borrowed the idea of human capital from the economics of Becker (1967, 1975, 1976) and Schultz (1961). In this formulation the educational achievement of children was understood as an investment which would pay off in terms of future income streams when the better-educated children got the better-paying jobs (since employers recognized the value of their human capital). The idea of human capital had originally arisen when economists had striven to make their basic theories a better fit with empirical data on labour markets, especially data 'at the boundary between economic and social phenomena' (Fevre, 1992: 39).

In Coleman's theory, the help and encouragement children received from their parents, siblings and wider communities were to be understood as *social* capital, a resource of norms and networks which individuals could draw upon to make a real difference to their life chances. In sum, a cohesive community with a strong commitment to an educational route to success, combined with vibrant social networks to help people access opportunities in the education system and the labour market, would produce children who behaved in the way that was necessary for a meritocracy to work well. Those children who lacked social capital and did not invest in their human capital would not behave in the same way.

Coleman learnt from the economists how to make culture and morality factors in an explanation of social inequality. In such an explanation, morality, like the economists' tastes and preferences (and the individual's utility function), would be reduced to the status of a clause in an argument. Thus in Coleman's theory social capital became the quintessential instrumental morality. As in the example of Granovetter's labour market theory (see p. 131), this sort of theory assumes that ideas about right and wrong are extremely valuable, not in themselves, but for their effect on economic behaviour.[3] In Coleman, for example, the morality of Catholic or Jewish families was useful because it meant that the children of these communities worked harder at school and eventually became more productive citizens. The space left for a consideration of the intrinsic value of the morality was reduced by the expansion of its instrumental function.

At the same time that Coleman imported notions of human and social capital into sociology, Bourdieu (1986) developed the idea of *cultural* capital. In some respects, Bourdieu and Coleman seemed to be saying the same thing in slightly different ways. Thus Bourdieu might have been describing social capital when he suggested that an individual's habits of thought were derived from their social environment (their 'habitus') and that these habits predisposed them to make certain sorts of decisions, including decisions about education, which reproduced existing patterns of social stratification and social divisions.

This has proved an influential view among those who seek to understand the reproduction of social inequality (see, for example, Hodkinson et al., 1996) but it appears to treat people's values, indeed their morality, in the same instrumental manner as Coleman. Yet, in other respects, what Bourdieu (1986, 2000) had to say on social and cultural capital and symbolic violence offered more to the sociology of economic behaviour than Coleman. Bourdieu described the way in which people were treated differently according to subtle distinctions which, even though the differences might have no relation to ability to do particular jobs, did affect labour market outcomes. This was more promising: in this view much of the inequality that Marshall et al. found they had to accept as an unpalatable consequence of the otherwise virtuous labour market could now be thought of as in some sense optional.

Further progress towards the sociology of economic behaviour occurred in the work of Phillip Brown. Brown (1990) argued that not only was the current system far from meritocratic (see p. 134), but the struggle to make it meritocratic had been abandoned. Perhaps because those who were less well off remained so unenthusiastic about education, Western governments had decided that meritocracy was an impossible aim. They had also decided that it was no longer economically rational to make such efforts to achieve it, for example it would never be possible to tap a hidden pool of working-class talent. The solution that most governments opted for was to legitimate what had been, for much of the time, the reality in supposedly meritocratic systems. They resolved to distribute educational resources according 'the *wealth* and *wishes* of the parents rather than the *abilities* and *efforts* of pupils' (Brown, 1990: 66). This basis for distribution was now to be made open and legitimate because these governments espoused an 'ideology of parentocracy' rather than the discredited ideology of meritocracy for the distribution of educational resources.

According to the new ideology, cultural prejudice against education among the working class was insurmountable and 'sensible' governments

141

would abandon the attempt to force all children through the same system. Instead the education system should be opened to more competition, and people who wanted a good education should be allowed to choose the best. This choice and competition would push up standards and strengthen the economy. The pursuit of the new ideology was in part stimulated by changes in political ideologies and voters' preferences. But Brown also pointed out that this suited the middle classes who had been attempting to corner the market in the certificates which were increasingly needed to get access to the better jobs, especially in a time of labour market uncertainty. In later work Brown built on these ideas in order to develop 'positional competition theory'.

This terminology originates with the economist Hirsch (1977), but in Brown's hands positional competition turned into a preliminary step towards the sociology of economic behaviour. Brown (2000) took as his starting point existing work on social closure (see Chapter 6) that suggested that groups tried to define the rules of labour market competition in a way that suited them best. He then drew attention to the way that individuals and groups also compete on the established rules and develop strategies to give them an edge in this competition. Brown wanted us to shift our attention away from the way educational credentials were sanctified as the proper mechanism of distributing resources (in a way that was convenient for the middle class who were so keen on education) to the sort of competition that went on once it was widely accepted that credentials played this role. Thus Brown described the way in which middle-class families in Britain and other post-industrial countries searched for extra bits of cultural capital to add to the familiar credentials and even sought out new credentials which they could deploy in different (and perhaps global) games.

'Positional competition theory' confirmed that meritocracy had been superseded and that no-holds barred competition had been put in its place. Brown made reference to Durkheim but it was not perhaps as clear as it might have been that positional competition was the fate of meritocracy under conditions of demoralization. This really was the war of all against all in which parents used every trick they knew to make sure their children stole a march on their classmates. The idea of getting everyone to the starting gate so that a fair race could be run (and the fairly established differences between individuals rewarded) looked quaint and hopelessly out-moded. There had been a further change in the legitimation of inequality. It could now be universally acknowledged that individuals – or groups or even countries – were not doing well because they were more able, but because they competed more effectively. This was the only remaining sense in which they deserved to win.

Progress towards the sociology of economic behaviour depends on understanding, and exposing to critique, the way that social groups construct the frameworks within which competition takes place. Brown's emphasis on positional competition may allow us to make progress in this way. Like Collins and Bourdieu – and unlike Marshall et al. – he did not take it for granted that the possession of credentials or cultural capital automatically signalled the possession of socially valuable characteristics. Indeed, his emphasis on parentocracy and positional competition told us that meritocracy was no longer considered by labour market actors to be necessary to legitimate the competition that went on. None of those middle-class families Brown wrote about seriously believed that the labour market was sorting people according to their ability (and, at one remove, their value to society). What was left was naked competition, competition as an end in itself, which apparently needed no apology.

Brown showed that society had entered, or was at least moving towards, a era in which the legitimation of privilege and advantage derived simply from the fact that individuals and families were competing for resources. As long as there was competition, then advantage and disadvantage were fully justified. This competition was of course driven entirely by the individual's desire for economic success and their readiness to use whatever means were necessary in order to give themselves, and particularly their children, an economic advantage. As in his other work (Brown 1995; Brown and Lauder, 1996, 2001; Brown and Scase, 1994), Brown was trying to give us a glimpse of the future by identifying the key trends that would soon become much more general and which we might want to put a stop to before it was too late. For this reason, Brown is also a useful theorist for social scientists who are interested in comparative work: Brown's theories can be used to compare one society with another and, particularly, to compare the rest of the world with the United States, the society which most closely accords with Brown's dystopian vision.

Brown's work makes a valuable contribution towards the sociology of economic behaviour but we also need to find ways to talk about all the observable variation of the present: we need to understand how the allocation of resources, and in particular jobs, works now as well as how it might turn out in the near future. The sociology of economic behaviour requires a sociology of labour markets that shows us all the different ways in which this allocation can be socially constructed. Brown made some contributions in this direction – for example, he discussed the distinction between membership, meritocratic and market rules for inclusion and exclusion – but we will now turn to an earlier, more detailed and comprehensive treatment of the same subject.

THE SOCIOLOGY OF LABOUR MARKETS

Marshall et al. (1997) remained trapped within economic sociology's limited world-view because they did not realize how little of their faith in the way the labour market sorts people into jobs according to their ability and competence was justified. To correct this mistake we need to pay attention to what the sociology (rather than the economics) of labour markets can tell us about the way they operate. The sociology of economic behaviour can expose the absurdity of the non sequiturs in the arguments that lead economic sociology to validate existing patterns of privilege and advantage because they are the product of hegemonic economic rationality. If we do this we will find ourselves in a position to develop a forceful critique of economic behaviour. If we undermine the belief in the superiority of labour markets which work according to economic values, we create the opportunity to expose the operation of labour markets to *real* moral judgement.

Despite their best efforts, in the final analysis Marshall et al. took a very similar view of the labour market to that held by other economic sociologists and even their critic Saunders. Herrnstein and Murray were more (in)famous proponents of Saunders's view that the division of labour reflects natural differences in ability. In Herrnstein and Murray we encounter a similar faith in the ability of the labour market to sort people into jobs according to their abilities and competence to that expressed by Marshall et al.: '[n]o one decreed that occupations should sort us out by our cognitive abilities, and no one enforces the process. It goes on beneath the surface, guided by its own invisible hand' (Herrnstein and Murray, 1996: 52).

What is this invisible hand and how does it work? The answer takes the form of a belief in the omnipotence of economic rationality:

> it so happens that the way to get the best possible work force, other things equal, is to hire the smartest people they [employers] can find. It is not even necessary for employers to be aware that intelligence is the attribute they are looking for. As employers check their hiring procedures against the quality of their employees and refine their procedures accordingly, the importance of intelligence in the selection process converges on whatever real importance it has for the job in question, whether or not they use a formal test. (Herrnstein and Murray, 1996: 88)

The notion that 'employers check their hiring procedures against the quality of their employees' quickly becomes ridiculous as soon as we begin to analyse even the most superficial evidence of what employers actually do.

In *The Sociology of Labour Markets* (Fevre, 1992) I explain why any real research on the subject shows just how difficult it is for

144

employers to work out how to recognize good work and, especially, good workers. This point will be discussed shortly but since the work discussed so far in this chapter has, in common with the rest of economic sociology, almost totally neglected the sociology of labour markets, there is some catching up to do first. In Fevre (1992) I define the key operations of labour markets and describe the way that innumerable labour market 'territories' are bounded one from another in all sorts of ways including geography, occupation, measures of social distance, and so on. I then map out the sociology of labour markets using three sociological projects: 'society', 'economy' and 'polity'.

Under 'society' we find the construction of labour market territories depends on two social principles – the social division of labour and social hierarchy – which have fascinated sociologists for over a century and a half. If labour is divided, this immediately raises the question of who should do what: how does it become acceptable that people are allocated to one job and not another, particularly when there are such potent consequences? From the founding of the discipline, sociological explanations of the legitimation of this process relied on the invocation of natural differences and the idea of specialization. But these conditions were not sufficient for the familiar system in which people and the things they do are assigned wildly differing values (degree of difficulty, value to society, and so on) if they are not combined with a widely accepted principle of social hierarchy: '[t]he belief in hierarchy leads to the acceptance of the idea that types of work and types of people are different, thus making the social division of labour – different people do different types of work – acceptable, even preferable' (Fevre, 1992: 52). The existence of labour market territories is proof of the way hierarchies of people and places in the division of labour have been created in different societies.

The two social principles of hierarchy and the division of labour are put into practice in the social groups, relations and institutions that sociologists generally consider as the locations of culture and power. One type of explanation of labour market and related behaviour looks to the effects of people's own choices, or perhaps those made by their families, as a result of membership of groups, relations and institutions. Under this heading we might find status attainment theory, and theories of the culture of poverty and the under-class theories. Large amounts of economic sociology could be categorized here, including much structural-functionalist sociology. Under the heading of labour market behaviour which results from the constraints and obstacles imposed on us by others, we find studies of social networks (now including much that is theorized in terms of social capital), and studies of social closure originating with Weber and developed by Parkin and Collins (see also Freedman, 1976),[4] and domination as refined by feminist sociology.

These explanations might help us to understand how hierarchies are created, but what are hierarchies based upon? Sociologists have considered a limited number of alternatives, all of which are based on assigning values according to specified social criteria. Labour market processes are in fact concerned with putting these values into practice. There are people-based hierarchies which refer to social differences like gender, religion, ethnicity, age and 'race'. In this view, types of work are assigned the value accorded to the types of people who do them. Then there are work-based hierarchies in which different values are assigned by reference to the work done. In Fevre (1992) I identified this view more exclusively with structural-functionalism, which commonly subscribed to the view that value derived from the degree of difficulty involved in the work, but this is not the only source of work-based value. For example, in the social mobility research discussed above, the value of the work done was determined by its usefulness to society. The people who do the work are then assigned a corresponding value – here people are judged by the work they do, or are capable of doing, rather than the other way round. Theories in this sub-category have therefore tended to assume that people are assigned places in the division of labour according to their competence to do the jobs they hold. As we have seen earlier in this chapter, these competences can be learnt or based on naturally occurring differences.

146

The final basis for social hierarchy that I considered was the market. Market values are one of the possible sources of value alongside work and people values, but whereas Marshall et al. (1997) saw supply and demand as indistinguishable from work-based values, there is no real reason why this should be the case. Market values can be completely independent and, according to some sociologists, this was actually what was entailed in the Weberian idea of 'market situation'. Under perfect competition market situation may be synonymous with relative scarcity – the types of workers for which demand exceeds supply will have the greatest value – but here relative scarcity plays nothing like the role it does for Marshall et al. (or Herrnstein and Murray). I also pointed out that, although this was rarely done, there was no reason why work should not be rated according to its 'market situation', just as workers were. Relative scarcity was one source of high value work (in addition to any value arising from its intrinsic merits or from the sort of people who characteristically perform it).

It is important to dwell for the moment on the implications of the analytical distinction being made here between work values and market values because economic sociology seems to have systematically conflated these two categories. In these matters, economic sociologists have simply followed middle-class thinking about the division of labour. Here it is commonly assumed that the jobs which are most valuable to society will be those that are most difficult to perform and for which the supply of qualified workers is relatively scarce. This is part of the process of legitimation of income differentials (see below) but it should not be imported wholesale into academic analysis. The distinction between legitimation and analysis has already been drawn in the discussion of the work of Brown above. Brown was describing a trend towards competition on the basis of market values alone. This increase in 'positional competition' threatened to undermine meritocratic legitimation that depended on people assuming there were more than market values at work. This would no longer be the case if people were believed to be getting jobs *only* because they possessed a piece of paper.

Now we can return to the bizarre idea that 'employers check their hiring procedures against the quality of their employees and refine their procedures accordingly' (Herrnstein and Murray, 1996: 88). At this point it is as well to remember that the agents of employers are usually human resource managers. In the previous chapter we learnt something of the limitations on the power and competence of such managers and of some of the incentives they have to give a false impression of their abilities (Gillespie, 1991). If we discount the ideological and self-serving accounts of managers, how do they really know what qualities are required for any job and how do they really know that one person has more of these qualities than any other? The sociology of labour markets suggests that managers decide on the basis of *social* values (people, work and markets) but to know how to enact this decision they must determine how these values are to be operationalized.

One way of operationalizing these values is to resort to *discrimination*, and related behaviours like favouritism and patronage that put people values into practice. (In the following discussion it should be remembered that there are two sides to the labour market and discrimination applies to the way workers – labour market actors too of course – choose jobs as well as the way employers choose workers.) If actors think that values which attach to people – in other words, those characteristics which are ascribed to them – are the right sort of values according to which labour markets should operate, then they will favour discrimination. Thus someone who thinks that the difference between races is socially significant, and wants this to inform the allocation of resources, will think racial discrimination a good way of distributing jobs.

Although plenty of hiring is still determined by discrimination, this is plainly not what Herrnstein and Murray had in mind. Without knowledge of the sociology of labour markets, they assumed that work values were operationalized in hiring procedures and, instead of discriminating, employers selected the best workers for the job in question. In *selection* the characteristics of the job will be paramount and workers will be sifted and screened for qualities that suggest they will be able to do the job in question (well). In this case employers are quite likely to choose workers according to their performance in aptitude tests or trial periods of employment.

There is a third logical possibility of operationalizing social values: putting market values into operation through *matching* the market situation of job and job-seeker. We need to bear in mind that these values occur in messy combinations in real life (for example, matching followed by selection with a dash of discrimination) but that we need to separate out the individual logical components before we construct equally complex explanations. So, matching on its own is simply the market's impersonal operation to bring the relative scarcity of the job into line with the relative scarcity of the job-seeker. Here the sifting and screening process may rely on previous experience or credentials. At this stage in the analysis previous experience or credentials are a measure of relative scarcity or 'market situation' (people without the credentials might still be perfectly capable of doing these jobs) but a way has to be found to screen the competition and credentials, for example, are an obvious way of using the market to do this.

In contrast to economic sociology, the Weberian work from which Brown draws, via Parkin (1979) and Collins (1979), has always been happy to see market values working alone. This was why so much attention was paid to credentials. They were unevenly distributed and acted as signs that indicated market value but could not be assumed to have any relationship with people's capacity to do a particular job. Of course, in practice, the use of 'credential' and 'credentialism' in economic sociology has been hopelessly corrupted for many years. It seems that academics with lots of credentials find it difficult to treat credentials simply as signs without assuming there has to be some 'real' value to them in terms of skills and abilities. Pure Weberian theory demands this but the corruption of this tradition can be traced to Parsons who elided work and market values in a way that incorporated a moral judgement of the division of labour (and the existing division of labour at that).

As Davis and Moore famously pointed out, the distribution of jobs according to the principles of relative scarcity was morally justified as being good for society and fair because it put the people who were capable of doing them into the difficult jobs (Davis and Moore, 1945). With minor adjustment this is the same confused reasoning we have already encountered in Marshall et al. To get the sociology of labour markets back on track we have to return to Weber and the idea that market values, like other values, must be treated independently in the first instance so that we can properly analyse the way that groups and institutions deal in power and culture to construct labour markets.[5]

Weber draws our attention to the need for legitimacy to be built in if this construction is to be successful and market values that can readily be sourced to the great modernist legitimations of rationality, legality and universalism, have provided an increasingly powerful source of legitimation as time has passed. We need to be able to *understand* this, not automatically approve of it and deprive ourselves of the opportunity of critique. When we do this we can see how the way market values and work values are yoked together (in the explanations of social mobility researchers or lay actors) turns them into very powerful legitimations of the existing distribution of resources. Our critique should be animated, rather than being disabled, by this power since we have taken a step closer to understanding the source and persistence of many stubborn social inequalities and to being able to mount a persuasive morally-based critique of the main argument that sustains them.

This is only one example of the way economic sociologists have routinely confused *discrimination*, *matching* and *selection* or, indeed, assumed that one served the other. In economic sociology it has usually been assumed that discrimination would not help employers to select the best people for the job whereas matching would. In the sociology of labour markets no such assumptions are made and each of these explanations are available to us to use singly or in combination to help us understand real, complex labour market behaviour. The alacrity with which economic sociology forgot this (and assumed that selection and matching were causally linked) can more easily be understood if we move on to the next plane of analysis.

149

Industrial capitalism brings with it a new layer of *industrial* values in addition to the social values (people, work, market) that form the basis of social hierarchy: 'industrial values as a whole do not provide the basis of hierarchies but ... theories of social hierarchies are not intended to explain all that can be explained in the sociology of labour markets' (Fevre, 1992: 97). The three types of values I consider are economic values, technical values, and organizational values. Economic values include the financial costs and benefits that affect the behaviour of job-seekers and employers. Technical values cover the workers' and managers' ideas about technology, work organization and skill (for example). Finally, there are organizational values which refer to authority structures and cultures like paternalism. When it comes to putting these 'industrial values' into operation, managers still need the social values and their associated vehicles, discrimination, selection and matching:

> If you are the manager of a paternalist firm, you will have a particular idea about the sort of workers you want and even about how they should be hired. You may want them, for example, to fit in with the family of the firm and even the process of hiring (an EILM[6]) can reflect

this wish. Here the labour market is shaped by your organisational values, but how do you actually make your choice of recruits? There is no other basis for you to make this choice than discrimination, selection or matching. For example, you may consider that using people values will allow you to find the workers who fit your requirements (which are derived from your organisational values). In this case you discriminate in order to make the decisions which are necessary in order to achieve the goals set by industrial values. 'Discrimination' describes the way in which the labour market works when, in this example, the labour market reflects organisational values arising from the economic division of labour.

This is, of course, only a hypothetical example, and there is certainly no one-to-one correspondence between particular industrial values and particular ways of describing the way in which labour markets work: organisational values do not always lead to discrimination. Thus an employer who values rationalisation and bureaucracy may be more likely to prefer market values above people values and so will engage in processes of matching rather [than] discrimination. Similarly, readers should not assume that employers who consider technical values important will always opt for selection, that is, for hiring and firing based on work values. (Fevre, 1992: 114–15)

As long as industrial values are put into practice through social processes like hiring and firing, employers and others are making decisions about how to make up the usual social hierarchies that allow them to run these processes and present them as legitimate ways of distributing valuable resources.

If an employer is prioritizing *technical* values this does not necessarily mean they will select their employees (as Marshall et al. or Herrnstein and Murray assume). Let us say that employers believe a particular skill is required in a job. They are at liberty to fill this job using any one of the three categories of social values. For example, if they are racists they may well discriminate against blacks because they believe white workers are easier to train. On the other hand, they may choose to see the worker in action so that they can select using work values. Finally, they may choose to ask for evidence of a credential that indicates the technical value would be satisfied.

We must bear in mind here that the credential is operating as a sign, and it does not guarantee that the person who possesses the credential also has the required skill (any more than the aptitude test or hiring a white person guarantees this). The employer is simply using a sign to stimulate the market to come up with the person they need. The particular sign used here, a credential, could also be used in pursuit of other values (see below) and, what is more, the credential is not the only sign that can be used in matching. Thus when an employer asks for previous experience in their job advertisement, this is also being used as sign and the employer has no guarantee that the market will bring them someone who can really do the job.

150

Just as in the case of technical values, organizational values have no predetermined relationship with any kind of hiring or firing process. For instance, an employer may discriminate against women who apply for promotion to senior management because it is believed by present incumbents that the admission of women would upset the 'atmosphere' (the formality of the organization might increase, for example). Another employer might think that the best way to represent organizational values was by getting potential recruits together in an assessment centre for a weekend to evaluate their behaviour in a setting that simulates work.[7] This evaluation leads to the selection of the recruits who will fit in best with prevailing organizational values. Finally, matching might be thought the best way of meeting organizational values. In this case employers might use credentials which they think would indicate the right sort of person – as in those organizations which prefer people from Ivy League schools or with prior military experience – or they can specify their preferences for 'fun-loving' people and 'extrovert personalities', for example, in their job advertisements.

Finally, economic values can also be pursued by way of matching, selection or discrimination. Let us say an employer is determined to prioritize labour costs above all other economic considerations (such as output, productivity, profitability, and the prospects for research and design). We might think an employer who wants the cheapest available labour has no alternative but to leave hiring up to the market and simply take the recruits who are willing to apply when the job is advertised. But the employer might be of the opinion (perhaps learned from bitter experience) that this sort of open hiring practice gives them incompetent workers who actually spoil the product. In other words, experience has taught these employers to use selection to achieve the satisfaction of economic values. Thus they may recruit by getting existing employees to bring in their younger brothers and sisters to work for a trial period rather than advertising their vacancies on the open market. Finally, an employer may have learnt that the workers who will respond to advertisements for low-paying jobs on the open market are quite likely to be young workers. If they consider young workers unreliable for some reason (for example, they are assumed to have poor time-keeping records, faster turnover and habits of pilfering, vandalizing and drug dealing on the premises), then people values will necessarily come into play. In these circumstances the recruitment of the cheapest available labour will take the form of discrimination in favour of others groups prepared to work for low wages like the retired.

We can now see exactly how complex our theories and models must be if we are to understand the variety and subtle shades of difference occurring in real labour market processes. We can also see that it is really an extraordinarily tall order for an employer to work out which

151

are the necessary abilities for any job and how these might be recognized among competing candidates (especially when there is such a tenuous connection between their abilities and the achievements employers might ask about in order to measure those abilities). Compare these insights drawn from an attempt to develop a proper sociological theory of the labour market with the best theories that are currently on offer in mainstream social science. Theories of bounded rationality have tried to grasp this sort of complex reality with a very limited universe of rational behaviour and a very limited repertoire of add-on solutions to the problems posed by real labour markets. These theories always see hiring in the same sort of way: filtering and screening, for instance, are to do with minimizing transaction costs and reducing the amount of information to be processed.

As Chapter 4 demonstrated, the prevailing ideology of management vastly over-estimates managers' knowledge, skills and ability to influence events by using chosen means to achieve defined ends. The way in which managers intervene in labour markets (together with limitations on their ability so to intervene) represents one of the prime examples where we continually over-estimate managers' knowledge, skills and ability to influence events by using chosen means to achieve defined ends. Sociology is well placed to make significant advances over theories which assume that any differences of opinion about what economic rationality is made of are simply the fault of imperfect information.

In fact, little empirical work has been undertaken with anything more than a very rudimentary sociological theory of the way labour markets work. One exception is Collinson et al. (1990) but, for reasons described below, this study involved a tremendous research effort with comparatively little to show for this effort in terms of findings. A much more recent example of labour market research shows how some level of understanding of the complexity of labour markets and the difficulties faced by those making hiring decisions can be put into practice on a shoe-string. In fact, theoretically informed empirical research on the way labour markets work is so rare that even research that is done on a shoe-string can quickly reveal findings which are quite different to those that might be expected from reading economic sociology (including the work of social mobility researchers).

As part of her PhD research, Jackson (2001) investigated the hypothesis of Increasing Merit Selection (IMS) against the contents of UK job advertisements (for further discussion of the IMS hypothesis, see p. 158). Advertisements for managers and professionals made much of *educational* qualifications whereas advertisements for other occupations were much more likely to ask for vocational qualifications. In addition, 'only 42 per cent of all advertisements contained a requirement for a qualification of any kind. If jobs truly are allocated only on the basis of exhibited qualifications, as the IMS hypothesis would predict, this is not reflected in the job advertisements studied here' (Jackson, 2001: 623).

Whereas we might quibble about Jackson's understanding of 'merit', her work does help us to evaluate the normal assumptions economic sociology makes about meritocratic labour markets. Jackson concluded that employers were more interested in ability and effort. These criteria also appeared in inverse frequency to mentions of qualifications. In addition, a substantial minority of advertisements demanded evidence (for example, previous experience) that employees could perform a specific task. This was especially common in intermediate class jobs but 82 per cent of advertisements mentioned experience or technical skills. Jackson concluded that employers were trying to find the skills needed on the job in question rather than screening for the ability to learn these skills. Again, there was an inverse relationship with demands for qualifications. Moreover, whereas 42 per cent of advertisements asked for qualifications, 54 per cent asked for social skills and personal characteristics. Jackson concluded that employers were finding other ways (than using credentials) of finding people who were suitable for their vacancies. We can conclude instead that her work demonstrates that there is very little that is easy or self-evident about the recruitment of the best person for the job.

The Sociology of Labour Markets suggests that an apparently simple idea like 'the quality of employees', so vital to Herrnstein and Murray's argument yet so unthinkingly deployed, falls apart once you develop a genuine sociology of economic behaviour. The construction of standards to measure quality is rather a matter of social negotiation, invention and even conflict using the various categories of value described above (and others, some of which will be mentioned below). Seen in this light, the apparent simplicity of the original notion can be reinterpreted as an ideological device: the power to hire and fire is self-evidently legitimate if those who exercise it are simply putting into practice commonly agreed standards (and everyone knows what counts as good jobs and good workers). This is why Herrnstein and Murray serve as a good example of the mistake that economic sociology makes: not only do they fail to question the status quo but they actually join in with the ideological work that maintains it. The fiction that employers could, never mind do, use cognitive ability to distribute people to jobs is a major plank in the legitimation of the existing division of labour and the behaviour of the actors who are responsible for it.

Uncovering the messy social construction of labour market operations is a deeply subversive act – just as we hoped it might be. It makes us look at assessment centres and psycho-social profiling in a very different light, for example. We no longer assume these are simply the latest refinements in the methods employers use to measure relevant cognitive abilities. We no longer abdicate the right to question ('these are hard-headed business people, they must have introduced these methods because they allow them to choose the right people for the job') because we know that we actually understand nothing until we find out what combination of values are being used to make labour markets work. Until we do the research to find out the truth, the assessment centres might be sophisticated engines of discrimination, and the psycho-social profiling all about prioritizing organizational values which conflict violently with some economic or technical values that the company holds dear.

Of course, social and industrial values do not exhaust the values that inform labour market processes, for example, in Fevre (1992) I discussed the legal-political values that inform the way that labour markets are influenced by their relationship with the state and other political institutions. For example, laws about equal opportunities put certain values into operation in labour markets as do state policies on education and training, work-life issues, and welfare. So far as empirical sociology is concerned, finding out how all these values (and many others) influence real labour markets is a matter for investigation. Does this employer discriminate, do they do it because they are pursuing organizational values (they think women will not fit in at higher management levels) and what success is the state having pursuing alternative equal opportunity measures designed to remove the glass ceiling? Finding answers to such questions is not a straightforward matter.

Part of the problem is that sociological researchers may only have access to the unreliable accounts of participants which are formed as part of their economic behaviour, indeed these accounts sometimes serve as the basis of their right to act at all (after all, every manager will claim they practise selection when they hire). People will have all sorts of reasons to make false claims about events. For instance, it is much harder to call the legitimacy of redundancies into question on economic grounds than it is on any other. For this reason management will usually cover up the organizational and technical values that may well have contributed to the decision to make workers redundant. Detailed empirical investigation is required in every case and frequently a lot of effort must go into finding out *who* is doing what even before research can try to determine which values influenced which decisions. In the case of redundancy, for example, there are other groups than managers – different groups of workers, trade union officers, trade union full-timers – who can have some influence on decisions about which workers are made redundant. As in all of these cases, empirical research must proceed by first finding out which groups are involved and which groups have the *power* to influence the way events turn out (Fevre, 1985).

154

To establish what is really going on, we have to find out which social relations and institutions and, in particular, which groups have the power to make their accounts the ones that matter. There may be all sorts of claims for the efficacy of family-friendly policies, for instance, but in order to assess the impact the values they represent are having on labour markets, we would have to know whether the policies had an effect on the groups which really had the power to change the situation. We have seen, for instance, the way that *voluntary* family-friendly policies have little effect on the behaviour of employees. To be effective such policies must be made to act on the employers – where the power lies in this instance – and this means making them compulsory.

At the most basic level we need to know how to explain the different mixes of values that we uncover in one labour market as opposed to another, but at a more sophisticated level we need to know about all the hidden and complex relationships between power and legitimacy (Bowring, 2000; Sayer, 2000b).[8] Employers have the power to stop family-friendly policies because this is seen as their legitimate right (and it is employees as much as politicians who grant them that right, see Chapter 2). The beginnings of critique require that these and other claims to the legitimate exercise of power are opened up to scrutiny. What values are really in operation here and why should they be privileged? For this reason it becomes absolutely vital to explode the idea that the market is synonymous with selection and, for instance, that technical and economic values can be satisfied together without messy compromises and trade-offs. All of this unpicking of the values that matter is vitally necessary to critique but it is also necessary that much more thought be given to the social groups whose behaviour is determined by these values and who use them, in turn, to legitimate their access to resources.

CLASSES AND INCOME INEQUALITIES

According to one persuasive theory, the labour market territories described earlier in this chapter are, in large part, the product of action taken by classes. In particular, the values of meritocracy and, subsequently, 'positional competition' have been associated with the middle classes. It is possible to infer patterns of class activity from social mobility studies such as those produced by Marshall et al. or by Prandy using a different approach influenced by Bourdieu.

Prandy (1998; Prandy and Bottero, 2000) was particularly interested in the significance for social stratification of the decisions people made in the course of routine social behaviour, especially their choices of friends and marriage partners. It was in these choices, and in the way that parents brought up their children, that stratification was reproduced and stable patterns of social mobility were maintained. According to Prandy, it was the unequal distribution of social, cultural and economic resources that gave rise to these variations in lifestyle, but the distinctive patterns of social interaction in friendship circles, marriage arrangements, and labour markets were necessary for these inequalities to be reproduced. In this view, the reproduction of inequality is the product of the action of members of classes.

Classes are also deeply implicated in the twentieth-century story of the way underlying patterns of social mobility were left largely unaltered by the replacement of ascription by achievement. With greater rationalization and bureaucracy there was a gradual movement towards using qualifications to establish competences. At the same time there were meritocratic reforms in education systems and the proportion of the population achieving educational qualifications increased. The remainder of this section consists of an account of the way classes adapted their behaviour to these changes. Over the course of the twentieth century some classes managed to set up a system for passing on places in the division of labour to their sons and daughters which had all the appearance of great legitimacy because it gave a central role to educational achievement.

156

Although Prandy's approach might be more suitable for this purpose, for the sake of convenience, we will persevere with the analysis of social mobility discussed earlier in the chapter. Marshall et al. (1997) showed that, below degree level, and comparing those born in the 1920s with those born in the 1950s, educational achievement increased at all levels of social class. Those born into the working class were particularly successful in achieving intermediate level qualifications (ordinary *and* advanced qualifications immediately below degree level). Indeed, the achievement gap between those from a manual working-class background and the rest got smaller although it did not close. For degree (and above) qualifications the pattern was different: here it was the routine non-manual and the salariat that benefited from the expansion of educational qualifications. For example, of those from the salariat born in the 1920s, less than 15 per cent achieved this sort of qualification, whereas for those born in the 1950s over twice this proportion did so. The increases in the proportion achieving degree level qualifications among those from a routine non-manual background were just as impressive with a particularly spectacular increase between those born in the 1940s and those born in the 1950s. For those from working-class backgrounds the changes were less marked. The strongest upward trend was for those from skilled manual backgrounds but for the rest of the working class gains were either slow or there was no change in the percentage gaining degrees or equivalent qualifications (Marshall et al., 1997).

In common with other social mobility researchers, Marshall et al. showed that, regardless of the qualifications achieved, those from higher class backgrounds were more likely to enter the salariat but that this influence has tended to get weaker over time. This weakening was particularly evident among the salariat, and especially the higher salariat. Over the course of the twentieth century, individuals were more likely to need a degree (or possibly some lower qualification) to enter the salariat and they were less and less likely to be able to do it on the strength of class background alone. *In effect, the connection between origins and destinations was increasingly mediated by that kind of education which favoured the middle class.*

The sons and daughters of the working class gained some qualifications as the century progressed but the big gains in the credentials (degrees) that were increasingly required to get into the salariat were made by those from the salariat and routine non-manual class. This meant the gap in these sorts of credentials (and the labour market access they give) actually increased. We should recall that between the 1930s and 1970s the number of manual working-class jobs, especially the unskilled jobs, declined. Over the same period individuals found it steadily more difficult to get into non-manual jobs with no or few qualifications. Changes in the occupational structure were reinforced by the shift towards achievement and made life *increasingly* difficult for those who did not perform well in school.

Marshall et al. (1997) showed that the percentage achieving intermediate qualifications and going into the salariat fell while the percentage going into unskilled manual work increased. Individuals might have got into the salariat with these qualifications in the 1930s but were much less likely to enter the salariat with these qualifications later in the century (they were also a little less likely to make it into routine non-manual jobs). It was at the level of these intermediate qualifications that the sons and daughters of the working class made their most significant gains (and not at degree level and above) yet it was precisely the qualifications that they had begun to gain that became less valuable labour market assets.

For example, less than 30 per cent of those gaining advanced level qualifications in the 1930s entered blue-collar jobs whereas well over half of the 1960s' cohort found a first destination in a blue-collar job. Looking at degree-level qualifications across cohorts Marshall et al. (1997) found that for all classes the proportions going into the salariat (and even skilled manual) dropped with the slack being taken up by unskilled manual. All the same, 60 per cent still went into salariat jobs whereas for people with intermediate qualifications the proportions entering the salariat fell much more dramatically. Using logistic regression, and controlling for education, Marshall et al.

157

showed the devaluation of advanced level qualifications over the period 1972 to 1987–92 which cut the advantage such qualifications used to give the men who held them (over those with basic or qualifications or none at all) in the competition for places in the salariat by half. The same analysis showed a slight devaluation of the power of a degree (or equivalent). For those in the highest social class, however, there was a slight increase in the value of a degree and here the devaluation of advanced level qualifications was less marked.

Of course all of this evidence argues against the 'Increasing Merit Selection' (IMS) hypothesis which would suggest a much smoother fit between qualifications and jobs. For example, the IMS would lead us to expect advanced level qualifications would increase in value as entrance to more and more occupations was tied to merit, whereas the opposite seems to have happened. Moreover, those with ordinary level qualifications have, by way of contrast, actually increased their chances of getting into the salariat over the period. It is hard to argue that advanced level qualifications are being squeezed out in favour of degrees when a higher proportion of those with lower qualifications are getting in.

Once we step outside the ideology of meritocracy and begin to understand the relationship between social mobility and educational achievement in terms of the joint action of a class, these data make a lot more sense since we would no longer expect a smooth fit between jobs and qualifications. For example, we can now argue that the middle classes made use of advanced level qualifications for the purposes of monopolization until the ideology of meritocracy began to affect the behaviour of some of those who were previously excluded. The usefulness of advanced qualifications for the purposes of social closure rapidly declined and, in order to restore the monopoly position (and keep social fluidity down to the same rate it had been up that point), the middle classes began to use degree-level qualifications for the same purpose.

Thus far we have paid very little attention to the resource implications of class action, in particular, the implications for incomes. Fevre (1992) specifically excluded the sociology of wage-setting from the sociology of labour markets but of course wage-determination cannot be excluded from the sociology of economic behaviour. We must extend the theoretical framework developed earlier in this chapter to explain income inequalities. The idea that values may have something to do with the setting of relative wage rates goes back at least as far as Durkheim:

> at every moment of history there is a dim perception, in the moral consciousness of societies, of the respective value of different social services, the relative reward due to each, and the consequent degree of comfort appropriate on the average workers in each occupation. The different functions are graded in public opinion and a certain coefficient of well-being assigned to each, according to its place in the hierarchy. According to accepted ideas, for example, a certain way of living

is considered the upper limit to which a workman may aspire in his efforts to improve his existence, and there is another limit below which he is not willingly permitted to fall unless he has seriously bemeaned [sic] himself ... A genuine regimen exists, therefore, although not always legally formulated, which fixes with relative precision the maximum degree of ease of living to which each social class may legitimately aspire. However, there is nothing immutable about such a scale. It changes with the increase or decrease of collective revenue and the changes occurring in the moral ideas of society. (Durkheim, 1897/1952: 249–50)

In contrast to the functionalists (for example, Davis and Moore, 1945) who thought we were paid what we were worth, here we are paid what we think others will accept as a reflection of what we are worth.

Economic sociologists have been unhappy with this approach, and have often contrasted it with the approach taken by economists (for which they have more respect). Thus Granovetter agreed with Phelps Brown that the 'sociologists' approach to pay determination' derived from the assumption that people act in 'certain ways because to do so is customary, or an obligation, or the "natural thing to do", or right and proper or just and fair'. Granovetter thought this justified criticism when sociologists indulged in over-socialized explanations of 'social influences' which had people following customs or norms 'mechanically and automatically, irrespective of their bearing on rational choice' (Granovetter, 1985: 485). On the other hand, more recent work in economics – and particularly the work of Blanchflower and Oswald (1994) – drew attention to the *moral* restraint which wage-earners exercise when unemployment is high (see also Etzioni, 1988). Indeed, research across the social sciences, including psychology and economics, suggested that morality lingered on in some unexpected places including the setting of wage rates (Dickinson, 1995; Dickinson and Sell-Trujillo, 1996).

159

Making further progress with the idea that we are paid what others think we are worth requires us to think about the values that others deploy when they decide how much we should get paid compared to an athlete or film star (say). The values used here – to give us a measure of what entertainment is worth, to help us factor in the millions who watch on TV – are very different to the values that we turn to in order to decide how much a day-care worker is worth. And, as with hiring and firing, there will be competing values and the key determinant of the outcome (in this case the level of pay) will be who has the power to make their values the legitimate ones.

Variations in the distribution of power and in the degree of legitimacy accorded to income inequalities will occur between one society and another. Thus there are large international variations in CEO salaries, for example, CEO salaries have been much higher in the USA than in Japan or Germany. The salaries of CEOs in the UK have traditionally been somewhere between these two levels but in the 1990s there was some upward drift towards US salary levels. In 2001[9] UK newspapers gave extensive coverage to the way CEOs of major Japanese companies had volunteered to cap their salaries (at levels like £100,000 per annum) and contrasted the morality of this action with the £2.2m payoff made to the ex-CEO of the failing Marconi company which lost 97 per cent of its value while he was in charge.[10]

We will return to conflicts over CEO salaries below, but we now return to the central focus of this chapter, the middle classes who engaged in joint action throughout the twentieth century to make the values of educational achievement increasingly important determinants of pay levels. Of course in this they were hugely successful. As Herrnstein and Murray (1996) explained so simply and forcefully, educational achievement had little to do with pay at the end of the nineteenth century and everything to do with it at the end of the twentieth century. The result was steadily rising pay for all those people who had been taking part in the joint class action, for example, professionals and managers. Using data from the New Earnings Survey, Johnson and Makepeace (1997) showed how in Britain in the 1980s, for example, the lifetime earnings of managers and professionals had forged ahead. While all groups increased the gap between their incomes and the incomes of the unskilled, the greatest growth was among the higher socio-economic groups, so inequality ('earnings dispersion') increased markedly.

All the effort that went into making sure that education, and particularly higher education, mattered more and more as the century progressed, paid off handsomely. It did not do so because people with degrees became more productive since we already know their educational credentials were often irrelevant to the work they were recruited to do. The extra income simply arose from the fact that everyone whose behaviour could have affected the incomes of the middle classes had come to accept the values of educational achievement. It was now agreed by those who mattered that these were the most legitimate values by which to judge the worth of middle-class labour. The possession of a degree was accepted as proof that the holder of it was worthy of the accepted premium paid for a graduate job.

The legitimacy of this premium was most widely recognized in the United States where very many citizens can put a figure on the premium and, indeed, where the size of the premium is notably higher than in other countries like the United Kingdom (Ashton and Green, 1996). Of course, most Americans believe that graduate pay is somehow related to relative scarcity or productivity and there are complex patterns of values at play here. The key point is that educational

160

credentials have achieved a pre-eminent position in the attachment of worth to a particular class of individuals and the work they do but that the exact degree of worth achieved in this way may vary from one country to another (just as Durkheim thought it varied from one point in time to another). In the 1980s and 1990s the UK government tried to encourage, with some success, the further association of pay differentials with educational achievement.[11] Most often this encouragement took the form of rhetoric but some key policy innovations could also be seen as attempts to make people accept greater pay differentials associated with variations in educational achievement (Keep, 1997).

Of course the demoralization that gives birth to 'positional competition' may ultimately undermine the legitimacy of the graduate premium or any other measures of worth founded on academic achievement. As we might infer from Goldthorpe's (1978) paper on wage inflation, when individuals cease to worry whether they are worth the pay they receive (or would like to receive), the legitimacy of their pay in the eyes of others will begin to decline. In time there will be calls from other groups for their pay rises to be restrained. In the situation described by Goldthorpe this proved to be a recipe for industrial, and even social, conflict that ultimately led to the fall of a British government and the transformation of British industrial relations.

Throughout the twentieth century there was a steady reduction in the contribution of genuine morality to (a) the founding of the values which people are prepared to act in pursuit of and, therefore, which define the interests they have in the market; and (b) the legitimation of market outcomes. One of the most notable outcomes of this process has been the rise of 'positional competition' (Brown, 2000) and another is increasing conflict over worth and legitimacy. In the UK, for example, there was much public debate over the 'inflated' incomes of CEOs and other 'fat cats' (Bauman, 2000). For example, with the help of campaigns in sections of the press, it was widely accepted by the public that the process of pay determination through remuneration committees was immoral. Particularly strong disapproval was expressed about the pay levels of the senior managers of privatized companies who had been appointed before privatization and appeared to have been performing poorly. As ever, the key question (for pay determination in this case) concerned the locus of power. Since the newspapers and ordinary citizens did not have the power to make their values count in respect of CEO's salaries nothing changed. The agents who might have made a difference – for example, institutional investors – did not share these values and usually did not believe CEOs were being paid more than they were worth.

CONCLUSION

According to Bryn Jones, sociology needs 'a more comprehensive theory which sees business and markets as a political sphere within which power and morality are competing but linked forces' (2000: 199). This chapter has tried to make a contribution towards this theory, and in particular, towards a theory of markets as surrogate political arenas (Jones, 1996). It has demonstrated that, far from being ruled by the invisible hand that automatically distributes resources to more productive uses, the labour market is highly political. Economic sociology has been an active participant in this politics, for instance, in the creation and validation of the economic rationalities that underpin the distribution of jobs and the determination of pay.

This chapter used my earlier book, *The Sociology of Labour Markets*, to expose economic, and particularly managerial, rationalities to closer scrutiny. In the process we saw how economic sociology had lent support to the ideologies that help groups to monopolize power and resources. The form of analysis offered in *The Sociology of Labour Markets* will also allow us to understand important changes in the relationship between morality and economic behaviour. This framework can be used, for example, to investigate the way that this behaviour reflects demoralization. Thus employers who recruited 'nice' middle-class women to work as cabin crew were using people values with the intention of recruiting employees who might be able to persuade customers they did not live in an increasingly demoralized world. We will need similar frameworks if we are to be able to pursue questions of power and morality outside the labour market. *The Sociology of Labour Market* shows that these frameworks will need to make values central to their analysis and be designed so that it is impossible to elevate economic values above other kinds of values (in the way economic sociology does) before any investigation begins. In *The Sociology of Labour Markets* the relative importance of various kinds of values in any example of labour market behaviour is determined entirely by empirical investigation. We need more frameworks of this kind to help us approach other types of economic behaviour in the same way.

The next chapter is intended to help us to mount a critique that will do more to level the playing field between economic rationality and other moral judgements (Gorz, 1989). This critique will be more far-reaching than the criticisms made by those such as Marshall et al. when they note that markets are economically rational but sometimes work by creating social costs, for example, in terms of social inequality or social injustice. The problem with this sort of criticism is that opponents can simply point out that prosperity for all cannot be achieved without some pain. To undermine such arguments we need a far-reaching critique that problematizes economic rationality. In the process we will see exactly why the labour market is so rarely understood as the arena for political conflict that Jones describes. In the next chapter we will find useful explanations for this conundrum in the subtle and complex field of identity.

NOTES

1 According to Parsons (1951: 94), it is possible for ascription and achievement to be systematically combined in the allocation of resources and prestige. In the 'German' type of social structure identified by Parsons, for example, people have to achieve things in order to become doctors but once they are doctors they can be accorded things – status, for example – simply because they are doctors. A recent discussion of achievement versus ascription cultures is provided by Trompenaars and Hampden-Turner (1997).

2 According to Ken Prandy (personal communication), fluidity may have been more constant in Britain than elsewhere and Prandy's work-in-progress is beginning to show some evidence of a slow trend towards greater fluidity in Britain over the last two centuries.

3 A related strand of social capital theory treats morality as part of the means by which valued political behaviour can be generated. In the work of Putnam (1993, 1995a, 1995b) democracy plays a parallel role to that played by meritocracy in the work of Coleman.

4 In his discussion of social closure Weber refers to the monopolization of 'offices, clients and other remunerative opportunities' by one group of competitors on grounds such as 'race, language, religion, local or social origin, descent, residence, etc.' (Weber, 1968: 341–2).

5 In Fevre (1992) the social groups, relations and institutions that determine the way labour markets operate include firms, trade unions, industrial relations, and collective bargaining in addition to families, pressure groups, political organizations, gender relations, the labour market institutions of the European Union, and so on. In addition, educational institutions have played a key role in the most significant social and economic changes described in this chapter (Schuller, 1996).

6 An Extended Internal Labour Market in which existing employees are required to assist in the recruitment of new ones.

7 Or, as in the 'ConsultancyCo' example discussed in Chapter 3, candidates can be interviewed on a charity fund-raising day when everyone, including their interviewer, is dressed up in costume.

8 'Often the advantages of one group and the exclusion of another are justified on the grounds that the former have and the latter lack the appropriate attributes, qualifications or "human capital", but of course these differences may also be precisely the result of those, and other, exclusionary mechanisms. Alternatively, the inequalities may be justified as functional for efficiency, but this too can be a way of trying to make right out of might, those in a strong position being able to insist on preferential treatment as a condition for carrying on their duties' (Sayer, 2000b).

9 11–13 September 2001.

10 *The Financial Times* (week beginning 10 September).

11 Presumably because it believed that this would encourage educational achievement and, therefore economic growth. As we know, this assumption – derived from Schultz (1961) – has been subject to considerable criticism.

six

identity and economic behaviour

The labour market is a political arena but, for the most part, individuals are not consciously engaged in an otherwise motiveless
struggle for power and resources. In fact they act as they do because
they believe what they are doing is right. The conjunction of self-interest and pursuit of the good has a long pedigree in the explanation of
action in sociological theory. The assumption that much behaviour
could be characterized in this way appeared in Weber's writing on
nation and nationalism (Weber, 1968) and lay at the heart of Marx's
theory of ideology (see Chapter 3). In Marx's theory of ideology the
pursuit of the good would be more productive for some classes than for
others.

Marx (1852/1934) described the ideology of the French peasantry in
the middle of the nineteenth century as a sort of armed nationalism
founded on gratitude towards Napoleon Bonaparte who, half a century
earlier, had made sure the peasants had their land. This ideology led
them to support the political ambitions of his nephew, Louis Napoleon.
Marx explained that this ideology put the peasantry at a disadvantage
and did not serve to protect and enhance their interests in the same way
that the ideology of finance capital or the industrial bourgeoisie could.
Because they were isolated – like potatoes in a sack – the peasants had
less of a worthwhile ideology than the proletariat but the proletariat
was also fond of ideologies that could not be relied upon to work in
their interests. In this chapter we will consider the idea that the working-class view of the world, unlike the middle-class view of the world,
often seems incapable of making morality commensurate with self-
interest.

In the previous chapter we saw that labour markets could not
function without values. When people internalize these values, they
frequently learn that the best course of action happens to be the one
that serves their interests. Internalized values do not always help people
to pursue self-interest, certainly not a narrowly-defined economic self-

interest, but they do help people define what makes sense, and what seems like a good idea. Thus they play a large part in determining whether the operation and outcomes of market behaviour are seen as legitimate, for example, whether there is agreement among those who matter that the middle classes 'deserve' their more interesting jobs and higher wages.

Most of the sense-making that goes on in the world is accomplished by social groups. This is how coherent systems of knowledge and belief are developed and, of course, different social groups make sense in different ways. In the writings of Marx and Weber, there is a correlation between the power and influence of a social group and the currency or salience of the sense-making it specializes in. Thus a group's hold over power and resources will be stronger the more widely held its view of the world is. Groups that learn to proselytize their view of the world, like the managers discussed in Chapter 4, have much to gain (Etzioni, 1988). A side-effect of this process is an inherent tendency to over-simplification and category mistakes within sense-making (Fevre, 2000b).

Marx's theory of ideology paid scant attention to individuals, but even in Weber's theory the way in which individuals learn to act in a way that ultimately produces the joint action of a group was sometimes obscure.[1] He wrote, for example, of the 'sense of dignity' individuals felt when they acted according to the values of their status group (Weber, 1968: 934). This suggests why the values appropriate to a group might exercise a hold over individuals sufficient to mould their behaviour, but the explanation is still incomplete. Why should it be that this becomes a matter of dignity to the individual and how do we learn to measure ourselves against these very particular standards? The missing piece in this puzzle is the way individuals assume identities. For much of the time it is through the assumption of identities that values and other ways of making sense get into people heads (where these values can motivate their behaviour).[2] The inequalities which were the focus of discussion at the end of the previous chapter are ultimately caused by people taking on identities which are fitting to membership of different groups. The identities we are particularly interested in are those appropriate to membership of social classes.

Very often there is nothing motivating economic behaviour other than a sense of what is right and this sense is almost entirely a function of one's social identity. This applies to those who grant others legitimate power over them (Dahrendorf, 1958; Grint, 1995) but also to those like Brown's (2000) middle classes who seem to set all the important rules of the game. In all of these cases, identities are the carriers of values – for example, the values of economic rationality – into the hearts and minds of individuals and, thence into the motivations that shape their behaviour. It is your social identity that convinces you that

165

you want to become a medical practitioner or the owner of a home cinema system. It is your social identity that gets you onto the plane from India to the USA or Europe as an economic migrant (Faist, 2000).

LEARNING AND IDENTITY

The importance of identity for economic behaviour will be explored in this chapter from several different angles. We begin by exploring the way in which economic sociology has treated issues of identity in relation to education and training (Fevre et al., 1999; Fevre, 2000a). This section will show how, in the work of Streeck, economic sociology in this field took a wrong turning. Streeck (1989) recognized the importance of identity when he argued that it affected your view of what counted as worthwhile training. He then firmly steered a course away from the classical concerns of sociology when he argued that identity should be seen as a means to the ends defined by economic rationality.[3]

For many years the German vocational education and training (VET) system, part of the German 'dual system' in which provision was made for both academic education and vocational training, was held up as an example to other countries. German firms had strong internal labour markets but training was treated as a public good and paid for by a levy. This situation arose out of a political compromise reached at the end of the nineteenth century in which training and careers for manual workers were presented as moral goals. The German trade unions lobbied for a political and financial settlement that would underwrite the position of respected, and self-respecting, manual workers (epitomized in the idea of *Beruf* and the identity of *Meister*) in German society. This goal was moral in many ways, not simply in terms of its implications for social justice but also for the moral constitution of society. For example, the character of the *Meister* was felt to be an important ingredient in social order.

Streeck argued that this political settlement, with its overt moral component, had the unintended consequence of allowing Germany to gain a competitive edge in high-skill, high-value-added manufacturing: morality was a means to an end defined by economic rationality. The key feature of the German VET system was that it made sure workers were trained in general rather than firm-specific skills; just the sort of skills, Streeck argued, that gave (West) German manufacturing its competitive edge, particularly when modernization was required. Training did not depend on employers' preferences but on the wishes of government, the chambers of commerce, the trades unions, the works councils and public opinion. Neither the state nor employers would have developed the necessary general skills, for example, employers would only have invested in firm-specific skills if left to their own devices. The German VET system meant that employers had no reason to try to protect their training investment against poaching by their competitors in this way.

So far as German workers were concerned, the motive for acquiring general skills was that this allowed them to become fully-fledged members of a community and, indeed, to assume a desired adult identity. Countries like Germany and Japan, with their 'heritage of community bonds', were better placed to create the skills needed for modernization than were market societies like the USA and the UK (Streeck, 1989: 91). Just as self-interested employers could not create such skills (but only firm-specific ones), so the self-interested behaviour of individuals would not lead them to acquire general skills. For Streeck the acquisition of these skills had to be seen as an obligation (ibid.: 93) and this was much more common in Germany and Japan than it was in the USA and the UK:

> It is no accident that the Japanese way of skilling and the German 'dual system', which a few years ago would have been regarded as remnants of a less 'modern' past, are attracting growing attention. Much to our surprise, 'premodern' institutions with their high mutual interpenetration of functions and social arenas often seem to perform better in a period of change and uncertainty than 'modern' functionally differentiated institutions. (ibid.: 99)

Thus, Streeck considered that: 'there is little doubt that in certain artisanal communities, where training and the rituals of examination and admissions are the focus of communal life and collective *identity*, a sense of moral obligation still plays a major part in the operation of industrial training' (ibid.: 100, emphasis added). The identities towards which young Germans aspired led them to acquire general skills which gave their country a competitive edge. The relevant identities were provided by social groups or communities.

Streeck's work on identities was confirmed and elaborated by others. Alan Brown researched the German VET system in the 1990s and his work added further detail to the roles of groups and communities in the transmission of identities (Brown, 1996). According to Brown, German workers were acquiring skills as part of their 'entry into a community of practice' and 'becoming skilled ... within a wider process of identity formation' where: 'recognition of significant achievement (and attainment of the status of experienced practitioner) is itself a socially mediated (or contested) process, dependent on others and a sense of self-worth' (Brown, 1996: 7).

By the time Brown was writing this, some researchers had begun to question the worth of the German VET system which was increasingly likely to be portrayed as inflexible and, indeed a major cause of the weakness of the German economy. Streeck's case began to look like an example of the misguided historical sociology criticized by Goldthorpe

167

(1996). It seemed that his adherence to European collectivist values of partnership and stakeholding had had more influence on his opinion about the role of the dual system in German economic success than any systematic evidence. This sort of difficulty tends to arise when morality is seen as instrumental and only to be justified by the economic benefits it brings. When it is no longer accepted that morality is beneficial in this way, and, indeed, might be harmful, then the case for having it is immeasurably weakened.

Polanyi (Polanyi et al., 1957) argued that class interests were much more likely to be social than economic. The most important of these social factors was social recognition. Honneth argued that such recognition underpinned our feelings of self-worth and guaranteed our well-being (Honneth, 1995, 1997; Petersen and Willig, 2002). If this recognition was denied to us, we suffered moral injury and a reduction in well-being. In Honneth's theory recognition was accorded not just to our labour – our contribution to society – but also to our social identities. Hill (2001) provided a simple example of the application of Honneth's ideas which (to begin with) underlined the contrast between this theory and one that made morality a means to an end.

Hill used Honneth's ideas of recognition to critique a conventional development model (as propounded by the World Bank, for instance) based on human capital theory and the assumption that people were driven by economic interests. These assumptions did not fit with evidence from poor countries of people failing to use the goods and services – for example, technology, credit or training – provided by governments and NGOs. In search of a better explanation, Hill began with Sen's 'capabilities' approach which 'requires that policy makers move from asking "What does a worker need to be more productive?" to "What is a worker actually able to do or be?"' (2001: 445). She compared this to Honneth's (1995) framework which made links between social recognition, identity and people's ability to take advantage of opportunities. Hill then applied Honneth's ideas to her own research on an Indian trade union. This trade union has a number of functions, including the provision of education and training, and 'by organising workers to come together to discuss common problems and possible solutions ... promotes self-recognition and worker identity amongst members which in turn empowers them to claim economic and cultural recognition in the public sphere' (Hill, 2001: 451).

According to Hill, it took recognition *as workers* (by employers and officials) for the women involved to be 'legitimised as citizens and empowered to claim the means of economic and social security' (ibid.: 451). She summed up her interview evidence this way:

When questioned about their experience of union membership many workers reported their experience in terms of the way it made them *feel*, and the positive impact that involvement in union activities had on their psychological well-being. Feelings of well-being and happiness were related to (i) the opportunity to work and meet other workers – the resocialisation of work; (ii) personal independence; (iii) participation in family, work and public life; and (iv) new-found respect and recognition from family and community. (ibid.: 453, emphasis in original)

Here, then, we have Streeck turned on his head. Instead of the morality of *Meister* and *Beruf* turning Germans into productive workers, here a moral end was produced by the recognition of Indian women as workers. Instead of morality being the means to economic ends, economic behaviour was instrumental in the pursuit of moral goals (also see Gorz, 1989: 140). O'Neill (1998) has explained why this might be problematic in market societies where social recognition becomes a positional good which derives its meaning from competition and comparison with the achievements of others. This kind of recognition is a travesty of worth measured by more enduring standards (see also Beder, 2000). Moreover, competition and comparison produce inequalities that undermine any possibility of a disinterested process of social recognition that has nothing to do with access to power and properly deserves our trust.

Hill, however, had no direct interest in such subtleties, being far more interested in development. This meant she was as keen on the pursuit of economic ends as Streeck or any other economic sociologist. She therefore concluded from her application of Honneth's framework to her own research that

169

Implicit to processes of collective action are the relations of mutual recognition that promote the self-realisation and identity upon which workers can make their claim for just treatment within the political economy ... it is positive change at the level of a worker's self-perception that underpins her ability to act and implement strategies of direct action and institution building. Identity-formation thus activates worker agency and enables workers to 'do' certain things that promote productivity and economic security ... Worker identity is therefore argued to be a critical determinant of worker agency ... Action that redresses moral injury and promotes worker identity is therefore essential to economic development and work life reform. (Hill, 2001: 460)

According to Hill, her case study showed 'the important role that the experience of love (friendship), rights and solidarity play in promoting work life reform amongst marginalised workers' and demonstrated 'the close relationship between the moral sphere of personal integrity and the material sphere of economic development and well-being ... strategies to promote well-being and economic security must address the cultural realm of moral injury' (ibid.: 461). I would argue that her evidence for this happy coincidence of moral ends and material goals is as tenuous as Streeck's evidence for the economic pay-off of the dual system and, once more, the argument for moral aims is made contingent upon these aims continuing to serve economic purposes.

For an example of sociological research on learning and identity that does not look for an ultimate economic benefit to flow from moral behaviour we can turn to some recent work on South Wales (Rees et al., 1997; Fevre et al., 1999; Fevre et al., 2000; Fevre, 2000a). This work describes the creation of the sort of learning community described by Brown (see p. 167) among Welsh coalminers at about the same time as the German dual system came into being. In the Welsh case this community did not transmit attitudes to training commensurate with the acquisition of a vocational identity[4] but encouraged *adult* learning in pursuit of a transformed adult (male) identity. In early twentieth-century Wales adults who were already in work began to question the nature of their adult roles. The end of this process was conceived as the production of the self-styled 'advanced man' who, having made himself a better person, was now expected to join with others to bring about the social and political changes needed to transform society.

The 'advanced man' would no longer rely on others to tell him what was in the books and pamphlets that told him how to understand the society he lived in – and how a better society could be made – and he was expected to interpret and make a contribution to the world on an equal footing with any one else. Later in the twentieth century this identity was subsumed within another which explicitly incorporated the aim of social mobility and included the positive evaluation of training and education which made this easier to achieve. But in the years before 1914 the minority of coalminers who considered themselves 'advanced men' were extremely distrustful of this sort of learning, and particularly of vocational training.[5]

'Advanced men' were not interested in the opportunities for learning which were geared to individual self-advancement within the coal industry through the acquisition of technical qualifications. They were interested in addressing much more fundamental questions about the colliery in which they worked, the company which owned it, the economics of the industry and the workings of capitalism. Such interests might lead them to see technical education in a negative light. In 1907 a small group of South Wales miners studying at Ruskin College opposed the idea that the South Wales Miners Federation, the miners' trade union, should contribute towards a new School of Mines at Pontypridd. Five years later A.J. Cook addressed the Pontypridd Trades and Labour Council on whether education was in the interests of 'the boss or the worker' (Lewis, 1993: 60; Davies, 1987: 18).

After the First World War the interests of the 'advanced men' were more widely embraced across the coalfield. While miners might once have been motivated to study commercial subjects or mine management, their interests now lay in other directions and there was a 'tense earnestness' in evening class students who had an increasingly urgent desire to get to grips with economics. Those miners' leaders who felt that technical education served the needs of business, and that the needs of business and workers were inimical, now articulated their views clearly. Almost from its inception in 1923 the *Colliery Workers' Magazine*, the new journal of the South Wales Miners' Federation, included articles which were critical of technical education which was said to be serving the interests of 'the quick witted magnate' for whom '[t]o subscribe to technical institutions is money well spent'. The author of this broadside returned to the theme a year later when, referring to technical education, he declared that 'objection is taken to any scheme which purports to increase production in order that capitalism may continue to further exploit wage labour'.

Archival data documents the coalminers' realization, around the time of the First World War, that education might be seen as a mechanism for increasing the rate of exploitation and even for maintaining wider capitalist social relations. It would be hard to make out the case for the economic benefit of South Wales miners learning to be 'advanced men' but this is not an unusual case. Social relations in capitalist societies do not always produce the identities that capitalism requires. But if such identities are lacking, then there is nothing to prevent employers and others attempting to manufacture new identities which are more fitting to the economic ends they have in mind. Seen in this light, much of the 'training' which takes place in modern corporations is really a matter of being drilled in a new identity (Beder, 2000) and we can now develop the discussion that was begun towards the end of Chapter 3.

In Chapter 3 some tentative steps were taken to suggest that employees were seen to be lacking in the morality that capitalism (and perhaps public service too) needs to do well. This might explain, for example, why for many years the number one complaint made by British employers about the preparation of school-leavers for employment was never their lack of literacy, numeracy or other skills but their inappropriate *attitudes* (Beder, 2000). It was once usual for people to leave school with very little education, and receive very little training in their work, but their socialization in family, church and community meant they had a degree of *inner direction* that made them good employees and workmates (Riesman, 1950). The types of training associated with the HRM model were, in contrast, tailor-made for *other-directed* individuals who, in a demoralized world, needed to be told how to *act* (Fevre, 2000b; MacIntyre, 1985; Riesman, 1950).

Chapter 3 discussed Hochschild's research on the way flight attendants were drilled in the 'niceness' which served as a 'necessary lubricant to any civil exchange' (1983: 167). It was suggested that

171

demoralization was the reason this sort of training had become so common. By the 1970s airline customers, for example, were no longer sure they could expect civility in public life and so airlines manufactured their own civility in pursuit of comparative advantage. Hochschild concluded that emotional labour made 'possible a public life in which millions of people daily have fairly trusting and pleasant transactions with total or nearly total strangers' (ibid.: 153). We can now see that much of this training – particularly the idea of 'deep acting' and other techniques designed to make employees internalize the values their employers think they should have – was concerned with teaching people, and persuading them to accept, manufactured identities.

It has already been pointed out that it is through the assumption of identity that values are carried into the hearts of individuals and then help to shape their behaviour. These can be the values of niceness or, indeed, of 'lifelong learning' (Coffield, 1999, du Bois-Reymond and Walther, 1999). In its heyday in the 1990s lifelong learning was conceptualized in the same terms as the learning community of South Wales described earlier in this chapter. In both cases it was the individual's duty to develop their potential, to keep themselves open to change, to serve society and perhaps even help to make a better society. In both cases learning was presented as something which benefited individuals because (in the language of the 1990s rather than the 1900s) it helped them to 'grow'. But the identity of a lifelong learner (as opposed to that of an 'advanced man') was generated by employers and governments who were anxious that the workforce should become more 'flexible'. We also saw in Chapters 2 and 3 how manufactured identities are not always discarded at the threshold of the workplace. Indeed, it is the express intention of many employers that these identities should be taken as seriously as any others. Perhaps fortified by their sense of the ridiculous, some individuals still seem capable of resisting this attempt to make them accept the identities manufactured by their employees as the real thing. Yet not all employees are equally capable of resisting and managers are particularly prone to full assumption of a manufactured identity with predictable, and far-reaching, consequences for their behaviour (Burns and Stalker, 1961; MacIntyre, 1985; Pattison, 1997). We will return to the behaviour of managers below but our next task is to deal with some loose ends left over from Chapter 5.

SOCIAL STRATIFICATION REVISITED

The previous chapter could not explain why people who are not middle class refuse to join in meritocratic or 'positional' competition. Even if the rules are not of their own choosing, what is to prevent members of the working class beating the middle classes at their own game? The short answer is that some do not see the point of the game, while others think the game is actually immoral, and that they feel this way because of who they think they are, in other words, because of their identities.

It was briefly mentioned in Chapter 5 that working-class members withdrew from competition because of their attitudes to education and training, but we now know that such attitudes could be transformed where working-class members aspired to certain identities (*Meister* or 'advanced man') and to membership of learning communities. The acquisition of knowledge could be an intrinsic part of working-class culture and identity but in this section we will see that working-class identity specifically excluded what were seen as cynical middle-class attitudes towards education, including those which led middle-class parents to 'push' their children to achieve educational success regardless of those children's aptitudes or abilities. While working-class identities have frequently been associated with the positive evaluation of useful knowledge, the acquisition of educational credentials in order to compete for economic ends was thought to be irrelevant to adult identity and perhaps even detrimental to it (Fevre et al., 1999).

Bynner (1989) identified the way the expectations and experience of employment conditioned the transition to work among the British working class. He argued that adult identity was so bound up with getting a job that learning was under-emphasized. Drawing on Bynner, Ainley (1991) argued that this was one of the main reasons why so many more people remained averse to education in Britain than in other industrialized countries. This aversion might also explain the finding of Banks et al. (1992: 47) that there was an *inverse* relationship between commitment to work and positive attitudes towards training among young people in Britain. Education and training were seen as a distraction from, or an obstacle too, the achievement of an adult identity. Formal learning kept people in their childhood role and frustrated their ambition to reach adulthood (Harrison, 1993; Taylor and Spencer, 1994).

The differences in working-class identity between the UK and (West) Germany, for example, were part of the explanation for variations in patterns of skill formation including differences in the proportion of firm-specific and more general skills. The pattern identified by Bynner helped to account for the fact that in Britain most training was paid for by employers (DfEe, 1995; Employment Department Group, 1994; Greenhalgh and Mavrotas, 1994; Park, 1994) and 90 per cent of people receiving job-related training were fully paid while they did it (DfEe, 1995). Education and training were seen as something that must be avoided or, if this was impossible, simply *borne* (Fevre et al., 2000). Research evidence from other countries also suggested that a similar pattern was developing there, for example in Finland:

173

Representatives of the oldest generation respected education in general, although they did not depict their own time spent in compulsory school attendance as at all pleasant. Representatives of the youngest generation found secondary school and the upper forms of comprehensive school (or the former intermediate school) boring, tiring and oppressive. (Antikainen et al., 1996: 62)

The British working-class aversion to schooling was documented in Nichols and Beynon's study of 'ChemCo' which was in many respects a forerunner of the new sociology of economic behaviour. Nichols and Beynon (1977) combined a classical focus on the true cost of *Living with Capitalism* with an investigation of the morality of the British working class. The workers they studied knew their lives were being wasted but they gave this waste positive moral weight by thinking of it in terms of self-sacrifice. More than twenty years later a study of American working men recalled some of the same themes.

Lamont (2000) found that American working-class men were much more concerned than their middle-class counterparts with trying to keep moral order in a demoralized world. Many workers still clung to religion and traditional morality and for some their concerns about demoralization had become entangled with racism. For present purposes, Lamont's most relevant finding is that American working-class men were much more likely to use income than education to measure people's worth and considered credentials less important than experience and informally acquired knowledge and skills. Lamont also suggested that American working-class men placed 'moral criteria of evaluation over socioeconomic criteria' because their morality was different and because they were seeking 'respect as human beings and workers' (2000: 129). In contrast to Hill (see p. 168–170), Lamont considered that self-worth was seen as an alternative to economic success and that living a moral life was seen as the best way to achieve this alternative goal. The identity of American working-class men required them to put morality before self-interest.

Lamont argued that morality gave these men dignity and that morality was therefore more important to them than the middle class who might share many of their values but could use other criteria to establish their self-worth. American working-class men put sacrificing for the family before the achievement of individual potential, and valued friendship instead of competition. They tended to place a high value on voluntary work with Black workers in particular adhering to collectivist values. Working men thought that people who were driven by economic rationality, ambition and competitiveness had poor interpersonal relationships and bought their success with insincerity. The middle classes, in contrast, attached a positive moral value to ambition and competitiveness as well as seeing their utility in achieving economic goals.

Despite these differences Lamont thought there was some evidence of convergence in the morality of working-class and middle-class American men. Indeed she found that the American working class sometimes had more in common with the American middle class than they did with working-class Frenchmen who totally rejected the idea of ambition and had real disdain for economic rationality. French workers thought stratification was based on real differences in competence – whereas American workers believed intelligence could be improved by education – but this did not mean they thought that stratification reflected morality. Indeed, French working-class men thought that moral worth varied inversely with economic success and that social mobility violated personal integrity and solidarity. Here ambition necessarily entailed moral corruption and in France even the middle classes were less enamoured of materialism and achievement (see also Lamont, 1992).

Lamont concluded from her study of working-class men in France and the USA that 'we need to rethink the nexus between respect, worth, socioeconomic standing, and social position in the community. At a minimum, we need to examine empirically whether the privileging of economic standards of evaluation found in much of the literature is justified' (2000: 116). Of course, much has already been done. We know that middle classes are prone to privilege education even when it is generally agreed that the content of that education has little or no relevance to job performance (Batenburg and de Witte, 2001; Livingstone, 1998). This would clearly be anathema to the working class. In the case of the middle class it is the credential, rather than any knowledge acquired, that is understood to be an intrinsic feature of middle-class identity, as is the middle-class occupation to which it gives access. Just as the working-class son needed to strain his muscles and risk his health and safety to earn his identity (Willis, 1977), and the teenage mom in the ghetto needed a baby of her own to become an adult (Fernandez Kelly, 1995), so the middle-class son or daughter needed a degree to join the adult world. During the twentieth century the key identity of the middle classes became that of *graduate*.

Members of the middle classes subscribed to credentialism because this was part of their identity, not because they saw intrinsic value in education or even because they made an accurate calculation of the economic benefits it would bring. There are wide variations in estimates of these benefits between different countries and some research suggests that these benefits disappear once the effect of family background is discounted (Greenhalgh and Stewart, 1987; McNabb and Whitfield, 1994). As we saw in the previous chapter, educational achievement mediated, or perhaps 'laundered' would be a better term, the influence of origins on destinations. At the end of this chapter we will see that middle-class values play an extremely important role in defining the content of the jobs to which they aspire. In other words, we should not assume that the quality of destinations should be exogenous to our theory because they are beyond the influence of class action.

For the present, we can think about the way identities underpinned the patterns (for example of social fluidity) observed in social mobility research. The study by Marshall et al. (1997) which was discussed in the previous chapter served as a kind of valediction for British research on social stratification and social mobility. With this study it seemed that a tradition of sociological research had reached a kind of (unsatisfactory) ending. For half a century or more there had been considerable agreement among researchers in this field about the nature of the problem that was being investigated (not enough meritocracy) and of the solution to this problem (more education). Most of the researchers' energy had gone into collecting and analysing the statistics which helped them to decide whether the problem was being solved. Up to the 1980s it was still commonly assumed that if *all* the barriers to educational achievement came down, the problem would disappear. In the following decade, however, the mobility tables continued to tell their story of little change in underlying patterns of social fluidity.

At this point mainstream mobility researchers found they were beginning to share some of the thoughts of heretics like Saunders (and, at one remove, Herrnstein and Murray). If the removal of barriers to educational achievement could not increase relative social mobility then, they wondered, perhaps the source of the problem lay with the working class themselves – if not in the limitations of their intelligence, then perhaps in the norms of their culture? In one sense this was a positive development but, without a thoughtful critique of meritocracy and the middle classes that both invented it and most reliably benefited from it, this amounted to little more than a lurch in the direction of the 'culture of poverty' thesis (Lewis, 1965: Murray, 1990, 1994).

Thus it did not occur to Marshall, Swift and Roberts (cf. Collins, 1979, for example) to wonder whether they should be sceptical about accounts of the operation of both the educational system and the labour market which conveniently justified every middle-class predilection together with all the inequalities which favoured them. Marshall, Swift and Roberts appeared to have no doubt that the better-rewarded jobs were simply more valued by society and required clever, well-educated people, even well-spoken people, to do them (of course they also assumed the creation of the quantity and quality of labour demand was entirely exogenous to the explanation, see p. 183). Most importantly, they did not seem to wonder about the reliable way in which, for generation after generation, the sons and daughters of the middle class happened to turn themselves into just the right people to fill their middle-class jobs. Marshall, Swift and Roberts might have spared a thought for middle-class identity.

As the twentieth century passed, and as a corollary of the process in which more and more of the connection between origins and destinations was mediated by education, the nature of middle-class identity changed. The changing values that underpinned this change in identity permitted the adaptation of the middle classes to new situations in which the old ways of reproducing and legitimating privilege were no longer so effective. Careful ethnographic work (for example, Roker, 1993) has shown how qualifications became central to middle-class identities. Of course this change in the specification of identity occurred at an earlier date in the United States than elsewhere. We have already noted that prevailing attitudes to education in the United States have reflected the greater approval of credentialism in American culture (hence the attention paid to it by Berg, 1971, and Collins, 1979, as well as by Dore, 1976, and Bourdieu, 1988).

When British working-class individuals started to value education in the same way as the middle class, they actually became middle class (Gorard et al., 1999). No matter how much the upwardly socially mobile individuals sought to deny that this had happened, there was no escaping the fact that they had assumed a new identity. This was the main reason why it was much easier for the sons and daughters of 'sunken middle class' families to make the upward journey (Jackson and Marsden, 1962). It was the individuals who adopted new middle-class identities who swelled the ranks of the middle class as the twentieth century progressed (Goldthorpe et al., 1987).

177

New recruits were not necessarily equal members of the middle classes, however (Brown and Scase, 1994). Junior members of the middle classes were less well equipped to find their way to more rewarding jobs because their parents only had working-class identities to offer them. Identities are a much less certain guide to values, and therefore to behaviour, if knowledge of them is derived at second hand. New recruits also found it harder to keep abreast of, and keep up with, the further evolution of middle-class identity, for example, the adoption into ordinary middle-class identity of selected aspects of upper middle-class identity. Brown and Scase (1994) refer to these – for example, private music lessons – as cultural capital but it may be more fruitful to conceive of them in terms of identity. Similarly, Hansen (2001) found evidence of the continued importance of cultural capital and social networks among Norwegian law graduates but this finding can also be understood as reflecting the difficulty new members of the middle classes have in respect of the transmission and acquisition of identity. Here we are reminded that middle-class identities are not simply a matter of educational achievement since they also school individuals in the behaviour needed to capitalize on their credentials in the labour market (see also Brown and Scase, 1994). This was also why Jackson and Marsden (1962) found, in Britain in the 1950s, that so many upwardly mobile sons and daughters of the working class could only aspire to become teachers: this was the only middle-class identity with which they had any familiarity.

To summarize, new and more marginal members of the middle classes, or those who still aspire to join the middle classes, have difficulty accessing the middle-class identities which will persuade them to acquire credentials and help them to cash out these credentials on the labour market. This 'identity shortage' is quite an unusual phenomenon in historical terms (Fevre, 2000a). In pre-capitalist societies, identities were derived from family, village and religion (and much more rarely from a craft or trade). In industrial capitalism occupational identity became paramount and, at the extreme, it determined all other aspects of culture (Beck, 1992; Beck and Beck-Gernsheim, 2001). There was a period of transition in which the rural-urban shift made many fates uncertain but in settled industrial societies, identity in the sense that the term has been used in this chapter came into its own. The communities of these societies transmitted the alternative identities to which one would discover one was equipped (or not) to aspire. The increase in absolute social mobility with the expansion of the salariat made certain that these identities became much less useful as the twentieth century progressed.

As time went by, more and more people who sought to leave the working class for the middle class were forced to rely on substitute identities for those offered by the communities in which they had grown up. Some of these identities were created and disseminated by bureaucrats like careers advisors (Strathdee, 2001) but others took the form of 'commodified identities' which were available on the open market. The principal source of information on such identities was television.[6] Where family and community provided no relevant information on the adult identity to which a young man or woman might aspire, the characters of television shows filled the gap. This goes some way towards explaining the subject choices made by large numbers of the students who benefited from the expansion of higher education in Britain in the late twentieth century. Without the influence of television's commodified identities, the popularity of courses in criminology and veterinary science, and indeed cultural and media studies, would remain a mystery.

At this point it is appropriate to return to positional competition theory (Brown, 2000). We must remember that one of the reasons why new members of the middle classes were disadvantaged was that the nature of middle-class identities – and the values and behaviour associated with these identities – continued to evolve. According to Brown, meritocracy would continue to be the dominant ideology so long as the expansion of the salariat continued but meritocracy was replaced by positional competition once this expansion ceased. In other words, the new members of the middle classes – already at a disadvantage because they relied on commodified identities – found that the rules of the game had been changed.

The allocation of places in the division of labour had been underwritten by an ideology of meritocracy in which value to society, relative scarcity, difficulty and educational achievement were all jumbled up. In meritocracy a credential clarified this confusion and marked an act of transubstantiation: it magically transformed the mundane allocation of labour into the fully sanctified recognition of merit. But if people are simply engaged in positional competition, they have given up any pretence that the credentials they earn are connected to the job they get in anything other than a symbolic way. In a meritocracy the least morally sensitive credentialist can still claim that their achievement of a less than relevant qualification shows they know how to learn (cf. Jackson, 2001) but in positional competition this kind of moral gymnastics is no longer required. It is apparently no longer necessary to demonstrate merit in order to justify one's occupation of a rewarding job since it no longer has to be justified, simply competed for. For example, those who succeed in this competition take a thoroughly *strategic* attitude towards learning (du Bois-Reymond and Walther, 1999).

Employers have been forced to adjust their recruitment practices to take account of the shift to positional competition and away from the justification of the allocation of places in the division of labour according to the values deployed in the ideology of meritocracy. These adjustments have occurred as part of the more general trend described at the end of the previous section where we reviewed the way employers set about manufacturing new identities to compensate for societal demoralization. Indeed, this may be why people do not take their new identities wholly seriously but nevertheless act in the way those identities require (Du Gay and Salaman, 1992). They are prepared to do so because this serves as a substitute legitimation (in place of meritocracy) for their access to rewarding jobs.

As we saw in the previous chapter, Marshall et al. (1997) wondered about the usefulness to employers of non-certified qualities like confidence and charisma. In positional competition it does not really matter if charisma is needed to do a job well, what matters is that an alternative solution to the problem of justifying recruitment decisions has been found (Brown and Scase, 1994). This solution involves the creation of a new identity for the successful middle classes and once again latecomers who do not realize the significance of the changes occurring around them are put at a disadvantage (Devine et al., 2000). This becomes evident as the new generation of recruitment auditions, assessment centres and personality profiling perform the work that was once accomplished by meritocratic means. Du Gay and Salaman (1992) were among the first to note the way these new institutions were used to convey to employees the necessity that cynicism should be covert and appearances should be marked by enthusiastic co-operation. This enthusiastic co-operation is the hallmark of the latest incarnation of middle-class identity.[7]

As new identities are created, old ones linger on in a twilight existence. The identities which dominated the labour markets of Fordist societies lingered long after they ceased to be of use (Portes, 1998). Problems of social exclusion were exacerbated where people, and particularly working-class males, continued to rely on them (Fevre, 2000a; Strathdee, 2001; Willis, 1977). What happened to the working-class people who stayed working class and adapted to the new situation characterized by the decline of working-class jobs (especially jobs for men), the loss of community and solidarity, the disappearance of all those sources of self-worth for working-class individuals? Working-class children could no longer be successfully socialized into a working-class identity by the family and community as they made the transition from school to work. The way that these children responded to the new situation as they grew into adolescents shows how working-class identity changed in response. These young people were in the vanguard, and many commentators noticed the change but it was Charles Murray who popularized the idea that these people were members of the 'underclass' (Murray, 1990, 1994).

According to Herrnstein and Murray (1996), structural changes reduced the number of jobs available for those with little cognitive ability. When people found out that, a result of the creation of a meritocracy, education mattered, all those in the working class with cognitive ability got themselves educated and became upwardly (and geographically) mobile. This left only those with low IQs and no stake in society marooned in islands of low-rent housing where the only values were those that derived from the culture of poverty. While the idea of the underclass is definitely useful, we can produce a much better explanation of its genesis.

The underclass was born as an alternative source of identity for working-class youth who found the traditional working-class route to adult identity closed to them. The traditional working-class idea of dignity had rejected the single-minded pursuit of money, indeed, this was seen as a component of *middle-class* identity (Lamont, 2000). Nevertheless, since well before Marx (1852/1934) was so disparaging about the *lumpenproletariat*, there had always been a deviant working-class version of identity. To take the obvious example, a criminal working-class identity valued economic rewards very highly. With the loss of any alternative traditional source of working-class dignity, such deviant identities ceased to be a marginal sub-cultural alternative.

The appearance of such identities in the mainstream of working-class culture was first noted in studies of Black Americans (for example, Rainwater, 1970). It was in the USA where the service sector grew most quickly and blue-collar jobs disappeared first. It was also in the USA that the Black migrants from the South to the North had been in possession of those working-class jobs for a comparatively short period. In addition, because of racism, it was less feasible for these working-class women and men to get by on the notion that they could aspire to a middle-class identity. With subtle variations, something like this pattern of identity reformation was followed amongst other groups at other times and in other countries.

Murray (1990) eventually found evidence of a British underclass: so uneducated as to be fit for nothing other than the most menial (and unproductive – therefore low-paid) work, yet greedy for material things and unscrupulous about how these things could be got. The archetype produced by this attitudinal complex was the teenage mother who set about having children of her own in order to become financially independent thanks to the state's welfare system. An alternative view which paid proper attention to the significance of identity was provided by Fernandez Kelly (1995).

Fernandez Kelly certainly found girls who 'present motherhood as a desirable condition, not as a calamity. In the light of expert judgements to the contrary, this is perplexing' (1995: 233). She concluded that:

> poor adults occupy with their children a similar position vis-à-vis labor market alternatives. In this context, motherhood represents the extension of responsibilities assumed at an early age and expresses a specific relationship with the labor market. That partly explains why, at seventeen, Latanya Williams can state with conviction 'I waited for a long time before I had my baby'. That's why she can ask, 'What's there to wait for?' (ibid.: 234)

For such young women the chasm in identity between children and adults had been bridged by the disappearance of the jobs that underpinned adult identities. The identity of mother was the only adult identity left to aspire to. But of course not all American Blacks remained unemployed and there were many who made it into the middle class.

When American Blacks, and members of other minorities, joined in the competition for middle-class jobs, they did not always compete simply as individuals. In Chapter 5 the rise of meritocracy was described in the familiar terms of the replacement of ascription by achievement. As meritocracy began to change once more (for example, in the direction of positional competition) later in the twentieth century, there were some signs that ascription was making a come-back as a result of the activities of members of largely professional, minority groups (see also Fevre et al., 1997). In a profoundly interesting development, these groups appeared to have a found a way of turning the rules of the game against the white middle-class incumbents of professional jobs.

Affirmative action is the most successful example for some considerable time of a social group coining a new social invention for the redistribution of resources from a more privileged group (for other examples, see Parkin, 1979). Many middle-class minority members got their jobs on the usual credentialist terms and many of them disapprove of affirmative action.[8] But this social invention was interesting precisely because it showed identity becoming part of the rules of the game in a new way. As Sayer (2000b) pointed out, in the last quarter of the twentieth century there was a volte-face in radical political sensibilities. Once it had been inequalities resulting from gender and ethnicity that were treated as inevitable or ignored. Attention used to be concentrated on inequalities which were 'identity indifferent' like unemployment and insecurity which might be cured with new economic systems.

While the use of ascriptive criteria remained controversial, by the mid-1970s US federal equal employment legislation and regulations covered race, colour, religion, sex, national origin, age, veteran status and handicap and affected the actions of government contractors, the recipients of government financial assistance and others. All of these agents had to demonstrate that they were taking action to correct under-utilization of ethnic minorities and women. This action would certainly include changes in recruitment processes so that women and minorities were represented on interview panels and all staff were trained in equal opportunities. Organizations also encouraged the broadening of the term 'qualifications' so that more people from the previously excluded groups could be considered (Edwards, 1987, 1995).

Sociological research found desperate employers tying themselves in increasingly theological knots trying to get more blacks and women on the payroll, for example, in this American police force investigated by Edwards:

> 'merit' is seen to consist of a wide variety of components, reaching far beyond performance on tests. There are many qualities required in a

policeman, including knowledge of, and sensitivity to, the community he or she will be policing. If that community happens to be predominantly black or Hispanic then being black or Hispanic may be a component of merit for the job ... [this] form of 'bending' occurs in promotion procedures. (1995: 135–6)

Edwards provides a business case for positive discrimination by arguing that it might lead to better service provision. Those who supported affirmative action programmes agreed and this allowed ascription to be put on a par with, or even on a level above, achievement. Edwards concluded that, '[i]f it is a matter of empirical evidence that better services will be provided if the provider is of a particular racial group (or indeed that the service cannot otherwise be provided), then a specification of that group becomes a reasonable and justifiable component of the job description' (Edwards, 1995: 210–11).

As noted at several points in earlier chapters, the provision of such empirical evidence may prove to be a difficult task. We now move onto consider some other questions of identity which arise in relation to the professions.

MAKING WORK

In the final section of this chapter it will be suggested that class competition involves the modification of the raw material of identity because it affects the quality and quantity of different places in the division of labour. Conventional social stratification research has rarely considered the existence or content of jobs, or the way they fit into organizations, as appropriate to its subject matter. As this section will demonstrate, all of these aspects of jobs are inextricably bound up with identity and, like any other aspect of identity, they can be subject to change.

The example that is used here is the way the identities of professionals in the public sector in the UK have been radically altered in the course of a workplace conflict with an increasingly influential managerial class (Dent and Whitehead, 2002; Pattison, 1997). The rising influence of managers could be measured by the way they demonstrated the power to make their views about what was right and necessary the ones that mattered. This resulted in a change in the quality and nature of the experience of public sector professional jobs which had further, and far-reaching, effects on identity (Dent and Whitehead, 2002; Exworthy and Halford, 1999). The most surprising example of these effects occurred when public sector professionals were made to behave as if market values were of supreme importance (Beynon, 1997). This experience was apparently so traumatizing to traditional identities that the only way it could be assimilated into economic sociology was by forming the mistaken assumption that *all* employment had suddenly become radically insecure!

The traditional sociology of the professions suggested that the least clear distinction between work and personal life was found among professionals and it was in the professions that people were able (since the classical period in some cases and the medieval in others) to insert morals into the world of paid employment which were in fact generated outside it.[9] We may have seen the final defeat of that enterprise and with it the demise of the professions proper. The replacement of professional morality was accompanied by efforts to tie professionals' salaries to some measure of, or proxy for, their output but the argument does not rest on proving the gradual extension of payment by results in the professions. Everything from staff appraisals through the huge variety of new auditing systems, and evaluations and league tables, to the introduction of internal markets and prices and budgets where none were needed before, was designed to meet this end (Exworthy and Halford, 1999; and see Chapter 4).

At this point it should be pointed out that all of these changes are equally open to explanation in terms of demoralization.[10] Just as the drilling of airline cabin staff in 'niceness' may have become necessary because we live in a demoralized world, so the domination of professionals by managers in the public sector may have resulted from an authentic decline in professional standards of behaviour. Since professionals were expected to regulate themselves, and resisted oversight by others, it is clear that the effect of demoralization on their capacity to mould their behaviour might have been catastrophic. On the other hand, and this may actually be more likely, it may be that the spread of demoralization meant that the politicians and managers in charge of the professionals no longer believed that anyone, even professionals, could be trusted to self-regulate in a demoralized world. In this, more subtle version, we can remain agnostic about the behaviour of professionals, and only need to know that the most saintly public servant is no longer trusted to apply professional standards away from public scrutiny.

In either version – subtle or less subtle – it was assumed that professionals could no longer be trusted to perform their jobs according to their own (moral) codes but must be supervised, audited and regulated. Moreover, like the cabin crew, they had to be made, through bureaucratic means, to produce the closest possible facsimile of the behaviour that was assumed to be typical before demoralization. Thus professionals had to make their workloads transparent and be accountable for their actions but they also had to be taught what their values were and why they were doing what they were doing. They subscribed to aims like service and quality and were then held accountable for achieving them.

As with cabin crew, professionals were trained, regulated and supervised (or audited) into behaving in the way that once came naturally to them.

In their seminal paper, Du Gay and Salaman (1992) described the way that the economic orthodoxy had changed from one in which bureaucracy made up for the shortcomings of markets to its opposite. In the 1990s markets were making up for the shortcomings of bureaucracy, and being actively introduced into administrative arrangements all over Britain, particularly in the public sector. Kevin Doogan (2001) showed that this intrusion of market *values* into the public sector made people question their identity and, more generally, made them unhappy. While there had been no real increase in insecurity in employment, the idea that the values which motivate and legitimate economic behaviour in this sector were changing made many people, especially professionals, feel deeply insecure. This feeling amounted to an existential crisis and it helps us increase our understanding of the relationship between legitimacy, motivation and identity. Doogan showed how we can begin to mount a critique of the intrusion of market relations into organizations as a moral rather than a material threat. In this way Doogan's work is a very useful example of a renascent sociology of economic behaviour.

According to Doogan, the statistical evidence suggested that the major research topics in the sociology of labour markets and social stratification at the end of the twentieth century should have been the increase in professional and non-manual jobs, upskilling, retention and ageing, and the narrowing employment differentials between men and women. Of course we heard very little about these topics and much more about the alleged increase in insecurity. On the basis of UK data for 1992 and 1999, Doogan disputed the ideas of increased short-term employment propounded by Beck, Castells, Giddens, Sassen, Sennett and many others[11] (Turnbull and Wass, 1999 also pointed out the paradox of stable job tenures and increased insecurity; see also Fevre, 1989).

The data Doogan used referred to current employment which had lasted for ten years or more (rather than average job tenure data which is affected by rapid recruitment). According to these data, average UK job tenure altered little over the study period while Long-Term Employment (LTE) dramatically increased. LTE increased most dramatically for women and, indeed, exceeded the rate of growth of all women's employment so that the rate of LTE for women rose from 21.2 to 28.5 per cent (cf. 35.5 to 36.7 for men). Analysis within industries with expanding employment over the period showed a rise in LTE for construction (from 30 to 40 per cent), education (34 to 37 per cent) and health and social services (25 to 32 per cent) (Doogan, 2001: 426).

185

Even the *declining* manufacturing sector saw a rise in LTE. Doogan concluded:

> it would appear that declines of long-term employment are more asso-
> ciated with institutional restructuring of formerly state-owned enter-
> prises which have resulted in large-scale closure programmes,
> privatisation, mergers, acquisitions and reorganisation. Contrary to a
> transformation of employment arising from the development of the
> 'information economy' or 'network society' it appears that the UK gov-
> ernment policy of privatisation has had much greater implications for
> long-term employment in the 1990s. (2001: 429)

There were large gains in LTE in some of the service sectors with lower levels of job stability and employing large numbers of women, young people and part-timers. In fact the rate of LTE among part-timers increased from 18.9 to 23.2 per cent. With the exclusion of younger workers (including students) who boosted the part-time figures, LTE part-timers more closely approximated the figure for full-timers. There was therefore no justification for citing any increase in the numbers of part-time employees as prima facie evidence of increased insecurity. LTE was positively associated with skills and qualifications and Doogan was dismissive of the idea of increased insecurity in the net-work society. In 'knowledge-based occupations' the trend seemed to be away from temporary contracts and '[t]he idea of individualisation rests upon the casualisation of employment and the constant changing of jobs and skills that comes with technological change. Yet, the evi-dence suggests that up-skilling leads to a greater degree of attachment and not dissociation from the labour market' (ibid.: 439). The increase in LTE has coincided with an ageing workforce but LTE had even gone up among the over-30s and (a little bit) in hotels, restaurants and cater-ing where there had been a steady fall in the average age of employees.[12]

Given all of this highly persuasive evidence of increased LTE, why was there such conviction, both within economic sociology and beyond, that employment had actually become much more insecure? Doogan noted considerable media coverage of redundancies while the media had virtually ignored the 'dramatic increases in long-term employment for women in clerical work or in the professions' (ibid.: 434). In the UK fear of redundancy was far in excess of any realistic expectation of experiencing it and Doogan suggested that people's false perceptions of their exposure to the risk of redundancy simply showed how dreadful people thought redundancy would be if it hap-pened. He concluded that this was largely a consequence of changing government policy on welfare and the trade unions and on the intro-duction of internal markets and decentralized budgets in the public sector: '[t]he "manufactured uncertainty" that accompanies the intro-duction of market forces in the public sector is of greater import than

186

the impact of technological change or the knowledge economy' (ibid.: 436). In addition, insecurity was fuelled by 'widespread concern over corporate restructuring' and Doogan quoted research by Burchill et al. that showed employees were much more concerned about mergers and take-overs than about redundancies.

Doogan concluded that in Britain in the 1990s there had been a widening gap between perceptions of societal insecurity and expectations of personal security as a result of generalized anxiety about market forces. He also thought this gap had been created as 'the outcome of a conscious strategy of government that arises from attempts to increase the productivity and competitiveness of the economy' (ibid.: 439).[13] We can suspend judgement on this point and still conclude that public-sector workers felt that their old, secure identities had been undermined by the increasing emphasis on market forces. In another sector this experience might not have been quite so traumatic but no sector was assumed to be as secure as public service, indeed, security was traditionally cited by those who worked, or wanted to work, in the sector as its most significant defining feature. This explains why public sector workers were so disturbed by the changes in their identity which the increased importance of market forces implied. If public sector workers' jobs were not havens from the seemingly arbitrary buffeting of market forces, what else were they?

Arguably, this also explains why so many economic sociologists were affected by the same paranoia about insecurity. After all, they were professionals in the public sector too, and also open to the increased scrutiny of managers and increasingly assailed by the language and values of the market place – there was no reason why they should be immune. Their feelings about the insecurity of their own identities became the foundation for a whole intellectual insecurity industry that manufactured a phantom menace.[14] Of course other individuals had identities that were better able to cope with insecurity, even when it turned out to be genuine. British television was one of those industries in which LTE really did decrease as a result of change in the contractual relationships between employers in the industry. Workers responded in a variety of ways designed to reduce insecurity including by leaving the industry (Dex et al., 2000) but some television industry employees coped much better with insecurity and evidence of employee preferences for flexibility has also been found in other industries (Gorz, 1989, 1999).[15]

Where Doogan had seen perceptions of insecurity rise with the intrusion of market forces into the public sector, Nichols (2001) described the way reports of stress among white-collar workers and the workers of the 'new economy' seemed to be related to the spread of the management techniques of private sector manufacturing to every other

187

kind of employment. These reports were not adequately supported by evidence of the physical signs of stress: 'the (social) complaint was not accompanied by the expected clinical condition' (Nichols, 2001: 196). Instead, this was a similar phenomenon to the one observed by Doogan. Because they had white-collar or 'knowledge worker' identities, these people had never expected that they would be exposed to the management techniques once applied only on the shop floor. Their identities equipped them with comparatively low pain thresholds for the sort of thing workers in private sector manufacturing had endured for years. The resulting reports of stress were really the consequences of the disappointment of their higher expectations of pleasurable work.

Further consideration of the relationship between identity and changes in job characteristics points towards one of the most exciting areas for future development in the sociology of economic behaviour. It is becoming clear that it is unhelpful to separate out competition over jobs from the creation of jobs, i.e. the activity of dividing labour. Nichols and Beynon (1977) and Blackburn and Mann (1979) showed how labour was divided in such a way that working-class jobs represented a waste of so many human lives, but we also need to know about middle-class places in the division of labour. For example, in Brown's (2000) theory of positional competition, the middle class simply compete over jobs, and do not have a role in creating the quality or quantity of labour demand or the tasks and products and services that jobs entail. But what sort of jobs might we imagine the middle class creating, or rather multiplying, if not the ones over which they already exert a monopoly (and which they think they can maintain), the jobs they think worthwhile, and the jobs they enjoy and consider essential to their identities?[16] This new theory can be used to extend the sociology of economic behaviour into a huge, and hugely neglected, area: the study of the economic behaviour which produces the occupational (and industrial?) structure. It is here that sociology promises to add a great deal to characterizations such as the post-industrial society (Bell, 1976), the network society and the information age (Castells, 1996/7), the knowledge economy and the age of the symbolic analysts (Reich, 1991). In so doing, sociology will show once more how little we understand if we ignore questions of power and legitimacy (Shenhav, 1999; see also Fevre et al., 1997).

For example, the idea of a 'knowledge economy' sounds very much like the wish-fulfilment of a million middle-class dreams of a new utopia of work in which the middle classes will be able to live out every aspect of their identities. Every facet of the new jobs will be tailor-made to ensure that the middle classes only have to do what they like to do, and are good at doing, but there is more to the ideology of the 'knowledge economy' than this. Even more than Reich's 'symbolic analysts',

188

the 'knowledge economy' establishes new justifications for the distribution of resources. It brings to the forefront the idea that all the best jobs of the future will be the ones the middle classes are good at but it also insists that these will be the jobs on which the future prosperity of the world depends (du Bois-Reymond and Walther, 1999). Not only must the middle classes get all the best jobs but it is legitimate, and indeed necessary, for them to be handsomely rewarded for doing the sort of work they have always wanted to do.[17]

The generation of sophisticated ideologies about the centrality of middle-class jobs to the future of our well-being and prosperity also necessarily entails the de-legitimation of the work that other people do. The idealization of symbolic analysts and the work of the knowledge economy goes hand in hand with the demotion in importance of all the more routine clerical jobs (Carnevale and Rose, 1998). As part of this ideological effort, received wisdom about the necessity for education and training in order to give access to middle-class jobs has turned into wild generalization about the necessity for everyone to be educated in order to justify their place in the new utopia. This further confirms the de-legitimation of other people's jobs (du Bois-Reymond and Walther, 1999). Since being highly educated was what made people important contributors, how could the work of those who sought to contribute without getting educated first be valued? In the way that Marx described, commentators and politicians have become convinced that these special conditions for the success of the middle classes have also become the general conditions for the success of everyone.

The battle-cry of *education! education! education!* recalls the phantom menace of increasing employment insecurity. In both instances economic sociologists were happy to join in the production of wild generalizations and they added their weight to the construction of models of the world, and especially the way the world was changing, that had long since parted company with empirical evidence. In both cases the personal identities of economic sociologists were deeply implicated in the way they let their imaginations run rampant. They were among the people who might face a lifetime of insecurity or – a happier thought – they were about to inherit the world as denizens of the knowledge economy. In either case, education was the thing and – again happily – as social scientists they all understood the importance (to them personally, at least) of education.

Since it has no investment in the dominant ideology, the sociology of economic behaviour is free to determine, through careful empirical research, the degree to which the value that is created by routine white-collar workers, and workers who labour outside the knowledge economy, sustains prosperity in the decades to come. Indeed, the idea

189

that technological change, and particularly the further development of ICTs, will necessarily lead to the creation of more and more challenging, and rewarding, middle-class jobs becomes much more doubtful when exposed to empirical enquiry (Apple, 1997; Neill, 1995; Selwyn and Gorard, 2002; Winner, 1994). Moreover, the sociology of economic behaviour will also investigate the way the ideas that were generated about the jobs of the future subsequently influence the re-interpretation of what it means to be middle class, for example. The basic raw material from which subsequent reincarnations of identity will be conjured is being created now. It consists of the way jobs are actually performed as well as the way they are perceived. What members of the middle classes do as they go about earning their salaries has a huge influence on the way they think, for example, on what they consume and what they aspire to. In order to understand the possibilities available for the identities of the future we need to understand more about the way the dreams of yesterday's middle classes shaped the work that their sons and daughters do today.

CONCLUSION

190

Persistent social inequalities require that people take on identities which are fitting to their membership of different groups, especially social classes. Identities work in this way because they carry values (including economic and moral values) which shape behaviour. Economic sociology failed to understand the significance of identity because it treated it as a means to the ends defined by economic rationality. This view of identity is itself class-based: it is identical with the view that the classes which have benefited from social inequality have proselytized, and profited from. Groups which hold to the alternative view – that economic rationality should be subordinate to an identity which can be defined in moral terms – have not fared well in times of increasing inequality.

The middle classes and business have an instrumental and amoral attitude towards identity. Not only is identity never an end itself, it is rarely taken seriously. Employers and others manufacture new identities fitting to economic ends and a considerable amount of the 'training' which takes place in modern corporations is really a matter of persuading people to take on these new identities. This explains much of the confusion in the research literature about the degree to which people take their new identities seriously. What is really required is that employer and employee conspire in the manufacture of identity. If employees complain that they are being asked to put on an act, they are not taking the necessary instrumental attitude. For the most part, employers and employees are very well aware, for example, that the 'lifelong learning' required for middle-class occupations is a travesty of the learning of autodidacts like the South Wales miners who read literature, science and philosophy because it made them better men.

The politics of identity help to account for the persistent lack of social fluidity which has meant that inequalities have been systematically reproduced from one generation to the next. The fact that the working class still tend to see identity as an end rather than a means, and still tend to see that identity in moral terms, has not served them well in times of increasing social inequality. The same observation holds where similar values exist in the middle classes, for example, among public-service professionals. The successful middle classes wrapped up their identities in credentials as the means to economic ends but keeping up with the competition increasingly meant adopting an evolving middle-class identity. The nature of this identity was revealed in the changes employers made to their recruitment mechanisms. Assessment centres, for example, were used to convey to employees the necessity that cynicism about the evolving identity should be covert.

The inequalities between those who adopted the evolving identities and those who could not abandon the old identities increased. Below the working class the demoralized underclass no longer aspired to the outdated identities. Above them middle-class minorities sometimes benefited from affirmative action which counted a range of new identities as the means to economic ends. But labour market politics and competition affect more than the cash-in value of any identity, they also affect the jobs to which identities are a means. It will be increasingly important for the sociology of economic behaviour to investigate the way the occupational structure is changed by the action of powerful groups. For example, the 'new' or 'knowledge economy' was tailor-made to match evolving middle-class identities.

Groups do what they do because this accords with their view of the world and, if they are successful, because this behaviour serves their interests and enhances their privileges. Once we are no longer required to see the world through the eyes of a particular, highly successful group, we can open the world up for more objective inspection and appraisal. This means much more than mounting a critique of the prevailing justifications for social inequality, and there must be more to the sociology of economic behaviour than the study of social stratification. In the next chapter we move on to consider questions of economic growth and development.

As we might expect, economic sociology has usually considered these questions from the point of view of people who have a particular interest in economic growth. In the following chapter we will take the advice of Deetz about how to mount a critique of current understand-

191

ings of such things: '[o]rder, efficiency and effectiveness as values aid the reproduction of advantages already vested in organizational form. Concepts of organizational effectiveness tend to hide possible discussion of whose goals should be sought and how much each goal should count' (Deetz, 1992: 24). Drawing inspiration from Critical Theory, Deetz finds that 'types of rationality, and the concept of profit are social productions. Each is produced as distinguished from something else' (ibid.: 28) and '[r]eproblematizing the obvious requires identifying conflicts which do not happen' (ibid.: 43). These ghostly conflicts have flitted in and out of our vision throughout the present chapter but will shortly assume more solid form.

NOTES

1 Social theory finds the mechanisms by which the individuals who comprise groups act in a way that makes joint action possible a perennial puzzle. The problems of co-ordinated action have even worried rational choice theorists but some of the more thoughtful solutions to these puzzles have been proposed within symbolic interactionism, a sociological tradition which has paid a great deal of attention to the question of identity. The relationship between identity formation and self-transformation was originally explored by Mead (1967).

2 Bourdieu and Foucault offer other explanations of this process (Deetz, 1992).

3 In this and other respects Streeck's approach is surprisingly close to that of Coleman, see Chapter 5.

4 Training and occupational socialization were achieved through an informal mentoring system (Fevre et al., 2000).

5 The remainder of this section is adapted from Fevre et al. (2000) and owes much to the work of Burge et al. (1998).

6 This may be one reason why Putnam is right to find television strongly implicated in the decline of social capital (Putnam, 1995a, 1995b).

7 In Brown's latest work (see, for example, Brown et al., forthcoming) the role of psychological profiling, recruitment auditions and assessment centres is explored within this context.

8 See, for example, Carter (1991) or Sowell (1990).

9 Gorz (1989: 144) suggested that within this process, and similar processes among some non-professionals, the morality of fair remuneration was subordinated to a morality of service.

10 Moreover, when government comes to believe it can no longer rely on the morality of public service and professionalism, and that economic rationality and self-interest rule, the obvious solution might be to bring in private sector management which is used to dealing with this sort of economic rationality.

11 Earlier examples of this literature date from the 1970s. On the basis of these sources, and predictions such as two-thirds of the workforce being in temporary work by the year 2000, Anthony (1977) argued that managers who experienced insecurity in work would no longer be so attached to it. In complete opposition to later writers, in particular those who emphasized the importance of employability in a time of increased insecurity, Anthony thought insecurity would mean people would make less of a fetish of work.

12 Doogan pointed out that this made the sector extremely unusual yet this age profile was barely mentioned when findings from this sector, for example, its flag-

ship company McDonald's, were generalized to whole societies (Ritzer, 1993).

13 An alternative explanation might begin with the difficulty of getting a relatively affluent population to make more money so that governments can raise more tax revenue. According to Davis, the state gains more than most from the generalization of the labour market and increased effort demanded in work and 'it is more fruitful from the revenue collector's point of view to have a large number of producers, in conditions of uncertainty, striving to produce taxable wealth' (1992: 72).

14 One of the tangible effects of this industry was the use of the ubiquitous assumption of increased insecurity as part of the marketing of financial services. Note also how this habit of seeing the world in your own image was already prominent in the work of Daniel Bell (1976).

15 Indeed, Gorz (1989) argued that our dislike of insecurity was the result of conditioning by the state and constituted further proof of the hegemony of economic rationality.

16 The next chapter considers the creation of 'false needs' in relation to economic growth and 'success'. Joint action also explains a great deal about consumption patterns, including leisure patterns, and the patterns of working hours (and work-family relations) described in Chapter 2. Remember that working-class males, despite their traditional views on the gender division of labour, share childcare responsibilities. Remember also that the sacrifice of personal and family time to the morality of work is an entirely middle-class phenomenon. It is completely different from the way working-class men and women extend their hours in order to boost their earnings in the only way they can: by working overtime or taking a second, or third, job.

17 And economic sociology was very happy to go along with this. Bell's vision was, more or less, of people like himself ruling the world, and the people who saw the Knowledge Economy as the future had very little to sell but concepts.

seven

competition, growth and development

Classical sociology was well aware that economic growth was becoming the central focus of human endeavour and it was concerned about the moral consequences of this process. This concern was pushed to the margins during the development of economic sociology but it had been central to Durkheim's sociological theory:[1]

> industry, instead of being still regarded as a means to an end transcending itself, has become the supreme end of individuals and societies alike. Thereupon the appetites thus excited have become freed from any living authority. By sanctifying them, so to speak, this apotheosis of well-being has placed them above all human law. Their restraint seems like a sort of sacrilege ... [s]uch is the source of the excitement predominating in this [business] part of society, and which has thence extended to the other parts. There, the state of crisis and anomy is constant and, so to speak, normal. From top to bottom of the ladder, greed is aroused without knowing where to find ultimate foothold. Nothing can calm it, since its goal is far beyond all it can attain. Reality seems valueless by comparison with the dreams of fevered imaginations; reality is therefore abandoned ... We may even wonder if this moral state is not principally what makes economic catastrophes of our day so fertile in suicides. (Durkheim, 1897/1952: 255–6)

There have been some recent attempts to revive sociological interest in the moral consequences of economic growth and development. Andrew Sayer (2000a, 2000b) urged sociologists to adopt the approach of Durkheim's contemporary, Hobson, and judge the morality of all economic behaviour. In this way sociology would help us to put the processes of development under conscious control and give us the space and time to find out what we really need and want. Other writers echoed Durkheim's concern about the way growth and development created wants that could not, and perhaps should not, be satisfied (Ekins and Max-Neef, 1993; Mestrovic, 1991). Some drew attention to the loss of happiness, and increase in depression, caused by the rising expectations that accompanied development (Lane, 2000).

Other sociologists wrote about the way that development caused ecological harm and entailed unknowable risks (Beck, 1992). Yet I wish to argue that none of this critical interest in growth and development meant that sociology was able to put in doubt the basic assumptions that identified economic growth as the source of progress. The preconditions for such a fundamental critique were lacking.

Within the idea of 'sustainable development', for example, no serious attempt is made to question the veracity of economic rationality. Instead a broader economic rationality is brought to bear against a narrower one.[2] The very idea of sustainable development is a profoundly economic one. An environmentalist critique of development judges its effects using ecological criteria but the theory of sustainable development begins life with the assumption that development is a good thing and then argues that the way development now occurs will ultimately prove self-defeating. The only way to *keep developing* is to take into account the environmental context of, and limitations on, development. In this way ecological values become means to economic ends and critique is emasculated into mere criticism in which one can only choose between competing economic arguments which differ only in scope, detail and time-frame.

'Anti-globalization' writing follows a similar route (Hertz, 2001; Klein, 2001). It has been a very long time since Baran and Sweezy (1966) first drew our attention to the over-weening power of global corporations. So far as the anti-globalization literature has anything new to say, its contribution tends to be limited to remarks about waste and the other economic costs of globalization. Wasteful transportation is a major theme of the literature and one of its major concerns is to make sure that these and other factors (especially other costs) which have mistakenly been left out of account are made visible when we draw up a balance sheet to assess the pros and cons of globalization. For example, we should understand that it is tax-free aviation fuel that makes it possible for affluent Westerners to eat fresh food in all seasons. To leave out such costs is not economically rational so, for example, ways must be devised to put a cost on damage to public goods like clean air. This literature does not press economic rationality very hard since it rolls out a broader economic rationality to criticize a narrower one. This makes the argument vulnerable if an even more fundamental, counter-argument can be conjured from economic rationality.

None of the criticisms of current patterns of growth and development were sufficiently robust to make headway against such persuasive economic rationality because they failed to make economic rationality their target. Instead they were happy to enlist economic values like waste and inefficiency in their cause and, in effect, found their criticism on economic rationality. Such criticism can always be trumped by another economic argument. This might be the argument made by Esping-Anderson about growth in the prosperous nations (see below) or other arguments that refer the situation of the less developed countries (LDCs). Theories of sustainable development and the dangers of globalization can be very easily portrayed as (perhaps unwitting) arguments for the maintenance of current global inequalities and even for arresting the development of the world's poorest countries.

If sociologists limit themselves to arguing about the most efficient use of resources, their criticisms of economic growth will always be vulnerable to fresh objections derived from economic rationality. Other sociologists, most notably Gorz (1989), have sought to draw our attention to the way the imperatives of growth dissuade us from raising questions about the criteria used to determine what counts as work and how much work should be done (Bowring, 2000; Stivers, 1994). When less and less real work is required, 'work-based morality' becomes 'possessive selfishness' (Gorz, 1989: 70). This kind of sociology is closer to a critique – and further away from economic sociology – than theories of sustainable development. Thus, Gorz (ibid.: 120–1) described growth as a normative goal which was accepted as an imperative in the absence of all evidence, and indeed all content. The supremacy of growth as a goal was taken entirely on trust and there was to be no possibility of dispute according to the evidence. One of the most powerful of objections to Gorz's thesis is the argument that any attempt to reduce the amount of work, or even halt the *growth* of work, would inevitably send an economy into a downward spiral towards penury.[3] Esping-Andersen (2000) presented this argument for the benefit of economic sociology when he explained that a reduction in working hours would damage job growth and that we have no alternative but to 'work ourselves to death' (ibid.: 766).

Esping-Andersen's particular concern was with mothers on low incomes who must be given work because that was the best way to raise their income levels. The concerns of those like Fraser (1989) and Sayer (2000b) who thought that it might be better for these women to spend their time doing the work of parents (with the aid of a care-giver's allowance) were misplaced. The key to the virtuous circle of growth was that the state should provide child-care funded by the taxes these employees would generate when they were in work. The virtuous circle would also be undermined if men took up domestic labour. If we reduced the amount of work we do, poor families would stay poor and fertility rates would continue to fall since families were no longer prepared to internalize the costs of childcare. Esping-Andersen noted that in Scandinavia, where these costs had been socialized, better educated women were increasingly likely to have the largest families.

196

Gorz's answer to objections which suggested reduced working time would lead to economic decline and sustained inequality took the form of the 'second cheque' or social wage which would be paid to people in lieu of the hours they no longer worked (there were also additional caveats about carefully phasing reductions in working time). For present purposes, the importance of Gorz's views on the social wage and, indeed, on wages for domestic labour, lies in the way he addressed the *meaning* of such payments (see also Chapter 8). According to Gorz (1989: 130–1), economic rationality had become so hegemonic that basic income guarantees seemed like the rare, captive survivors of extinct species of sense-making. Such schemes had come close to challenging economic rationality in the early days of the factory system (see pp. 228–230) but to mount this sort of challenge now something far more radical was required. This was why Gorz was so insistent that the second cheque should be seen as payment for hours surrendered and not for domestic work such as child care. Gorz (1989) thought wages for child-care anathema because applying economic rationality here was, in effect, a category mistake. We should oppose the limitless expansion of economic rationality which turned all our free time into money and it was wrong to turn our domestic labour into jobs for the poorest (like the mothers who concerned Esping-Andersen). Gorz alone explored the moral significance of inviting quasi-servants to do our domestic work and likened it to South Africa before the abolition of apartheid (1989: 156).[4]

197

Following the lead of Gorz and others, a revitalized sociology of economic behaviour could help us put morality back into our decisions about growth and development on an equal par with economic rationality. The last section of the chapter will demonstrate how this might be done by exploring the possibilities for critique using the idea of *cheap labour*. Concepts such as cheap labour help us to make the moral element inescapable, but we must first deal with the problem we have been bequeathed by economic sociology: our apparent inability to break out of the habits of thought taught by economic rationality whenever we think about growth or development.

We can only free ourselves from these fetters if we become convinced that economic values are fungible. If something is fungible, then it is perfectly acceptable for another similar thing to stand in its place. If economic values were fungible, then other values could serve us instead. The first section of this chapter shows that economic sociology consistently turned its face against this possibility and thus deprived sociology of the chance to build a critique of growth and development. Thus there have been numerous opportunities for sociologists to realize that the way capitalists changed the way they organized production demonstrated the fungibility of economic rationality. The key example of a missed opportunity that is discussed here concerns Marx's idea that the concentration and centralization of capital were supremely economically rational. Such changes in organization made capital more productive and gave capitalists a competitive edge. Later in this section we will consider more recent suggestions that the trend towards centralization and concentration has been *reversed* because it was economically rational do so. From another point of view, however, there is nothing new about these arguments and current intellectual competition simply rehearses debates between alternative economic rationalities that pre-date the Industrial Revolution.

The chapter then turns to that branch of economic sociology which considered non-economic norms might be the key to successful competition and economic growth. Of particular interest here is the work of Dore, Etzioni and Fukuyama (an enthusiastic convert to economic sociology). The approach that they exemplify can be understood as a curious combination of Weber and Durkheim. It bears some similarity to the work of Streeck discussed in Chapter 5 and, as with Streeck, this approach makes morality the means to economic ends and leaves the supremacy of economic rationality unchallenged. The sociology of economic behaviour requires that morality should not be treated as the means to economic ends. The final section of this chapter will pursue some ways of doing this by building on the conviction that economic values are fungible. Unlike ideas like 'social capital' which preserve economic rationality's aura of inviolability, the idea of cheap labour offers a genuine possibility of developing a critique of economic growth and development.

ORGANIZATION IS THE SECRET OF SUCCESS

The three volumes of *Capital* (1867–94/1954–9) remind us how fascinated Marx was by the effect of new forms of capitalist organization on the way people lived. Perhaps the most obvious change in organization was the transition from domestic industry to the factory system. Marx concluded this was only the initial step in a process of evolution that would eventually lead to the transformation of capitalism. Without necessarily sharing Marx's view of the inevitability of this transformation, subsequent economic sociology took the same wrong turning, even when dealing with evidence that seemed to be entirely contrary to the evidence Marx had sought to explain.

It is well known that Marx saw the organization of production in mid-nineteenth-century England as the product of specific social relations but Marx decided that this pattern of organization was a necessary stage on the way to transformation. As it developed further, capitalist organization would assume the social forms required after transformation: social labour, separation of ownership and 'the labour of superintendence', socialization of capital, co-operation, and so on. Every development in capitalism that tended in this direction was progressive. The progressive logic of capitalism as dictated by the laws of capitalist accumulation also fulfilled a progressive function for socialism.

Marx undoubtedly saw domestic industry as an obstacle to progress that capitalism had swept aside. The domestic system was the antithesis of the concentration and centralization of capital: production was (very) small scale, workers usually owned the means of production, they organized and supervised themselves, and so on. This system had to be swept aside because it was backward in every sense.[5] Capitalism would simply out-compete the small-scale competitors of the domestic system. Any production process that had been temporarily farmed out to domestic workers as 'outwork' would soon be absorbed into the factories where it would become part of the grand socialization of labour. This was how economics paved the way for socialism: by building the foundations for the new society while making profits in the manner established by the old one.

The mechanics of the actual transition illustrated the inevitability of the changes in organization. The domestic system began with small producers working on their own equipment with materials they owned and sold. In the outwork system that marked the beginning of the transition to the factory system, these producers no longer owned the materials but laboured on them for others. Some might not even own the equipment they needed to perform this labour even though they continued to work in their own homes. For Marx, all of the following were essentially progressive, and wholly necessary, developments: the bringing of all own-account producers into dependence on the factory for outwork, the increased supervision of domestic workers as they laboured on materials that did not belong to them, and the eventual removal of one process after another to the factory.

If it would not have occurred to Marx to question, for example, whether capitalist anxieties about embezzlement were sensible justifications for doing away with outwork and much the same was true of his successors. Marx's view of the transition to the factory system was adopted by economic sociologists (see, for example, Marglin, 1974 in Chapter 4). With their acceptance of what they believed to be the facts of this transition, sociologists and others also accepted Marx's explanation for them: the transitions from domestic system to outwork to factory system happened because they made economic sense. Let us deal first with the 'facts'. Berg (1985), Hudson (1981) and others modified the orthodoxy once unchallenged among economic historians. They argued that, contrary to Marx's view, the domestic system had not simply been swept aside with outwork lingering as a form of making-do until the victory of the factory system was complete. Rather, the domestic system was the foundation of capitalism and outwork was a vital part of the process of industrialization. Outwork helped the factory system to develop.

In the view of Marx and many others, outwork succeeded the domestic system and (then) outwork was absorbed into the factories because this made economic sense. Basically, these changes in organization permitted factors of production to be moved to more productive uses. Yet if this were true, the economics of the transition to the factory system produced surprisingly diverse results. The way in which industrialization occurred in each of the different textile industries (woollen, worsted, cotton, linen, jute, knitting, and so on) of industrializing Britain was remarkably different. While it is fairly widely known that spinning and weaving went into the factories in different orders in the Lancashire cotton and Yorkshire wool textile industries, there were several other variations. There was considerable variation in the pattern of industrialization in South and North Lancashire and between the worsted and woollen branches of wool textiles. There were also regional and international differences in the way that organization changed that had little to do with the type of textile being produced (Schremmer, 1976). Such differences put in doubt accepted wisdom that variations in patterns of industrialization should be explained by differences in the rate of technological change in the various textile industries. But the most persuasive evidence on the side of a less orthodox understanding of economic history comes from the period prior to mechanization.

In the sixteenth and seventeenth centuries the wealthy woollen producers of the West Country of England were implored to move their production out of their factories in order to compete with the rising Yorkshire domestic system (Mann, 1971: 116). While they had no power, these *manu*factories were early examples of the centralization and concentration of capital yet an economic case was made for something that Marx would have seen as a senseless backward step. Contemporaries explained the success of the Yorkshire industry, which eventually eclipsed the established West Country competition, in terms of the economic advantages of *not* having production concentrated in one place (Fevre, 1990).

On the basis of the evidence to hand, Marx decided that there was only one template for economic development, and according to this template production moved *from* the domestic system *to* the factories. The limitations of this view also account for Marx's extraordinary blind spot in respect of the joint stock companies which he took to be the very latest development in the process of concentration and centralization which presaged the transformation of the mode of production. Joint stock companies were the wave of the future, sanctified by economic rationality to ensure that capitalism paved the way for socialism, in this case through making sure profits assumed a social character:

> The result of the ultimate development of capitalist production is a necessary transitional phase towards the reconversion of capital into the property of the producers, although no longer as the private property of the individual producers, but rather as the property of associated producers, as outright social property. On the other hand, the stock company is a transition toward the conversion of all functions in the reproduction process which still remain linked with capitalist property, into mere functions of associated producers, into social functions. (Marx, 1894/1959: 437)

With the benefit of hindsight, Dahrendorf (1958) found Marx's opinion that the joint stock companies were the harbingers of socialism quite absurd. He used its absurdity to suggest that Marx had always been mistaken to attach so much importance to property. Dahrendorf argued that property was only a particular form of power and that, so long as capitalists retained their power over the producers, it was quite ludicrous to see the joint stock companies as stages in the socialization of the ownership of the means of production. As part of his rebuttal of Dahrendorf, Nichols (1969) argued that Dahrendorf had misunderstood Marx who actually thought that joint stock companies allowed the opposition between capital and labour to stand out in sharper relief and therefore hastened the final dénouement. This dénouement had, of course, failed to arrive and Dahrendorf and Nichols wrote from the vantage point of an age in which public limited companies had long become the accepted vehicles of capitalist development. For our purposes the point is not that the joint stock companies proved to be such a success that they ensured the apparently infinite survival of capitalism. The point is rather that most of the first generation of joint stock companies which bore the burden of Marx's hopes were ghastly failures (Pollard, 1965). In complete opposition to Marx's expectations, these companies proved to be uneconomic disasters.

By the beginning of the twenty-first century the publicly owned corporation was once more established as the development vehicle *nonpareille* but in the 1990s this position had been seriously questioned. Inspired by the success of the German and Japanese economies, and subsequently the spectacular performance of some smaller Asia-Pacific countries, many economic sociologists decided that the secret of success lay in alternative forms of organization (Cooke and Morgan, 1998). In Germany local and regional banks worked hand-in-hand

201

with the companies of the *Mittelstände* to make high quality goods with cutting-edge skills and technology and a strategic approach to research and development (Hutton, 1996). Asian capitalism relied on debt arranged with the much larger banks which were apparently under the complete control of the debtors yet this unorthodox approach seemed to be able to work economic miracles, first in Japan, then in the rest of the region.

While the USA was suffering from Japanese and German competition, and the UK was set on a path of irreversible decline (see Chapter 4), the self-evident superiority of shareholder control became questionable. According to many, the problems of the Anglo-American economies could be traced directly to their leading companies' dependence on shareholders and stock markets. In the UK this dependence was so extreme that it condemned the UK to terminal decline because companies were never able to rise above the short-termism imposed by the pre-eminence of their share price and thus were unable to take a strategic approach to research, product development or marketing (Coates, 1994; Hutton, 1996).

These new certainties were soon belied by the protracted crisis of the Japanese economy, the Asian financial crisis of 1997, the failure of the German economy to recover from reunification, the revival of the British economy, and (for a short period) the dot.com shareholding bubble. As this last example indicates, none of this should be taken as proof that the modern heirs to the joint stock companies which raised their finance on the open market were naturally superior to their competitors elsewhere in the world who relied on other means. The lesson to be learned from these reversals of fortune is rather that any commentator who thinks they have found the organizational solution to succeeding in capitalist competition is making as big a mistake as Marx did before them.

Such mistakes litter the pages of the literature of economic sociology which devoted its energies to keeping true to the pre-eminence that Marx (and Weber) had given to economic rationality while having to cope with increasingly contradictory and confusing evidence about changes in patterns of organization. In the 1980s economic sociologists began to wonder whether outsourcing might now be the key to success in capitalist competition. In the UK this suggestion first arose as the (Conservative) government of the day put out to contract the activities of the public sector including nationalized industries like steel. Sometimes this was done as part of preparations for full-scale privatization, while at other times contracting out acted as an alternative means of transferring public assets to the private sector (Fevre, 1989).[6]

Within a short space of time the wisdom of 'outsourcing' processes and services was being preached globally and the link with the privatization programme of a particular government had been largely forgotten (Fevre, 1990). By the time outsourcing was being advanced as the panacea for all sorts of organizations (Harrigan, 1985), this apparently infallible secret of successful competition had found its place in a genre of economic rationality which Marx would have found bewildering. This genre had been born a few years earlier with the idea of flexible specialization (Brusco, 1982; Piore and Sabel, 1984; Sabel, 1982) and it consisted of a general *volte-face* in almost every certainty which Marx had held to. Everything he had thought progressive, especially every aspect of centralization – things were not quite so clear-cut with concentration – was now being portrayed as archaic. That what had been thought of as progress had become regress showed (to those who had eyes to see) just how fungible economic rationality was.

In common with some more short-lived examples of this genre (for example, the 'new times' of Hall and Jacques, 1989), flexible specialization offered a true mirror image (in which objects appeared to be back-to-front) of the world Marx had tried to make sense of. In Sabel and Piore's Emilia-Romagna region of Northern Italy, highly skilled workers undertook rewarding work in conditions of considerable autonomy while they were employed in small firms with a reputation for innovation and marketing acumen. These small firms gained strength from their inter-relations with each other, and from the sympathetic assistance of leftward-leaning local governments, and this form of organization represented the key to success in a new era of niche markets. In Sabel and Piore's opinion, capitalism was finally turning out alright because the key to capitalist success appeared to be a form of enterprising socialism in which fulfilled workers produced desirable things in a way that was completely responsive to subtle shifts in the wishes of discerning consumers (see Bowring, 2002, for a persuasive critique of post-Fordist work and consumption). Every dream that Sabel and Piore might once have had about an industrial utopia turned out to be, amazingly, the secret of successful competition in the 1980s (for more delusion that whatever was not Fordism must be utopia see Wajcman, 1998).

In the decade that followed, flexible specialization was jumbled up with the ideas of the 'flexible firm' , 'just-in time production' and lean manufacturing in a portmanteau labelled as 'post-Fordism'. Of course there were still many who were prepared to defend the rationality of Fordism or, at the very least, to assert that the economic rationality of post-Fordism was not as popular amongst capitalists as its cheer-leaders suggested (Williams et al., 1987). This point can be illustrated with the arguments that were constructed to show that outsourcing was not as economically rational as the fashion of the day claimed. For example,

Fevre (1986, 1989), Hurstfield (1987a and 1987b) and Ascher (1987) described the hidden economic costs associated with the outsourcing which occurred with privatization in the UK. These included the longer-term effects of reduced attention to routine maintenance, deleterious effects on health and safety[7] and increased opportunities for fraud and embezzlement. In later years, similar points were made by other researchers (Bach, 1999; Farnham and Horton, 1993; Hay and Morris, 1991).

Mackenzie's research on British Telecom (BT), a privatized utility company, suggested that the process of contracting out much of the company's work was 'riddled with internal contradictions' (2000: 711). As in the case of British Steel/Corus (Fevre, 1989), the work that had been contracted out was performed by ex-employees who took voluntary redundancy in very large numbers and were then re-employed by the contractors. When the labour market tightened, this strategy began to falter as contractors who could no longer recruit labour found it difficult to fulfil contracts. BT helped their contractors by attempting to even out major fluctuations in workflows. Mackenzie pointed out that this response threatened to undermine one of the key advantages of contracting out since it amounted to 'a direct inversion of the notion of flexibility' (2000: 717).[8] All the same, contractors were often unable to do the work that was needed and BT was increasingly forced to rely on an agreement with its Irish counterpart, Telecomm Eireann, to use the Irish firm's employees on a contracted basis. Telecomm Eireann provided directly employed staff on rotating secondment to BT. Of course this arrangement was only effective because Telecomm Eireann was *not* a contractor but made this work part of its own core business.

Where BT continued to rely on genuine contractors, there were increasing problems of labour quality which appeared to be related to dilution of the contractors' workforces with employees who had not been made redundant by BT (see Fevre, 1987, 1989, for a similar process in steel). BT then set about encouraging, and often facilitating, contractors to do their own training. BT mounted a registration scheme for BT-approved training activities and was planning a national accreditation scheme for everyone working within the BT network (whether or not they were a BT employee). Mackenzie described all this as 'the attempt to assert stability over the external environment despite the logic of externalisation' (2000: 722) and referred to BT's need to retake 'the role of regulation wrested from, or surrendered by, traditional instruments and agents associated with direct employment' (ibid.: 723).

Examples of conflicting economic rationalities could be found elsewhere, for example, in the research which contributed to 'flexibility debate' that was mentioned in the previous chapter (Atkinson, 1984; Doogan, 2001; Fevre, 1991; Pollert, 1988, 1991). Research

like Mackenzie's, which painstakingly constructs alternative economic rationalities to those currently being advanced to explain fashionable economic behaviour, is useful because it adds to the evidence
which shows us how fungible economic rationality really is. Like the
comparison between Marx's understanding of the economic rationality
of centralization and the economic rationality of flexible specialization,
it should help to persuade even the most obdurate of economic sociologists that economic rationality is fungible after all. Indeed, it is frequently the case that one or more of the conflicting economic
rationalities that inform the 'debates' of economic sociology are simply
the resurrected orthodoxies of an earlier age.

Some of the economic disadvantages attached to the use of contractors by Fevre (1989) and Mackenzie (2000) echo the points that Marx
made when he declared the domestic and outwork systems were backward forms of organization. At this point the reader will recall the pleas
made to the West Country clothiers of the seventeenth century to adopt
the outsourcing solution that appeared to be such a successful strategy
for their upstart Yorkshire competitors (p. 200). Fevre (1990) drew
attention to the similarities between this case and the exhortations of
contemporary management gurus and social scientists to increase
outsourcing to remain competitive. It was apparently just as easy to
reconstruct the economic rationality of the sixteenth century in the
twentieth as it was to forget all the advantages that Marx once found
in centralization and concentration.

We can conclude that there was no cut-and-dried case against outwork in the nineteenth century just as there was no cut-and-dried case
against centralization and concentration in the twentieth century. We
will find a way to build an alternative to economic sociology on the
basis of this new information in the final section of this chapter but, for
the moment, we must consider one more historical comparison of
forms of industrial organization. It is not just in respect of outsourcing
that big corporations have found completely different economic rationalities persuasive at different points in history and twentieth-century
orthodoxies were overturned in favour of organizational forms that
were even more *outré* than subcontracting. We must begin with history
once more and thereafter we will find more evidence of how fungible
economic rationality can be.

Within the textile factories of nineteenth-century Britain there were
forms of industrial organization that looked very much like stop-gaps
and false starts that would disappear as the full potential of the factory system was realized. These included the internal subcontracting
systems of the cotton industry and bizarre hybrids like the 'room and
power' tradition of the North of England in which a part of a factory
was leased to a small-scale capitalist who manufactured on their own

205

account (Fevre, 1990). Generations of economic historians considered such hybrids to be historical accidents and curiosities which would never to be repeated, part of a palimpsest in which old and new, and transitional, arrangements existed side by side. Thus, a factory which hosted 'room and power' production might also have workers employed by the factory owner to work on material that was owned by a third party. The third party might be known as a 'manufacturer' ('without looms') and their primary interest was in trading and specu-lation in the prices of raw materials rather than production. Beside them, or more likely *underneath* them on a lower floor, one might find a genuine example of the factory system, although some employment might be taken care of by the overseers who acted as internal con-tractors. In addition, numerous additional processes which were required for the production of the finished product were conducted under a variety of different arrangements in other factories or by domestic industry (Samuel, 1977). These and other bizarre organiza-tional palimpsests were actually typical of the early factory system (Littler, 1979) and, it now transpires, they are typical of the twenty-first century too.

Volkswagen's 'modular production system' in Resende, Brazil, was an example of a modern-day parallel to 'room and power' and 'manu-facturers without looms' (Abreu et al., 2000). The details of this system were as bizarre as anything ever organized in a West Yorkshire factory. The major auto companies were manoeuvring themselves into the role that was once occupied by the old speculators and merchants who employed nobody who was involved in production and neither owned nor directly controlled the means of production. Whatever *outré* eco-nomic rationality that motivated those Bradford manufacturers was now at home in the minds of the auto company strategists. Where they once staked success on centralization in clones of Henry Ford's Baton Rouge plant, then on multi-sourcing in parallel facilities (Beynon, 1974), and latterly on the just-in-time model of their Japanese com-petitors, the auto companies now considered that the secret of success was the Resende solution.

If one was not interested in economic history it might be fairly easy to surmise that there was an avant-garde economic rationality behind this 'new' form of organization.[9] If one later learned of the way prior incarnations of the Resende solution were seen as quaint features of the early industrial palimpsest, one might respond by searching (no doubt successfully) for the other factors (perhaps technology, or skill levels, maybe patterns of ownership and control) that explained why eco-nomic rationality produced such contradictory solutions in two differ-ent cases. This is the way of economic sociology – when it comes to the fundamentals, it does not deal in falsifiable propositions.[10]

Earlier in this chapter it was suggested that a variety of different criticisms of current patterns of growth and development simply pitted one economic argument derived from a broader economic rationality against a more narrowly-based economic argument. These criticisms were therefore open to challenge from further economic argument. We have now seen how just such a process has apparently operated in the decision-making which informed major changes in patterns of organization at various stages of industrial development. For example, taken together, the arguments of enthusiasts for outsourcing and the arguments of their critics suggest that the possibilities of persuading people of completely opposing economic rationalities are inexhaustible. The same could be said in regard to the strategic planning of the people who ran VW and Ford. Capitalists decided to be manufacturers who did not actually make anything but tomorrow they might be persuaded by another economic argument and return to concentration and centralization.

This is just the sort of insight we need if we are to progress beyond criticism to develop a proper critique. In large part because of the salutary lessons of historical comparison, we are much less likely to think of the latest innovation as being a brilliant discovery in the ongoing *refinement* of economic rationality. We are much less likely to imagine that capitalists are making progress towards ever greater rationality and much more inclined to think of all ideas about organization as equally worthy (or worthless). We therefore make the breakthrough that economic sociology has avoided since Marx because we recognize that economic rationality is infinitely fungible.

To conclude this section we might attend to some loose ends. If capitalists do not change patterns of industrial organization because they choose a superior economic rationality over an inferior one – but only because they are persuaded by a *different* one – why do they bother to change at all? Once this question has been framed, we can see there are a great many possibilities for us to explore. Indeed, we can begin to see that the search for answers to this question will be a major preoccupation of a revitalized sociology of economic behaviour. There is such an enormous opportunity for future research precisely because we have only just asked this question.

We might begin by making the practical efficacy of the economic rationality an open question. When it comes to defining 'efficacy' we encounter some further, interesting conundrums. If the world's stock markets expected car companies to adopt the Resende solution, they might punish any companies which demurred, yet this would not mean that the Resende solution really moved resources to more productive uses. Needless to say, most 'empirical' proofs of the economic rationality of one or another organizational change do not bother with such subtleties.

Once the practical efficacy of economic rationality becomes an open question we can consider other reasons why people might be persuaded to shift from one rationality to another. The sociology of economic behaviour will be forced to take very seriously the possibility that people are persuaded by economic rationality independently of its efficacy. There will be many opportunities to develop explanations which refer to the way individual decision-makers copy the behaviour of other members of their group. There will also be opportunities to explore the way in which individual and group interests are tied up in changes from one economic rationality to another. A company that is focused on mergers and acquisitions will not look for evidence of the failure of this strategy and will be locked into it because the instrumental means to achieve these goals (the CEO's bonus package for instance) creates individual or group interests in pursuing it (Mannheim, 1935; Michels, 1911/1962). If a CEO's remuneration package makes it more lucrative for her to buy companies rather than make widgets, the economic rationality of mergers and acquisitions will make more sense to her than the economic rationality of research and development. What is true of the behaviour of CEOs can also be true of banks, shareholders looking for short-term gain, pension funds and other institutional investors, management consultants and accountants (Hayes and Abernathy, 1980). Thus we begin to see how the economic rationalities discussed in this chapter can function in the same way as the class ideologies which were discussed in Chapter 6.

The propagation of economic rationalities that serve the interests of individuals and groups may have far-reaching consequences. In the mergers and acquisitions example, take-overs affect everything about the company: what the firm sells and how it makes or provides this, the size of its constituent units and their location, the structure of ownership and control, and so on. We will have to understand that this sort of behaviour applies to much more than mergers and acquisitions. It also applies to all sorts of other behaviour which affects decisions about what to make or buy, decisions about the size of firms or plants, the degree of horizontal or vertical integration, the shape of technology and work organization, and so on.

Such possibilities were well beyond the purview of economic sociology because economic sociology did not perceive a change from one fungible economic rationality to another, just ever more rational behaviour which was hardly in need of explanation since the reasons for it were so self-evident. Economic sociology's best efforts were devoted to the kind of thinking that was exemplified by the work of Streeck in Chapter 6. To beat the economists at their own game, economic sociologists tried to show how the tastes and preferences that economists thought so marginal to the explanation of economic behaviour actually contained some of the secrets of success. Economic sociology concentrated its best efforts on exploring the way in which the non-economic norms which influenced economic behaviour might be understood as the crucial ingredients that gave companies and countries a competitive edge.

NORMS ARE THE SECRET OF SUCCESS

As ever, economic sociology was obliged to bring morality, and more general norms like trust and reciprocity, into its arguments in the category of means rather than ends. Chapter 5 recalled how Weber identified the norms of economic rationality (the 'rational ethic for the conduct of life', and so on) as components of the culture that allowed capitalism to flourish in the West and not the East. The development of capitalism was obstructed in the East by, amongst other things, irrational law and 'ideas and institutions connected with magic' (1981: 322–3). It is less well known that Weber also thought that non-rational norms could also hinder development within Western societies. In his Freiburg inaugural address (Weber, 1895/1989) Weber explained that part of the blame for the arrested development of capitalist agriculture in Germany lay with the norms of the German workers who were migrating out of the agricultural regions of Prussia. He described these norms in terms of 'primitive *idealism*' and the '*magic*' or '*spirit* of freedom'. Although the German workers might be advanced according to the terms of *The General Economic History*, development could still be hindered by non-rational norms in unexpected ways.

209

Dore (1973) offered an explanation of the motivation of economic behaviour in non-economic terms. He shared Weber's interest in the identification of the norms that hindered, and aided, capitalist development. On the basis of his comparative research in Britain and Japan, Dore simply turned Weber's conclusions on their head and declared that it was the non-rational norms[11] of Japanese workers that lay behind the faster growth rates of their economy. Dore assumed that the non-rational commitment of Japanese workers to their firms helped to explain their superior productivity and the success of their employers. This made sense in the economic competition of the 1960s and 1970s when Japanese firms were clearly much more successful than their British counterparts. If Dore had been able to foresee the economic situation of Japan in the following decades he might have wondered whether Japanese employers who recognized a reciprocal moral relationship with their employees would be extremely reluctant to let economic values excuse their employers from their obligations within that relationship. Perhaps Dore would have predicted that these employers would wish to subordinate economic values and ask the banks to lend them more and more money to stay in business (with ultimately disastrous results).

For all the criticisms that can be made of Dore, it is a matter of regret that his work was not more widely recognized. Much greater recognition was achieved by Etzioni and it is his name that is generally associated with the idea that community and its associated morality functions as the secret of business success. For example, Etzioni (1988) argued that giving workers dignity would make them work harder and reduce turnover and absenteeism (see also Hodson, 2001). Dore was also responsible for some of the earliest work on the economic significance of trust relationships between, as well as within, firms. Although economic sociology was capable of discussing trust relationships in other ways (Lane and Bachmann, 1998), it frequently used the framework of social capital theory to discuss trust and reciprocity. Social capital is the characteristic example of the way economic sociology has taken recourse to the concepts of economics in order to cast morality in an instrumental role (Fine, 2001).

The idea that social capital in the form of social networks and their associated norms could make a vital contribution to economic growth and prosperity has been central to the social capital literature since Coleman (1990). Within the social capital literature we hardly ever encounter the idea that economic growth has an effect (good or bad) on networks or norms. The focus of writers like Woolcock (1998, 2000) and Portes (1995a, 1998) is firmly directed in the other direction, towards the effect of norms and networks on development. In the work of Fukuyama (1995, 1999) there is, at least, some recognition that development might have a deleterious effect on social capital. Of course, Fukuyama concludes that this is not really a problem or, more strictly, not a problem that requires intervention, because instinctive human sociability guarantees the spontaneous regeneration of social networks.

Fukuyama found an explanation for this spontaneous sociability in the characteristics of human nature that biological science was discovering (game theory showed how this worked out in terms of norms). While few economic sociologists shared his view, critics commented on the elective affinity between the ideas of socio-biology and those of some economists and economic sociologists (Fevre, 2000b; Fine, 2001; Fine and Green, 2000). A previous chapter discussed the contribution of Herrnstein and Murray to economic sociology but this was only one example of the way in which reductionist assumptions about the biological roots of human behaviour fit similarly reductionist assumptions about the economic causes of this behaviour. Moreover, economists have been as happy as biologists to assume that the actions of optimizing individuals solve the 'problem' of social order. Both disciplines shared the heritage of nineteenth-century utilitarianism and this heritage appeared to include a determination to put morality in an instrumental role. For example, evolutionary biology and the economics of Gary Becker shared the conviction that altruism was merely an adaptation that served the atomized self-interest of the individual (or gene).

Earlier in this chapter, historical material was deployed in order to shed light on the provenance of more contemporary economic rationality. Fukuyama, by way of contrast, made the effort to remove the complications of real history from the picture and replace it with the more amenable idea of evolution. In *Trust*, Fukuyama declared that 'a society's endowment of social capital is critical to understanding its industrial structure, and hence its place in the global capitalist division of labour' (1995: 325) although 'the causal relationship between social capital and economic performance is indirect and attenuated' (ibid.: 321). In his later book, *The Great Disruption*, Fukuyama took up Durkheim's interest in the morality underpinning social order. Unlike Durkheim, he was sanguine about the way this morality, and the social order on which it depended, periodically broke down as a direct result of the process of development. Adapting Schumpeter's view of economic change, Fukuyama portrayed development as a form of creative destruction which had a disruptive effect on social capital: '[t]he bonds of social reciprocity that facilitated production in the earlier time period become obstacles to production in the later one ... To continue the economic metaphor, social capital can be said to be obsolete and needs to depreciated in the country's capital accounts' (Fukuyama, 1999: 18–19). But, just as morality was remade, and order reconstituted, after the creative destruction of the industrial revolution, so also was Western society at the end of the twentieth century witnessing the benign effects of the reconstitution of social order in the wake of the birth of the information society. The proof of this evolutionary adaptation could be seen in the falling crime statistics of both periods.

211

In *Trust* the process by which social capital was renewed had been mysterious but, in Fukuyama's later book, renewal was guaranteed by our 'very powerful innate human capacities for reconstituting social order' (1999: 282). If we chose not to share his faith in the sociobiological solution to the problem of social order, we might conclude that social capital could be destroyed by economic development and not be reconstituted at all. As we saw earlier in this chapter, such a view might accord more closely with historical evidence but the instrumental role that is accorded to morality in Fukuyama's work meant that this evidence was irrelevant. Since development continued we were urged to conclude that social capital must therefore have been remade.

Fukuyama's work is instructive because it offers an ahistorical view of the relation between social capital and economic development but the fundamental fault in his argument still lies in the primacy it gives to economic rationality over morality. The questions that should be central to sociology have simply been wished away (Fevre, 2000a). Indeed, the social conditions that are the most important stuff of people's lives – their loves and friendships, all that they hold most dear – are not considered an appropriate subject matter (Beder, 2000; Gorz, 1989; see also Chapter 5). Because people will find a way of making the new social capital that is needed, there is no problem here that requires investigation. Since the most important purpose of social capital is to underpin economic development, we have no reason to care about the fate, and even the misery, of individuals.

If we find this neglect shocking there is no special blame attached to Fukuyama. It may be that since he was a late convert to economic sociology Fukuyama was not quite as adept as others when it came to glossing over some of the less palatable implications of the approach. (Indeed, this is one of the most important reasons why space has been devoted to Fukuyama's work here.) In any event there are some hopeful signs that others are not so happy to learn from economic sociology how they should treat morality in their explanations of social phenomena. Such signs can be found in Beder (2000) and in papers by Sayer (2000a, 2000b). For example, Sayer (2000b) recalled the work of Bowles and Gintis which summarized empirical evidence on popular morality that suggested people recognized the necessity of support for the needy but expected reciprocity in human relationships and strongly disapproved of free-riders (see also Nichols and Beynon, 1977). Sayer noted that such opinions might well legitimate social inequality. Self-sufficiency earned through the market was not an option for everyone because it was founded on unequal access to employment and an unequal burden of responsibilities (for domestic and care work, for example). Sayer added that (heavily influenced by US precedent) the UK government had made such self-sufficiency the cornerstone of their social policy (Barry, 1998; Holden, 1999).

Sayer paid particular attention to conflict between morality and market relations, and this has been a theme of several other sociological works.[12] In the previous chapter we learnt of the work of those like Lamont (2000) and Bynner (1989) on working-class disregard for the values of the market. With a variety of colleagues, Nichols has investigated the extent to which the conflict between morality and market relations is perceived by individuals varies with their socio-economic group. As we might expect from Chapter 6, managers are more likely than other employees to apply economic rationality alone. Nichols and O'Connell Davidson (1993) explained employee resistance to privatization within the health service and public utilities, and services provided by local authorities, in terms of their morality. Employees refused to evaluate the organizations which employed them simply according to economic rationality. Nichols et al. (1998) also suggested that a moral element was underpinning the different views of privatization taken by workers in Turkey and the UK.

Waddington et al. (1998) compared the fate of two UK coal mines which were now owned by their employees according to 'collectivist' rather than market criteria. They found that:

> what distinguishes Tower so markedly from Monktonhall is its over-riding commitment to ensuring the satisfaction, safety and well-being of its employees, even at the expense of forsaking potential markets and enhance profitability ... Tower's adherence to collectivist ideals is undoubtedly a reflection of the long socialist tradition of its NUM lodge. (ibid.: 343)

Discussion of similar values – more typically described as 'community' than 'collectivist' values – has appeared in sociological studies of local exchange trading schemes (LETS). A UK study of LETS conducted by Seyfang (2001) recalled some of the findings of Hill's study of an Indian trade union (Hill, 2001, discussed in Chapter 6). As well as finding evidence of increased feelings of self-esteem arising from economic activity (see also Offe and Heinze, 1992), Seyfang uncovered a further, moral dimension:

> Most members (72 per cent, and 80 per cent from low-income house- **213**
> holds and 79 per cent of those not engaged in formal employment)
> enjoyed the ways that doing business on LETS was unlike the cash
> economy: the most commonly reported benefit of the scheme was that
> people were 'more friendly and informal', 'more helpful', 'trusting'
> and 'patient', 'more cooperative and equal', and LETS interactions
> were thought to have 'fewer social barriers' and 'a caring element,
> with more communication' than trading in the cash economy. The
> LETS then became a cherished space for the expression of compas-
> sionate and human-centred values normally crowded out of the com-
> petitive conventional economy: 'There is an assumption of values
> other than money' ... Local money systems like LETS offer a unique
> opportunity for experimentation with different value systems.
> (Seyfang, 2001: 588)

This last remark was informed by the knowledge that LETS partici-pants thought their system fairer mainly because there was one hourly rate of reward and this made all participants feel equally valued. Seyfang compared these findings to research on people's judgements about the value of various kinds of work. For example, Schumacher (1979) defined 'good work' as providing necessary, useful goods and services, enabling people to put skills and talents to good use, and working both in service to, and co-operation with, others. It is to fur-ther discussion of the way that different values can be attached to labour that we now turn.

CHEAP LABOUR AND ECONOMIC DEVELOPMENT

The discussion that concludes this chapter capitalizes on the fact that we have now learnt what Marx did not – that economic rationality is infinitely fungible. If there is never a watertight case for economic inevitability, we can bring morality into our deliberations as an end not a means. Once this is done, the trump cards of economic rationality, for example, the one that Esping-Anderson refers to as the necessity to work ourselves to death, no longer seem so irresistible. But to give morality an equal presence to such arguments requires some conceptual invention. *Cheap labour* is one of those important concepts that allow us to operationalize moral concerns so that they can be put on a par with economic rationality.

Cheap labour is clearly not simply a matter of low pay but we are perhaps not conscious, in the normal course of events, of the sort of judgements the idea of cheap labour allows us to make.[13] Since the concept represents one way of introducing the idea that there may be some types of work that are less morally defensible than others, it must obviously allow the generation of criteria that distinguish these different types of work. Cheap or 'sweated' labour is often thought to involve particularly unpleasant or intense labour, or simply very long hours of work, and work which is designed to be insecure. For the purposes of sociology, however, the term can most usefully be applied to work which does not receive the rewards normally expected for the type of work in question.

Chapter 5 introduced a theory of a morality of wage-setting in which people were paid according to their *worth*. The term cheap labour applies to those situations in which people are receiving significantly less than their worth. Whereas within positional competition – and according to campaigns against inflated rewards for 'fat cat' executives – this morality was over-ridden by powerful groups acting to monopolize resources, the people who perform cheap labour are in an especially powerless position. It is not simply that they are unable to monopolize resources (Weber, 1968). Very often the workers who provide cheap labour are unable to access other forms of work because of legal or linguistic barriers or because of some form of discrimination. In some cases cheap labour is provided by workers who are physically compelled to do it and in other cases by migrants who find its meagre rewards are relatively attractive when compared with wages in their country of out-migration (Fevre, 1984). In the latter case workers are caught between the moralities of wage-setting which apply in two different cultures and their employers benefit accordingly.[14]

The idea of cheap labour sometimes appeared in the economic sociology literature with the qualification that economic rationality

214

clearly showed that cheap labour was a mistake, a relic, or a backward step, which would actually retard development or even put it into reverse (Corrigan, 1977; Miles, 1987). We have already found an early example of economic sociology's mistakes in the Freiburg Address. As German workers migrated out of the agricultural regions of Prussia, so Polish peasants were imported and for both reasons the productivity of German agriculture suffered:

> *It is chiefly German day-labourers who move out of the districts of progressive cultivation; it is chiefly Polish peasants who multiply in the districts where cultivation is at a low level.* But both processes – here emigration, there increase in numbers – lead back to one and the same reason: *a lower expectation of living standards*, in part physical, in part mental, which the Slav race either possesses as a gift from nature or has acquired through breeding in the course of its past history. This is what has helped it to victory. (Weber, 1895/1989: 192, emphasis in original)

Weber saw the Polish peasants as cheap labour and the result of the replacement of German day-labourers by this cheap labour was that the development of agriculture (both its productivity and its output) was retarded and even reversed.

As became customary in economic sociology, Weber did not consider the possibility that cheap labour might actually represent the way in which development was occurring. This would be a step too far from the idea of progressive economic rationality. In simple terms, if economic development was a self-evidently desirable thing, and cheap labour was undesirable, it would be much too inconvenient to find that the former fuelled the later. Much the same conclusion was reached in later examples of economic sociology in which the idea of a secondary sector dedicated to inefficiency and low productivity and which made use of cheap labour was used to denote the antithesis of the technologically-sophisticated development pole (see pp. 112–113). If their objection to cheap labour was simply that it had a negative effect on development, how could economic sociologists find grounds to object to cheap labour if evidence to the contrary was found?

Economic sociology might be happy to accept that cheap labour was a drag on development because it muted the incentive to increase productivity through technological change. Evidence that suggested that prohibitions on the use of cheap labour would undermine the competitive advantage of developing countries might make economic sociologists, including those who were critical of globalization, less comfortable (cf. Kenyon, 1972). In what follows we will see that it is equally possible to construct an economic rationality that will allow one to argue that cheap labour can stimulate growth rather than arresting it. Similarly, getting rid of cheap labour can be portrayed as damaging to the people of less developed countries as well as being beneficial to them.

215

Prohibitions against the employment of children in nineteenth-century Britain did not appear to stall development, nevertheless the British textile industry, in particular, periodically resorted to other forms of cheap labour such as the labour of migrants from poorer countries, in subsequent generations. On many occasions cheap labour was introduced in order to facilitate technological change (Fevre, 1984). In this important industry cheap labour was never a relic of a bygone age. Sassen (1988) collected considerable empirical evidence from a variety of sectors in different countries to suggest that cheap labour of this sort, including the labour of illegal immigrants, had become an integral component of development in the cities of the advanced economies at the end of the twentieth century.

We will only find such evidence to be an embarrassment if we are tied to an economic rationality that sees cheap labour as a drag on economic development. Once we leave economic sociology behind, we no longer handicap ourselves in this way and we can judge cheap labour as wrong simply because it is morally wrong, i.e. we promote morality to the status of self-sufficient end rather than a means. We are no longer required to ignore evidence that suggests cheap labour can accompany development in order to oppose it. Throughout the nineteenth century textile employers planned their investment in technology in the knowledge that their new machines would be worked by children (for example, Ure, 1835/1967). Towards the end of the nineteenth century they did the same with women (Pinchbeck, 1930; Walker, 1979), but child labour was the main support of technical change. In the worsted branch of textiles, for example, the proportion of children increased with the spread of the powerloom (Clegg et al., 1964; Pinchbeck, 1930; Ure, 1835/1967). There may well be all sorts of economic arguments for having branded sports goods sewn by young children but the idea of cheap labour puts the moral objection to this form of labour on a par with any economic case for it. Moreover, the moral objection to cheap labour has much more chance of having an effect than any economic argument.

As we will see later in this section, the economic arguments for and against cheap labour tend to be deployed by groups with diverging interests in a similar way to the ideologies described in Chapter 6. Researchers face all sorts of difficulties when they try to determine which argument best represents the truth. Moreover, as the interests of groups shift, so do their arguments. It is often forgotten that the core of the Luddites' complaint against their employers was the labour 'dilution' that accompanied technological changes, in particular the introduction of shearing frames in the textile industry. The idea of dilution of labour was short-hand for an economic argument against the introduction of cheap labour. The complaint against the use of women, children and other 'unapprenticed' labour in place of craftsmen was founded on the conviction that the quality of production would necessarily suffer (Fevre, 1984).

Workers all over the world used the labour dilution argument on many occasions in subsequent decades but there was nothing automatic about this response to cheap labour. For example, when organized labour did not perceive that members had an interest in the work which was to be performed by cheap labour they were much more likely to be persuaded of the employers' arguments in favour of it: this was the only way to get a proper return on new capital investment, this was the only way to beat low-wage foreign competition and so on. In such cases organized labour typically tried to negotiate an agreement with employers or the state which would ring-fence the jobs their members currently held against dilution and provide for cheap labour to be removed in the future if labour market conditions changed (Bohning and Maillat, 1974; Castles and Kosack, 1973; Fevre, 1984). As we saw in Chapter 4, conflict between economic rationalities is usually determined by the distribution of power. The economic arguments wielded by organized labour to dissuade employers from using cheap labour have only prevailed where workers have the power to impose their wishes on their employers (Fevre, 1985).

217

All of this demonstrates how foolish we would be to rely on campaigns based on economic rationality if we wished to do something about cheap labour (Gorz, 1989). When Shaftesbury, Foster, Oastler and all the other British nineteenth-century reformers and philanthropists argued the case against cheap labour they did so on moral rather than economic grounds (Driver, 1970). In effect, they acted as moral entrepreneurs (Becker, 1963). If they had not done so, the cause of factory reform would have been lost. As the Commissioners on Child Employment established, it was not enough to tell the facts about the employment of children, there had to be moral interpretation of these facts (Wing, 1967). It was this interpretation that earned the Commissioners a reputation for exaggeration and perhaps fabrication but this was of course why they were effective. The simple, and most important, point to grasp is that the argument for factory reform would not have succeeded if it had been founded on economic rationality. It only worked because it was shot through with morality (of every kind). Indeed, it was simply a component of a much wider cultural revolution, a society-wide move to re-moralize the first industrial nation (Himmelfarb, 1995; for the American equivalent see the summary in Barley and Kunda, 1992).[15]

The prototype organizations of industrial society operated with varieties of cheap labour provided, as a result of legal compulsion and physical coercion, by prisoners and paupers (Melossi and Pavarini 1981; Pollard 1965). The labour of many thousands of very young 'pauper apprentices' shipped from the parishes of the South of England supported the industrialization of the northern towns (Pollard, 1965). The first 'free' labourers of the factory system were children and women who had not been in the poorhouse and factory labour was constructed as the appropriate form of work for this estate. It was some time before this morality was so reconstructed that it was thought immoral for children and, eventually women, to be employed in certain forms of paid employment. It was the continued attempt to re-moralize Victorian Britain – a sort of permanent revolution in morality – that led the philanthropists and reformers to campaign for the Ten Hours legislation and the Factory Acts. Most famously, it was their concern for the sexual dangers posed to children that led to the 1833 Factory Act.

The textile industries of Britain continued to rely on child labour in the twentieth century. In 1901 children under 12 were barred from the mills, but full-time employees between 12 and 18 years of age made up 21 per cent of the wool textile workforce. There had, however, been a reduction in the number of half-timers: the numbers of 12- to 14-year-old half-timers were less than a third of the total ten years before and made up only 3 per cent of the total workforce (Clapham, 1907). It was a long, slow process that led to the removal of children from the factory system but it was the development of a tradition of moral entrepreneurship (abetted by Kingsley and Dickens) that led to the creation of the idea of childhood. By the 1880s the trade unions were playing a role in moral enterprise. Whereas the early combinations had made various arguments against the substitution of 'unapprenticed' child and female labour for the labour of men, the mature industrial trade unions elaborated a moral argument in favour of the nuclear family with one male breadwinner supporting a wife and children on a family wage. It was on the basis of this morality that the twentieth-century masculinization of work proceeded (Liddington and Norris, 1978) but the economic effects of removing children and women from the factories were not straightforward.[16]

The argument for a family wage implied that the women and children who were saved from factory work were the same women and children that the family wage would provide for. This was not always the case. For much of the nineteenth century the families that sent their children and women to the mills had no other involvement in the textile industry (Thorpe, 1973). If men in that industry received a family wage it would not be of immediate benefit to the families of displaced child workers and the prohibition of child labour might well undermine these families' economic survival. The acute dilemma presented by

218

child labour was illustrated by Ure's pronouncement that the low wages very young children received were a cause for satisfaction because their removal from the factory would have less effect on their parents' finances (Ure, 1835/1967).

Such complications have not disappeared with the passage of time. In their research on Turkey late in the twentieth century Kahveci et al. (1996) discovered families which were supported by child labour. Both the children and their parents believed that child labour was wrong but could not afford to live by this morality. On the other hand, Chapter 2 showed that, among the middle classes, incomes which far exceeded modest expectations of a family wage did not entitle children to parental care during working hours. According to Lamont (2000), American working-class men were much more likely to continue to use the ideal of a non-working wife as a moral signifier which very few of them would ever achieve because they would never earn a family wage. She speculated that this might reflect their acute awareness of their demoralized surroundings and the dangers entailed in giving over the care of their children to non-family members. This contrasts sharply with the middle-class professionals (but not the lower-paid employees) who Hochschild (1997) found were prepared to leave their young children home alone. Chapter 2 suggested that British working-class men also arranged their lives so that they could take care of their children when their wives were working. As in the American case, these men still aspired to the family wage and non-working wife that very few of them would ever achieve.

219

The effects of ideas like cheap labour are complex and unpredictable but if we choose to do without the kind of moral levers that proved so powerful in the nineteenth century, we not only reduce our capacity to take effective action but we diminish the sphere of the changes we might think possible or even desirable (Bauman, 1993). In the nineteenth century, campaigners used moral arguments when trying to change the relationship of various social groups to work and employment. These moral elements allowed campaigners to formulate a thorough critique of the status quo and to imagine a very different society to the morally dubious one they saw coming into existence all around them. At the start of the twenty-first century, campaigners who wanted to put education in place of employment found that the only way in which they could argue for an extension of the school leaving age or increased participation in higher education was in terms of the economic imperatives of investment in human capital (Coffield, 1999; Fevre et al., 1999; see Chapter 3). This confirmed the status quo rather than challenging it and there was no possibility in this limited economic logic of imagining a different kind of society.

We will conclude this chapter with a final illustration of the possibilities for mounting a moral critique of economic behaviour using studies of international migration. We already know from Weber's Freiburg address that this topic has long been the focus of economic sociology (for typical later examples, see Portes, 1995b). There is an economic rationality for importing cheap labour, just as there is an economic rationality for exporting jobs to the East so that the sports goods can be sewed with (possibly indentured) child labour. With the idea of cheap labour we can reveal that both of these decisions are actually moral ones (and that the same goes for the decision to export jobs) although this fact is usually hidden from us. In other words, cheap labour – and some other basic concepts of the sociology of economic behaviour – show us that decisions about where to put production are always economic *and moral*.

On p. 216 we encountered Sassen's theory about the centrality of the cheap labour provided by migrants (both legal and illegal) to the economies of advanced (post)industrial nations, and particularly to their cities. For many years, at least since the idea of the 'new international division of labour' was popularized by Frobel, Heinrichs and Kreye et al. (1980), economic sociology had assumed that there was every (economic) reason to expect that jobs which required cheap labour would be exported overseas or would simply disappear in the face of competition from counties with lower labour costs. Sassen (1988) suggested that the presence of cheap labour was simply too useful to the advanced economies for these jobs to disappear. Many of these jobs (for example, those in the service sector) could not be exported for technical reasons and these reasons were part of a complex economic rationality which meant that the development of the advanced economies was helped rather than hindered by their retention. Sassen's migrants clearly met the classic criteria of cheap labour and if we therefore judge their employment on these terms to be wrong, and if moral considerations matter to us, then we determine to change this. For example, we might argue for the setting of a minimum wage at a level which means these workers are no longer providing cheap labour and we may demand that the position of illegal workers is regularized.

It is important to note that none of this depends on predicting the consequences of putting a stop to cheap labour for the workers concerned (cf. the discussion of different types of moral consideration in Etzioni, 1988). For example, without a moral context, arguments for minimum wage legislation quickly get mired in conflicting economic rationalities. It can argued that the real purpose of minimum wage legislation is to reduce immigration (*South China Morning Post*, 14 January 2002) and that the people who

220

have provided cheap labour will suffer by it but such arguments are spurious to the moral imperative that arises when we apply the category of cheap labour.

The moral context for the application of the idea of cheap labour in the nineteenth century was provided by Shaftesbury, Dickens and all the other Victorian reformers. In our current demoralized condition we have a great deal of work to do to provide a similar context. For example, we are able to raise an objection to the use of child labour in other countries because we can rely on the fact that the immorality of child labour is underpinned by statute in our own societies but, when it comes to applying the label of cheap labour to a new category of work, we are much more timid and uninspired compared to the great Victorians. For example, the idea of a care-givers' allowance might make the employment of women on poverty wages unnecessary but we would generally prefer that the government provide day-care facilities which allow care-givers to work, even if that work amounts to cheap labour (Fraser, 1989; Sayer, 2000b).

CONCLUSION

Judicious application of the idea of cheap labour, and of other concepts which allow us to operationalize morality, is essential for policy-making purposes. Consider the example of *skilled* labour migration from a less developed country to a more developed one. Because this migration entails a regressive redistribution of training investment, it might be a very effective way of making sure that the gap between rich and poor nations does not narrow too much. Nevertheless, the lack of a moral context to make sense of this kind of migration means that it is largely invisible to those who criticize current patterns of growth and development, for example, the anti-globalization writers. We can begin to correct this blind spot by thinking of this 'top-end' migration as cheap labour too.

We limit the usefulness of the idea of cheap labour if we only apply it to work which takes place in a sweatshop. Skilled migrants who move from poorer countries to richer ones constitute cheap labour to the extent that their wage expectations are heavily influenced by their experiences in their countries of origin. In this they are no different to the Polish peasants of the Freiburg Address. They may also face restrictions as a result of special immigration arrangements including those which tie them to particular employers, and even to particular jobs. We need to deploy the idea of cheap labour to help us make judgements about such migration and develop a critique of patterns of growth and development which appear to rely on it.

221

There are a number of very obvious case studies which could be used to develop such a critique. These include the recruitment of highly-trained medical personnel from LDCs to staff the hospitals of European countries and the recruitment of Indian computer software engineers to work in the United States in the late 1990s. In neither case did the migration lead to significant moral concern but only to the predictable arguments on behalf of competing economic rationalities. Thus labour unions saw the migration from India to the USA as the employers' solution to rising wage increases in a tight labour market. The employers argued – in the media and on Capitol Hill, and to very good effect – that special immigration arrangements should be made for these workers because they were vital to America's further development.

The United States has long been dependent on massive immigration to fuel economic growth and development and many of these migrants have been skilled workers (Erickson, 1957). The American road to development was paved by cheap labour which was periodically renewed. So soon as one cohort of migrants had become accustomed to the expectations of its adopted country, and was therefore less likely to provide abundant cheap labour, a new source of immigration, perhaps from a country which had not supplied immigrants before, was found. Because it had the room to do so, the United States could continue to absorb new generations of immigrants and so develop at the pace required to maintain the gap in wage expectations that makes it possible to recruit cheap labour from other, less developed, countries.

In complete contradiction to the view of development propounded by Schultz (1961), the American road to development also required that the short-comings of an ineffective system of education and training system would be compensated by skilled labour provided by other countries that were less prosperous. Every so often national attention was focused on the short-comings of American education and training but the continued possibilities of a cheap labour solution to shortages of skilled labour ensured that nothing really changed. This, in turn, helped to preserve another key characteristic of the American political economy: the antipathy towards government intervention in the economy (Rostow, 1960).

At least so far as education and training were concerned, the luxury of doing without government intervention in the process of development was made possible by the recruitment of wave after wave of skilled immigrants. For example, *laissez-faire* meant that in the United States there was very little chance of a national skill *standards* policy, let alone a national skill *formation* policy. The continued opposition to such solutions – which were seen as fundamentally anti-democratic and anti-American – was only sustainable with immigration as a back-stop when the inevitable skill shortages arose. Without immigration the opposition to a national policy and government intervention would have been defeated long ago.

We will return to some of these ideas in the next chapter when we consider the meta-level relationship between social and economic change and the condition of morality in society. For the moment we should note that, in order to provide sound foundations for the sociology of economic behaviour, we need more of the concepts (like cheap labour) that operationalize morality.

NOTES

1 Durkheim's ideas, like Simmel's (see Chapter 1), owed something to Schopenhauer and in *Suicide* Durkheim developed Schopenhauer's ideas about the generation of insatiability (Mestrovic, 1991).

2 In the terms of Fevre (2000b) environmental costs are 'nature-knowledge' that must be *translated* into economic values in order to be made to count in 'human-knowledge' calculation.

3 This objection to any plan for the 'organised diminution of work' (Russell, 1932/1999) also applies to plans to reduce or limit our demand for goods and services.

4 Although Gorz did stumble occasionally. See (Gorz, 1989: 141) where he seemed to go along with the idea that there might be a valid economic argument for contracting out child care. Also see (ibid.: 194) where he talked of reducing higher-value work because the quality of the work would be improved.

5 Compare to Calhoun (1982) for whom domestic workers were definitely not backward in this sense.

6 See Chapter 6 on the connection between privatization, marketization and feelings of insecurity.

7 This proved to be a recurring theme in subsequent commentary on outsourcing, for example, a report by the UK Health and Safety Executive on the Dounreay nuclear energy facility in September 1998 concluded that the organization was too dependent on contractors and that it did not have management control and lacked managerial and technical expertise. These weaknesses contributed to the risk of major incidents at the plant.

8 BT also used their contracts to stop contractors poaching labour from each other.

9 Several years ago, Littler drew attention to the dangers of the 'ahistorical ... nature of most organization theory and analysis' (1979: 1).

10 For examples of very similar arguments, consider the work of Edwards (1979) or the 'contingency theorists' (like Pugh and Hickson, 1976) discussed in Chapter 4.

11 Of course these norms were also heavily implicated in questions of identity. Dore's work could just as easily have been discussed in Chapter 6.

12 By way of contrast, in Fukuyama (1999) there are obstacles to 're-norming' like moral individualism and more relativism (and the associated 'miniaturization of community') but market relations and capitalism are never the problem – they only cause good (albeit that the unavoidable side-effects are sometimes –

223

temporarily – inconvenient).

13 'Even the bourgeois intellect understands' cheap labour according to Marx (1867/1954: 240), but sees it as low pay. Marx also discusses the 'dishonourable' or 'sweated' trades, as did his contemporary Fielden (1836/1969) – see also Samuel (1977) and Thompson (1974).

14 Faist (2000) shows that such migration is unusual where there are no big differences in income levels. In Europe the historical examples of cheap labour import from other European states have been comparatively rare (Fevre, 1998).

15 Etzioni (1988) and Fukuyama (1999) refer to similar trends in the United States at a slightly later period.

16 I am indebted to Keith Grint for bringing this point to my attention.

eight
conclusion

E conomic sociology's rigorous prosecution of the agenda defined by economic rationality only makes sense if it is coupled with a mistaken notion of the capabilities of social science. In reality, there is no compensation for economic sociology's neglect of moral considerations because the goals it defines for itself are unattainable. Indeed, economic sociology does further damage to morality because it treats it as a means to economic ends. If morality can only be valued when sanctioned by economic rationality, this cannot help but demean and distort it. This certainly makes it impossible for us to imagine a different kind of society to the one we live in. To do this we would need to hold morality to be equal with economic rationality and not subordinated to it.

When economic sociologists feel that moral considerations matter, they never pit morality against economic rationality but argue instead that the morality they favour also happens to be economically rational. Morality is allowed an instrumental role when the moral means to economic ends seem to chime with the convictions of the sociologists concerned. In Europe, for example, economic sociologists have argued that the desiderata of a left-leaning social democracy also happen to make organizations and countries more competitive. A similar point could be made in respect of claims that a lifelong commitment to learning is at the root of the comparative advantage of individuals and states; or arguments about the economic advantages of equal opportunities or family-friendly policies.

DIGNITY AT WORK

Nichols and Beynon (1977) described how, no less than in Marx's time, British capitalism was capable of creating working-class jobs which nobody could do with dignity. To further strengthen their moral evaluation of this kind of job creation, they used the idea that workers' lives were being wasted. In Nichols and Beynon's hands these ideas of waste and dignity allowed them to operationalize morality but these concepts do not serve, on their own, as an antidote to economic sociology. Nichols and Beynon (1977) was one of the workplace ethnographies which Hodson (2001) deployed in order to investigate 'dignity at work'. Like Etzioni (1988), Hodson maintained that the dignity of workers was also good for companies but Hodson did not simply assert that the values he favoured were the means to greater business efficiency. Instead he produced a mass of qualitative and quantitative evidence derived from the ethnographic studies to prove his point. On the basis of his analysis of this evidence, Hodson identified mismanagement rather than overwork and insufficient autonomy as the root of threats to workers' dignity. If incompetent management was the cause of lack of dignity, it was fairly obvious that what was bad for workers was also bad for companies.

Hodson's argument was much more sophisticated than the familiar, naïve assertion of the congruence of moral and economic values but it required that dignity at work be defined in a particular way. It was a necessary condition of dignity at work that workers had to be able to 'operate purposively and effectively' (Hodson, 2001: 237) and it was therefore not surprising that incompetent managers turned out to be the biggest obstacle to the achievement of dignity at work. Other necessary conditions of dignity at work included the successful achievement of goals like 'job satisfaction, a liveable pace of work, and creativity and meaning in work' (ibid.). None of these are deontological values which defy the need for reasoned justification (see Chapter 2), indeed, they are just the sort of values which frequently appear in texts which instruct managers on the best way to treat their 'most valued resource' in order to embed quality and encourage innovation. These other necessary conditions of dignity at work (as defined by Hodson) are closely related to the idea that workers achieve dignity if they 'operate purposively and effectively'.

Hodson defined dignity at work in a way that made it inevitable that what was good for workers was good for managers. Even when workers tried to maintain or achieve dignity by acts of resistance, including sabotage and theft, Hodson argued that they only resorted to this behaviour because incompetent or abusive managers were forcing them to do so. A productive and efficient workplace would not produce this aberrant behaviour because workers would not have to fight for every scrap of dignity left to them. When workers were well managed, they would do nothing in pursuit or defence of their dignity that would undermine the economic goals of their employers. Indeed, the reverse of this was true. According to Hodson, workers everywhere were naturally 'eager to be active and positive participants in their organizations ... This reservoir of positive citizenship is a potentially powerful force for productivity' (ibid.: 236).

Hodson concluded that the 'workplace of the twenty-first century' needed 'greater employee participation in order to run efficiently' (ibid.: 258–9). Long-standing research evidence (Blumberg, 1968; Vroom, 1964) would lead us to treat this claim with extreme scepticism. Examples like this suggest that, even though economic sociology internalizes economic rationality and the economic imperative, it carries a vague memory of the classical period in which moral concerns were paramount. But in economic sociology the morality that has no economic purpose has no point: if lifelong learning or social partnership or equal opportunities or employee participation were not economically efficient, then what grounds would economic sociology give us for promoting them? In classical sociology an attempt was made to understand how economic behaviour might influence morality but economic sociologists only ever ask this question in reverse.

Economic sociology is increasingly likely to borrow the approach and concepts of economics in order to deal with morality in this instrumental way. This happens in rational choice (or exchange) theory and, of course, social capital theory (Fine, 2001). The application of these theories absorbs much of the energies of economic sociologists but it is not only through social capital theory, for example, that economic sociology hopes to find out how to make organizations and economies more competitive. For example, along with psychologists and other social scientists, many economic sociologists spend their time finding ways to make management more effective. Their misunderstanding of the possibilities for perfecting management replicates the misunderstanding which leads them to over-estimate the efficacy of applied social science. Yet the delusion that economic sociology and managerialism share about their capabilities legitimizes the authority with which they both direct our attention away from moral ends. In fact, social science has only been effective in this way through its (often unwitting) contribution to the cultural invention that has been found necessary in order to replace the values that have been stripped from economic behaviour during demoralization (Anthony, 1977). Beginning with Elton Mayo, economic sociology's major impact in the real world has been in the invention of substitute, or *ersatz*, moralities.

Thoughtful writing on economic behaviour (including Du Gay and Salaman, 1992, and Kunda, 1992) has been increasingly likely to draw a distinction between genuine and manufactured norms and moral conditions. For example, Hardy et al. (2000) described the construction of 'façades' of trust in order to minimize conflict resulting from organizational change (also see Knights et al., 1993). In this book I have argued that neither economic rationality nor the wider category

227

of sense-making from which it flows (common sense) are capable of authoring a genuine morality. Moral rules for behaviour flow from beliefs of various kinds rather than from knowledge (Fevre, 2000b). It follows, therefore, that the morality *of* work (leading to the compulsion to prioritize work over other values), and all other moralities created by corporations, are inauthentic.

CAPITALISM AND MORALITY

It is not possible to account for the development of economic sociology unless we refer to the displacement of morality in wider society as a result of the increasing hegemony of common sense and economic rationality. Economic sociology is a footnote to a much more important narrative of the way different kinds of sense-making became privileged, while others were demoted. These shifts in sense-making have been deeply implicated in major trends in the development of capitalism. According to Jones (2000), 'when moral needs confront prevailing powers the history of capitalism suggests it is morality which gets discounted' but things were never really quite this simple and it is not possible to deploy simple notions of cause and effect to understand the relationship between morality and capitalism. Changes in the character of morality have been linked with major developments in capitalism including the factory system, Fordism, new management orthodoxies and development, flexible specialization and globalization.

The Industrial Revolution would have 'annihilated' society 'but for protective countermoves' against the dangers of 'a self-regulating market system' (Polanyi, 1944/1957: 76). Polanyi's insight helps us to recognize a contradiction of the type later noted by Daniel Bell in which industrial capitalism helped to undermine the cultural conditions which were required for it to thrive. Although it was not the only cause, capitalist industrialization contributed to demoralization and demoralization posed problems for capitalism (Barley and Kunda, 1992). Thus we have learnt that companies must now train their employees in the verbal and non-verbal ceremonies which, following Durkheim, Goffman (1959) understood to be the characteristic form of modern social interaction.[1] Those who were committed to the ends defined by economic rationality decided that synthetic substitutes must do the work of the absent morality. But there is a lot more to the relationship between capitalism and morality than recent attempts to train employees to be courteous to customers.

Evidence that capitalists were concerned about, and responded to, demoralization dates back to the early days of the factory system (Anthony, 1977). At the beginning of the Industrial Revolution, English society had little in common with the Puritanism of Baxter that so impressed Weber: consider, for example, the way embezzlement loomed in the minds of those who organized the domestic system (Marx 1867/1954). Josiah Wedgwood and Robert Owen are perhaps the best-known examples of the different ways in which factory owners responded to demoralization in advance of the remoralization that would occur in the Victorian era. Pollard (1965) described the way Wedgwood made iron virtues of good time-keeping, care and cleanliness, and heinous sins of wasting materials and drinking. A long list of rules ensured that behaviour met these standards with fines (and ultimately dismissals) for their infraction (also see Engels, 1845/1958). While Wedgwood pioneered bureaucratic methodologies for *controlling* the worst effects of demoralization in the workplace in a way that anticipated F.W. Taylor, Owen was an early moral entrepreneur who wanted to remoralize a whole society. The workplace was the arena over which he had immediate authority but he also attempted to remoralize social life outside the factory beginning with the model communities he established for his employees.

Of course, the distinction between this effort to control the effects of demoralization and Owen's attempts to remoralize society is rather too tightly drawn. Owen made sure the output of his employees was publicly judged at the end of each day and there were other mill-owners – for example, Titus Salt – who, like Owen, built model villages for their employees but also enforced lists of rules and fines as long as Wedgwood's. It is also noteworthy how important all of the factory owners considered the elimination of the vice of drunkenness. They blamed drink (even more than godlessness) for demoralization. Salt did not allow a public house to be built within his model village and all of them, including Robert Owen, were determined to dismiss a worker who was found drunk.

Since Weber, sociologists have become accustomed to thinking of this morality as an optional extra. The only ethic that really mattered to capitalism was the work ethic and if factory owners were obsessed with punishing drunkenness this was simply because gin and the work ethic did not mix. In fact, their obsession suggests that the factory owners were preoccupied with societal demoralization (for a summary of the evidence of this preoccupation in the USA, see Barley and Kunda, 1992). They may have been quite wrong to identify alcohol abuse as a cause, rather than a symptom, of demoralization,[2] nevertheless their anxiety about the morality of their employees shows that they were beginning the task of creating a morality out of the ashes of secularlization. This task was largely completed by the Victorians although the vehicles of remoralization such as the YMCA and the wider Temperance Movement continued to exert an influence well into the twentieth century (Barley and Kunda, 1992; Himmelfarb, 1995; and see the discussion of J.Q. Wilson in Etzioni, 1988).

229

In another contradiction between capitalism's aims and its cultural effects, temperance played an important role in the development of British socialism and social democracy (Thompson, 1974). Indeed, from the early days of the factory system, elements of remoralization became a central part of the mission of the social movements which intended to transform industrial capitalism into a good society. Some capitalists even shared their intentions. There were factory owners like Richard Oastler who were less well known than Robert Owen but who made significant contributions to the reform of the factory system (Driver, 1970). Like Shaftesbury and several other reformers, Oastler was one of those Tories 'who was not dominated by the transcendent economic ethic and still able to oppose it from the independent basis of spiritual or traditionalistic values' (Anthony, 1977: 62). From the 1830s, in Britain, the exclusion of children (and then women) from successive places of employment, the extension of the education of working-class children, reductions in the maximum hours of factory workers and rudimentary regulation of health and safety became intertwined with the other missions of a society which was increasingly concerned about the effects of demoralization. As noted in the previous chapter, the Victorian reformers mounted a critique of the capitalist system which was founded on their conviction that present arrangements encouraged immorality. If they had not mobilized morality in this way it is very hard to see how their campaigns could have been as effective as they were.

230

The morality that was in decline at the end of the twentieth century was the morality that had been created in the second half of the nineteenth century. This is evident in Sennett's (1998) account of the corrosion of character with its careful attention to the bonds of mutuality and in Lamont's (2000) study of working-class men.[3] One of the most obvious effects of this morality on economic behaviour was the practice of enforcing socially inspired, and sanctioned, output norms – the very same norms that inspired F.W. Taylor to create Scientific Management (1911/1972). It has often been said that Scientific Management was intended to turn workers into machines but it might be better to think of Taylor's aim as the inculcation of common sense. Workers who were motivated by economic rationality and had no care of collective values would leave their norms at home and leave off social, and indeed moral, behaviour while they were at work. The techniques of Scientific Management were designed to prevent workers polluting the economic with the moral and therefore establishing non-technical or non-physical limits on productivity gains. Workers were meant to leave their consciences outside the factory gates and the 'drill' and payment systems that Taylor insisted they should be subjected to were intended to fulfil this purpose. The characteristic consequence of Scientific Management was therefore the promotion of demoralization in the workplace.

One of the first to recognize the consequences of demoralization for capitalism was Henry Ford himself. The function of the 'Sociological Department' at Ford's Highland Park plant was to make clean-living and right-thinking Americans out of the immigrants who came to work for the Ford Company. As in Wedgwood's time, a premium was placed on cleanliness and drunkenness was not tolerated but the Sociological Department only really came into its own with the $5 day. Ford was terrified about what his employees might do with this money if they did not treat it as a family wage (see also Gramsci, 1971). The Sociological Department's job was to vet and monitor workers to make sure they were thrifty and spent their $5 in the right way: supporting families and other dependants (Batchelor, 1994). As the first head of the Department, J.R. Lee, explained in 1916:

> It was clearly foreseen that $5 a day in the hands of some men would work a tremendous handicap along the paths of rectitude and right living and would make some of them a menace to society in general and so it was established at the [start] that no man was to receive the money who could not use it advisedly and conservatively. (quoted by Batchelor, 1994: 49)

231

The Sociological Department made sure that those who did not qualify for the $5 day on these criteria only earned 34 cents an hour instead of the 62.5 cents an hour which made up the $5 day (Batchelor, 1994). It was not widely known that even two and a half years after the $5 day was introduced, nearly a third of the workforce (including any women workers) were not deemed worthy of it (Serrin, 1973).

In the harsher economic climate of the 1920s the Department's activities were scaled down and it soon came to resemble a normal personnel department. The moral element of Ford's labour relations was replaced by 'strong-arm tactics' with 'gangland' overtones (Batchelor, 1994: 53). From the 1920s Fordism followed the path of Taylor rather than that of J.R. Lee. Chapter 3 discussed the link between Fordism and the spread of common sense and economic rationality through the manufacturing workforce. Fordism subsequently struggled to cope with the behaviour of a demoralized workforce. It did not offer capital reliable protection against workers who periodically gave in to common-sense motivations unfettered (to a greater or lesser degree) by morality (Gorz, 1989; 1999). The biggest Fordist factories became arenas for struggles between capital and labour in which strikes were simply collective bargaining by other means.

Chapter 4 showed how engineers proselytized a form of common sense that gave American management its aims and its characteristic language (Shenhav, 1999). Engineers created the reality managers acted towards and gave them the tools to deal with it, especially the idea of *system* which they offered as a panacea for industrial conflict. Shenhav showed that the incidence of strikes coincided with the introduction of such systems-thinking and suggested that this pattern lay behind the diffusion of Scientific Management itself (ibid.: 180). But by the time the engineers' contribution to American management was being forgotten, it had become increasingly clear that there were limits to the possibilities of coping with the effects of a second wave of demoralization using the traditional solutions that Fordism had put in place (to cope with the demoralization it promoted). Society-wide demoralization could not be dealt with by innovations in work organization and technology alone. Instead, it required that managers take on the task of manufacturing the morality that wider society could no longer assure. In Gillespie's account, welfare capitalism was the first attempt to deal with demoralization in a Fordist environment. It was then superseded by the human relations approach which was presented as the systematization of the hard-won lessons which had been learned through the application of a scientific method to the 'human element' in the workplace (Gillespie, 1991:26).

232

Rather than have people leave their consciences at the factory gate, Human Relations wanted to remake them. Clearly it was of no help to Western Electric or any other business if workers were encouraged to behave according to the morality of mutuality and socially-inspired output norms. This must be replaced by a morality customized for the needs of business. While Taylor wanted to make sure that people got no opportunity to collaborate to enforce their group norms, Mayo, Roethlisberger and Dickson wanted to put the idea of the informal social group, with its norms and sanctions, to good use and this meant reconstituting these informal social relations under managerial control.

Human Relations and Human Resource Management had very similar missions but they can be distinguished by the circumstances in which they appeared. Mayo and the others were responding to the difficulties of managing workers in large manufacturing enterprises in which management methods had previously encouraged demoralization. Human Resource Management came into being at a time when wider, societal demoralization had become even more widespread. Here the focus of managerial attempts to remake morality was as likely to be skilled or clerical workers – and subsequently even professionals – rather than the blue-collar employees Mayo had in mind (Barley and Kunda, 1992). If industrial relations problems gradually became more and more acute within Fordism, so the newer enterprises, for example, the chemical plants with their continuous-process production, were a far more dangerous proposition for managers to control if they were engaged in guerrilla warfare with a demoralized workforce (Gallie, 1978). Such workplaces really required workers with an element of inner-direction (Riesman, 1950). The same remained true of more skilled jobs and the professions but it was precisely the appearance of other-direction among white-collar workers which Riesman described.

The components of a new, manufactured morality for these workers were summarized in the Harvard Analytical Framework (dating from the 1980s) where the longer-term outcomes of HRM were defined in the familiar terms of Mayoism: 'individual well-being', 'organisational effectiveness', and 'societal well-being' (Storey, 1995). As befit the different occupations of the workers, learning and development were given a central role in HRM/HRD whereas Mayoism had relied on a form of counselling. The full credo of HRM included the belief that human resources gave a competitive edge, that corporations needed to go beyond employee compliance to employee commitment, and that employers needed to carefully select and develop employees. The key levers of HRM included the aim of managing culture (which was more important than managing procedure), integrating the traditional functions of selection, training and development and developing employee responsibility and empowerment through restructuring and job re-design (ibid.).

We will return to employee empowerment in a moment, but first we should note a key consequence of Fordism's promotion of demoralization. It is often suggested that Ford's $5 day was the (economically rational) solution to serious problems of labour turnover. For a time Ford thought that making the tie between workers and employer a matter of pure economic calculation might be dangerous for employers but there were also unanticipated advantages in the new relationship. Because it did not rely on morality, Fordism made it theoretically possible to severe the connection between the community and the factory that Owen and others had fought so hard to establish. Drawing on the legacy of Taylor (with Ford's experiment with the Sociological Department now long forgotten), Fordism had no stake in the morality created outside the factory gates and this morality was definitely not welcome within the workplace. (Mayo did nothing to fundamentally change this new situation because his ersatz morality was manufactured entirely in the workplace and there was no need for the link with community to be reinstated). Fordism therefore created the possibility of capital becoming footloose for the first time and from this point in the development of capitalism, industry slowly began to realize the possibilities for strategic relocation in other places and, subsequently, other countries.

Economic sociologists like Dore have sometimes suggested that the demoralization of Western culture signalled a crisis for Western capitalism

233

alone. For example, in the early 1990s several economic sociologists compared the rampant individualism of ailing economies in the West with the successful economies of the Asia-Pacific which were apparently reaping the benefit of Confucian virtues. This thesis was made to look a little silly by subsequent events. Theorists who were interested in the relationship between culture and economy would have been much better advised to pursue the links between demoralization and the new international division of labour and subsequent globalization. As ever, we are likely to find economic sociology looking in other direction when important economic changes are occurring (Doogan, 2001). Chief among these was the expansion of women's employment in the second half of the twentieth century, a phenomenon that was deeply implicated in demoralization and the associated hegemony of economic rationality.

Chapter 2 suggested that demoralization undermined mothering because it replaced sentiment (which valued mothering) with common sense and economic rationality (which did not). Demoralization made mothers feel that their worth was not recognized and they responded by seeking recognition in paid employment instead (Fevre, 2000b). Hochschild (1989) captured the relationship between this aspect of demoralization and capitalist development when she referred to the women who went to work in their millions as the 'urbanizing peasants'. She also described three stages of American fatherhood: in the agrarian stage, fathers socialized their sons into employment; in the nineteenth century they left child-rearing to their wives and became distant and stern; from the 1950s, as women began to work outside the homes, fatherhood was rediscovered. Hochschild concluded that '[t]oday most families are in the third stage of economic development but in the second stage of fatherhood.' (1989: 187) and she summarized the shift in the moral expectations of mothers in this way:

> If, in the earlier part of the century, many middle-class children suffered from overattentive mothers, from being 'mother's only accomplishment', many of today's children may suffer from a parental desire for reassurance that they are free of needs. Throughout the second half of the nineteenth century, as women were excluded from the workplace and the woman's role at home expanded, the cultural notion of what a child needed at home expanded as well ... doctors and ministers once argued strongly that a woman's place was at home because her children needed her there. As economic winds have shifted, so has the idea of a woman's proper place – and of a child's real needs. (Hochschild, 1997: 229)

As Hochschild (1997) explained, the women who took up an increasing proportion of the jobs in the second half of the twentieth century

234

were among the most prominent beneficiaries of HRM and HRD (see also Townley, 1994). Chapter 6 suggested that the emphasis on human resources was a part of a general movement towards training (or 'development') in the attitudes that employers found were no longer displayed by the staff they recruited in a demoralized culture (Beder, 2000). In particular, employers wanted their staff to display the right sort of attitudes towards their customers and set out to train them in attributes that might once have been identified with everyday civility but were now conceived in terms of customer care and responsibility for quality.

When its proponents said HRM would empower employees, they meant it would make them morally responsible for their own actions at work. Where they argued HRM developed potential and showed people how to assume more responsibility, we might think it trained them to act as if they were inner-directed and monitored them to make sure they kept up the act. All sorts of training, but especially training on the HRD model, were tailor-made for cynical other-directed types who needed to be told how to act (Beder, 2000). In Chapters 6 and 7 we also saw that this training could involve explicit training in ethics. Among professionals, training in ethics often took the place of the values of the professional learning communities and their particular version of inner direction (Maclagan, 1998).

235

Despite its interest in teamwork, HRM placed little importance on social groups or Mayo's belief in our 'compulsive sociability', and the ideology of individualization fitted neatly with the characteristics HRM aimed to inculcate. Moreover, within multi-national companies HRM permitted the production of packages of ready-made ersatz morality that could be delivered anywhere in the world. This made globalization more feasible and of course HRM paved the way for delayering. With HRM in place as a response to demoralization, it apparently became possible for companies to introduce flat hierarchies. The management layers that were constructed with Fordism were now assumed to be redundant.

TRANSFORMATION AND REMORALIZATION

What is the relationship between demoralization and the conventional idea of a second great divide (Piore and Sabel, 1984)? Demoralization can be very clearly linked to the idea of a transformation in the direction of post-industrial society, post-Fordism, disorganized capitalism, and so on (Casey, 1995). All of these attempts to describe the transformation are rather mesmerized by technological change, but what if the real divide that they were trying to grasp lay between capitalism with morality and demoralized capitalism? Perhaps the technological changes were themselves affected by this more fundamental transition? In this view, the idea of a second great divide might really be about the sorts of production, marketing, work organization, management *and technologies* which were thought necessary in order to continue capitalism with demoralized workers and consumers (Casey, 1995), not to mention demoralized suppliers and bankers.

Beder (2000: 233) cited Macdonald and Myers (writing in *New Internationalist*, November 1998) for the interesting idea that we only earn the right to be treated with manufactured courtesy if we pay for it as consumers. Our conventional understanding of the role of consumption after the second great divide can be considerably enriched by the idea that we only get the illusion that we do not live in a demoralized culture when we shop. These ideas must clearly be pursued in further research. More research is also needed in order to explore the relationship between demoralization and the changing position of public-sector services. Chapter 6 raised the possibility that when governments came to believe they could no longer rely on the morality that once underpinned the sector, and that economic rationality and self-interest were as common there as elsewhere, they (naturally) felt that the route to better public services lay in private sector solutions. This raises an issue which requires clarification.

236

In Chapter 1 I did not fully explain my reasons for disagreeing with Durkheim's idea that whatever created solidarity qualified as morality.[4] Groups, along with institutions, are the key to the social construction of morality but groups and institutions also make other kinds of sense (including common sense, economic rationality and science) and associated rules and guidelines for action (Fevre, 2000b). These include highly instrumental rules, for example, those which are helpful in excluding others and monopolizing power and resources. Some sociologists (for example, Wolfe, 1989) do not employ a distinction but I suggest that these rules should not be confused with the (deontological) moral principles which a group may also produce. There is nothing intrinsically moral about the sense and rules which create solidarity and nor do moral principles necessarily bolster group solidarity. Moral principles may enjoin us to have thought for others but these others are not necessarily members of our group and following such principles may violate the rules created by a group to enforce solidarity. In sum, even if we agree that all forms of morality are rooted in membership of groups of one kind or another, we must not confuse how morality is created with what morality refers to.

We can now return to the question of public services. A morality of public service was created in post-war European welfare states but the culture produced by groups and institutions in these welfare states was not free of sectionalism or, indeed, economic rationality. Nevertheless, just as nineteenth-century remoralization produced a long legacy of morality, for example, in the culture of working-class respectability, so the moral invention of the welfare states produced a variety of moral attitudes towards public service and public goods (Jordan, 2002). The demoralization thesis suggests, however, that groups and institutions in Western culture are no longer capable of making or reproducing morality. Of course, the thesis does not suggest that any of the other sense- and rule-making which goes on in groups has come to an end. The construction of economic rationality, for example, continues and, even expands, where groups and institutions no longer care to make morality. As part of this process, the morality of public service has been neglected, indeed, it had been undermined by an economic rationality which declared the provision of such services was better left to market arrangements.

The post-war welfare states were certainly possessed of economic rationalities but the groups and institutions that subsequently pursued the ideals of free-market liberalism had a much more tenuous association with the production of any sort of (deontological) morality. Morality played a much smaller part in any of the sense- and rule-making they accomplished because the space that morality might have occupied was taken up by a very powerful economic rationality. As I have argued throughout this book, economic rationality is intimately connected with the legitimation of power and inequality and this was particularly obvious in the case of free-market liberalism. Where deontological morality got a mention, it was the embalmed, traditional kind which played no part in the cultural invention and renewal that was going on except in so far as it garnered votes. In addition, free-market liberalism featured its own lexicon of supposedly moral concepts (like freedom of choice) which underpinned the arguments made for the optimum social and political conditions needed to allow economic rationality free rein. These principles recalled the morals of Benjamin Franklin that I suggested Weber found disgusting (see Chapter 2) in that they were thought good because they were useful in their consequences (for example, increased prosperity).

Some of the economic rationality espoused by trade unions has been hostile to morality but this does not mean trade unions cannot help to create moral thinking. Trade unions played a key role in the creation of the morality of the welfare states and for some thinkers it is only revitalized trade unions that can challenge the way labour is seen as a means to an end and never valued in itself. Thus Gorz (1989) argued that the unions' original purpose was to challenge economic rationality and, in particular, to dispute the way capitalism had turned labour into an economic resource like any other (as suggested by Polanyi, 1944/1957). The trade unions' most subversive demands, the ones which necessarily

237

entailed a critique of economic rationality, were those which involved a limit to the amount of work which could be demanded of people. Bowring therefore suggested that 'the contested features of post-Fordism may furnish the basis for the radical reassertion of the labour movement's original purpose and goal: namely, the *refusal of paid work* and the *reconquest of time*' (2002: 165, emphasis in original).

Trade unions have put forward other demands than a reduction in working time and Casey (1995) pointed out that by valorizing the work people did, and giving them a social identity, the unions had once helped to create the morality (for example, of working-class respectability) needed to make up for the demoralization that capitalism had helped to bring about. By the end of the twentieth century the unions had been so weakened that they were no longer capable of performing this function. In this way capitalism had created new problems for itself and been forced into the business of making morality. We are now accustomed to the way in which capitalism periodically creates the most unexpected contradictions of the type first identified by Bell. We are familiar with all the innovations introduced to fill the gaps caused by capitalism's cultural vandalism: HRM, TQM, empowerment, the illusion of insecurity, the audit society, and so on. Is it possible that, given time, these ersatz moralities might, in turn, form the basis of the real, new ones (Casey, 2002)? Michelle Lamont's working-class moralities (as well, perhaps, as working-class racism) can be traced to the remoralization prompted by the capitalist and intellectual elite of the nineteenth century. This represented a genuine attempt to reverse societal demoralization and the efforts that were made to inculcate and reward morality were not part of a calculated and manipulative charade designed only to make the lives of capitalists and other powerful people easier. Management gurus like Peters and Handy are genuinely concerned about demoralization but perhaps it is too fanciful to suggest that some of their followers will turn out to have been the midwives of a new morality?

Management ideas were implicated in an earlier attempt at remoralization and it might be quite logical for them to be central to another. Pattison (1997) showed that American management ideas had particular religious origins which prefigured the later association between management and morality. Thus Pattison found within the writings of Tom Peters both a theology and an overarching moral order. This was very good for managers – it made them feel better – but management could also be seen as a 'Christian heresy' which was dangerous because it had no sense of its own limitations:

> when reality is over-simplified, or important aspects of it are downgraded, excluded, denied or ignored, then there is every prospect that harmful effects will ensue. The single-minded, clear adoption and

pursuit of one kind of 'good' or truth to the exclusion of other goods and truths is likely to give rise to at least some serious negative outcomes. Indeed there is no more sure way of corrupting or tainting good than by pursuing it too narrowly and too vigorously. (Pattison, 1997: 86)

Just as it over-rated its own effectiveness, so management underestimated its power to produce evil. Pattison concluded that the Christian tradition could still provide a rich source of ideas that might help management be more balanced and more self-critical.

Other writers have given voice to less specific anxieties about any new moralities that might be emerging in our corporations. Grugulis et al. (2000) found the way the distinction between work and non-work was being blurred to be 'totalitarian' and 'disturbing'. Jones (2000) found totalitarianism in the compulsion to adhere to certain business ethics. Hochschild and Casey found disturbing totalitarian tendencies in Amerco and Hephaestus. This understandable distaste might be a sign that the ersatz moralities are being inserted so deeply and insistently, becoming so familiar and intruding so far into our non-work lives, that we will finally forget they are ersatz and turn them into the real thing. This is not so far-fetched: after all, corporations are putting a great deal of effort into trying to make this happen and some of the initial cynicism and scepticism about ersatz morality is a transitional phase that we can see is passing even now (see Chapter 4). The workers who first encountered the ersatz moralities could compare them with a memory of an authentic morality that was still fresh – and the comparison would not be flattering to management's efforts – but more and more workers have no traditional morality to use as a benchmark (Sennett, 1998).

It is possible that the ersatz morality produced by capitalism could be turned into a belief system in the category of sentiment that could give rise to a genuine new morality. Elsewhere (Fevre, 2000b) I have argued that a new sensibility will require some element of 'recombination' of ideas drawn from the ways of making sense that have now come to dominate out lives. If we now begin to take the manufactured morality to heart we may begin to find morality persuasive enough to allow it to influence our actions once more, but it is by no means certain that this will be good news for capitalism. We have only to remember the way some of the workers discussed near the end of Chapter 3 turned the ersatz morality back on their employers and of the way really caring for your customer might mean refusing to sell them something they did not want to buy. The point about remoralization is that, whatever its origins, it allows us to put moral ends first. The particular point about remoralization of economic behaviour is that we will put moral ends before the goals of economic rationality.

239

History sometimes shows that are dangers for capitalism in the creation of moral workers (especially workers who are moral at work). As we saw in Chapter 6, the 'advanced men' of the South Wales coalfield rejected the vocational training that they thought was only in the interests of their employers and spent their time learning how to imagine an alternative, and altogether more moral, society instead. A morality gives people an opportunity to judge their own society – and its prevailing economic arrangements – and to find it wanting. In the end, it may not matter whether this is a morality passed down by tradition or a glimpse of the morality of the future in some banal and self-serving managerial injunction to assume our share of responsibility for other people's comfort and happiness. All those companies which behave like Hephaestus, Amerco and ConsultancyCo might just be giving their employees ideas of what a better society might look like (Gorz, 1989: 60; Parker, 2002).[5]

CONCLUSION: THE NEW SOCIOLOGY OF ECONOMIC BEHAVIOUR

As we were reminded in the previous chapter, the first task of the sociology of economic behaviour is to show that economic rationality is fallible. For example, it helps business decision-makers to make *systematic* mistakes and yet, at the same time, legitimates their power to make decisions and justifies the outcomes of those decisions. Values legitimate economic advantage and domination and in the twentieth century it was economic values that came to be the only values that did this in a reliable way. We must learn to critique the economic rationality that justifies middle-class advantage in the labour market and the workplace (where the future of work is determined). We must debunk the magic of their credentials and the other ways (assessment centres, psychosocial profiling) in which their advantage is justified. We will not accept that labour markets put people in the right jobs and that managers make the best of all possible decisions in the best of all possible worlds.

Chapter 5 showed that when the economic efficiency claims of meritocracy were put in doubt, this opened the possibility of reapplying the criteria of social justice to the way labour markets distributed resources. The way in which the quality of candidates for vacancies is appraised was shown to be a matter of social negotiation, invention and conflict (Fevre, 1992). The insistence that quality was self-evident or easy to measure was now understood as an ideological device which legitimated privilege and advantage in the labour market and the power of managers within the workplace. As we saw in Chapter 4, the sociology of economic behaviour must see the workplace as intensely political (as Deetz, 1992, suggests, management is like any other, earlier

240

form of domination in this respect) and every kind of market as a political arena. For the moment, at least, the actors in the workplace and the labour market are understood to be members of classes and it is the joint action of class members that is thought to be the most important form of political action.

Identity is crucial to the construction of such joint action. Chapter 6 discussed the overt use of identity within affirmative action by the more advantaged members of previously marginalized groups. Groups compete in the production of alternative sense-making just as they compete in other respects. Identity also allows us to understand why individuals are prepared to make their contribution to these competing constructions of the world in the way they behave as well as the way they think. Without identity would they accept the privileges or privations that came their way with such alacrity? The political explanation of credentialism is strengthened by the addition of identity to an explanation which looks weak when it assumes that credentialists think of education in the same terms as human capital theory. Chapter 6 discussed the way working-class identity excluded the behaviour (notably, success in higher education) needed to access the resources monopolized by the middle class. Middle-class parents took great care to encourage this behaviour in their children and made them think it the key to their assumption of a middle-class identity.

241

Chapter 6 also suggested the potential new recruits to the middle class are handicapped by having limited access to middle-class identities. They may only aspire to those few middle-class occupations of which they have any reliable knowledge and these are likely to be the less well-paid middle class occupations (for example, teaching). Moreover, their notion of middle-class identity may be a somewhat impoverished one which does not include the enthusiasm and social skills which are now seen as essential in many more rewarding middle-class occupations (Brown and Scase, 1994). As with Hochschild's cabin crew, a confident, outgoing niceness long associated with middle-class identity has now become a qualification for all sorts of jobs. In Chapter 6 we encountered the idea, originally credited to du Gay and Salaman, that selection by way of assessment centres and the other fashionable recruitment paraphernalia of large organizations requires successful candidates to display their enthusiasm and social skills and make sure these appear genuine. They must seem to be fully-integrated aspects of their personality and any suggestion of cynicism or acting would be fatal to a candidate's chances of success. Another way of expressing this would be to say that organizations are specifying character as part of their recruitment criteria.

While in some situations pretending is not enough, in others it appears that all that is required is that we are not overtly cynical about the roles we perform (Casey, 1995). In order to navigate our way around this extremely complex field we need to be able to rely on more potent distinctions than that between 'deep' and 'surface' acting (as deployed by Hochschild, for example). The sociology of economic behaviour will need to pay careful attention to the distinction between identity and role, and between character and competence. Sennett (1998) found it hard to take capitalism's attempt to produce substitutes for character seriously. The reality of teamwork was that everyone was completely indifferent to who the other team members were. Their character was irrelevant and all that mattered was how well they could act.

The sociology of economic behaviour will also have to make use of the notion of category errors (Fevre, 2000b). Thus in Chapter 2 people's feeling of a being under a moral compulsion to sacrifice their marriages, and their relationships with their children, to their work was analysed as a category error. At the instigation of our employers we substitute sense-making according to sentiment when we should apply common sense, and vice versa. Du Gay and Salaman (Chapter 3) described this as business aligning different spheres of our lives (see also Shenav, Chapter 4). The explanation was then elaborated to show how companies engineered (deliberate) category mistakes in order to combat the effects of demoralization. Gorz (1989) elaborated criteria that can help us to determine where economic rationality is appropriate and where it is corrosive and destroys meaning. For example, Gorz argued that economic rationality should not be applied to actions which were 'consonant with their meaning if the time they take is left out of account' (ibid.: 137). Such insights would repay further development.

Perhaps the most exciting area for future research within the sociology of economic behaviour lies at the overlap between work on identity and work on the political aspects of economic behaviour. In particular, we need to turn our attention to the way that any social groups that are capable of joint action play a part in constructing the very rewards that they compete over. The constitution of places in the division of labour should not be taken for granted any more than wage-setting should be. There is a great deal of research to be done on the way jobs are created and the way their content is specified. It is by no means self-evident how we have ended up as arbitrageurs and social workers and investment analysts and personal shoppers and software engineers. Nor is the further specification of the tasks required in each of these occupations simply a technical matter. Each of the jobs, and, within them, the disparate expectations of the behaviour that is needed for these jobs to be done well, are in large part the outcome of a political process. The distribution of things to do, just as much as the distribution of income, is a function of the distribution of power (Gorz, 1989; Shenhav, 1999). Groups which have the power to influence the shape of the division of labour can create jobs which match, *or indeed enhance*, favoured identities. For example, it now goes without saying that it is expected that middle-class jobs should be made as rewarding (in every sense) as they can be but it is simply accepted as unavoidable, and perhaps quite natural, that working-class jobs are both badly paid and awful to do. A key field for future research on middle-class jobs will clearly be managerial occupations and we need to know much more about managerial identities and the way managerial tasks are constructed (Hochschild, 1997).

So far as business decision-making is concerned, it would be hard to under-estimate the use that can be made of good historiography to help us put contemporary economic rationality in context (Littler, 1979; Thompson, 1976). We will also need patient and careful research – as exemplified by Mackenzie's work on contractors in the previous chapter – to help us look beneath the appearances of contemporary economic rationalities. Since we will discover (from historical comparison and contemporary research) so many equally plausible, alternative rationalities we will then need to do more research to explain how people make choices between them. This branch of the sociology of economic behaviour parallels work on politics and identity in the labour market and the workplace. It will require political explanations of shifts between rationalities, and perhaps classes will also figure prominently in these analyses. For example, when we know that it is possible to construct equally plausible economic rationalities for and against the retention of junior managers, we start to understand the removal of these layers of management as a part of a political struggle.

We also need to pay special attention to the construction of explanations of organizational failure in terms of the mistakes made by bad managers (Grint, 1995). Ideas of management omnipotence and omniscience are widely held, and provide the foundation of managerial authority, but both the ideas and the authority they support can only be preserved if cases of failure are explained as Frederick Taylor recommended: as the fault of incompetent managers. If there were no manager on earth who could have averted failure, then we might begin to wonder about the basis of any manager's authority. The price we pay for maintaining this authority is the hugely expensive (if only in terms of golden hellos and golden handshakes) turnover in managerial personnel that occurs as blame is meted out to 'bad' managers and faith in managerial authority is renewed with every new broom (Pattison, 1997).

Nichols (1986) considered another explanation of the problems of British industry, and particularly its manufacturing sector: the recalcitrance of its workforce. In fact, Nichols did rather better than Grint when it came to raising fundamental questions about the causes of economic success. He showed that different kinds of worker behaviour were not related to variations in productivity in the straightforward way that most economists imagined they were. British industrial relations might be different to American industrial relations but it was not safe to conclude that British workers were the cause of low productivity or that the Thatcher Government's assault on the trade unions and on manufacturing had brought about the productivity gains that were claimed for it.

In this way we will develop our own critiques in the style of Marx when he exposed the economic rationality which justified the consequences of economic behaviour as surreal and absurd. The exposure of all of these economic rationalities to scrutiny is therefore valuable in itself but it has been repeatedly stated that the crucial advantage of the sociology of economic behaviour (over economic sociology) is that it returns to the classical mission to make the investigation of the moral consequences of economic behaviour an end in itself. In order to do this we have to be able to evaluate economic behaviour against moral criteria. It is only in this fashion that we can, for instance, decide what new forms of work or industrial organization mean to us. But how do we then escape a similar criticism to the one that has been levelled against those economic sociologists who import their own values into their accounts of productivity and competitiveness? While we are no longer including morality in an instrumental role, surely we are picking our values in just the same unreasoned and unsupportable way?

This is of course the only way to pick values (Bauman, 1993) and the sociology of economic behaviour makes this explicit rather than pretending, as economic sociology has done, that we can pick our morality according to some higher (economic) rationality. The whole point is that we debate what values matter to us from the start – what sort of lives we want to lead, what sort of society we want to have – and then we judge the sort of economic behaviour that goes on all around us against these values. This is precisely the enterprise that Marx was engaged in when he enquired about the real cost paid by those who labour. But where do those values come from? If we simply seek to apply the values of wider society, what do we do when we find working-class moralities tied up in racist beliefs (Lamont, 2000)? There is also an even more fundamental problem: where can we find values to judge economic behaviour when we live in a demoralized age?

We have found evidence throughout the book of sociological research that suggests people do have moral values and feel that particular economic behaviour fails or even violates them. Yet we have also discussed cases in which it is clear that people are no longer able to act on their values. Thus, Chapter 2 discussed Hochschild's findings about the way people knew their morality gave them other priorities than the ones they pursued day after day. In Chapter 6 we learnt that people have now become so unaccustomed to judging economic behaviour against their values that they have a kind of psychosomatic reaction to their violation in the form of false perceptions of increased insecurity or stress (Doogan, 2001; Nichols, 2001). In other places we have seen that people are so unused to applying moral judgement to measure economic behaviour that the only judgements that are made on their behalf are those applied by their employers.

Once we take away the ersatz moralities created by our employers we see that, because of demoralization, the oughts that matter in our lives are now few and far between and we are much less sure of what moral ends might be. The morality on which the founding fathers of sociology could rely is now considerably diluted and our consciences are frail (Bauman, 1993). Because the economic values of efficiency, moving resources to more productive uses, accumulation and so on, have assumed such hegemony, it cannot be a straightforward job of taking up where classical theory left off. Perhaps by levelling the playing field between economic values (and all the other desiderata of common sense) and morality, we will make it a little easier to grow more oughts and get back our faith in the values that do not involve calculation and the estimation of increased productivity or improved competitiveness (Shenhav, 1999). But we need to remoralize many aspects of economic behaviour and this means finding concepts that people can choose to believe in and from which we can derive our moral criteria. This is not strictly a task for sociology but (Gorz, 1989) the further development of the sociology of economic behaviour will be impossible if it is not performed.

In particular, we need the concepts that will operationalize morality in order to organize the research agenda for the sociology of economic behaviour. Of course we may still find we can make use of existing ideas of social justice, fairness and just desserts when they are separated from the economic rationality in which they became entangled. We can also try to breathe life back into the collectivist values that were once part of a robust resistance to the spread of market relations, but we need so much more than this. We need, for example, to find a way of operationalizing the moral value of human relationships and interactions.

For Sennett (1998) the teamwork which modern corporations prized created superficial ties between individuals that were a grotesque caricature of real solidarity and friendship. Grugulis et al. (2000) found it *'morally* problematic' that normal 'innocent' social interaction, including friendship, was being commodified. We need to be able to measure economic behaviour by its effect on friendships and on relationships between parents, and between parents and their children, and on all other forms of solidarity (Beder, 2000; Gorz, 1989). In Chapter 7

245

it was suggested that the sacrifice of social relationships in periodic gales of 'creative' destruction should not be accepted in the stoic way that Fukuyama recommended. We need to find a way of making the moral end of preserving community a measure of economic behaviour. This is the kind of conceptual creativity that the sociology of economic behaviour requires in place of the ideas of human, social and (even) cultural capital that economic sociology relied upon and which allowed Granovetter, Coleman and others to deal so coldly with friendship and community. We need to be able to make friendship and neighbourliness ends rather than means. As was pointed out in Chapter 5, the sociology of economic behaviour could mount research to establish the effect on forms of solidarity of their use in labour market behaviour. For example, and in direct contrast to Granovetter, we could ask whether this strengthens 'ties' or compromises them.

When it comes to the moral evaluation of work and employment we need to develop ideas of good work, payment according to worth, self-worth and recognition, cheap labour, wasted lives and dignity at work. As the example of dignity at work suggested earlier in this chapter showed, we will need to be careful about the way we introduce these concepts into sociology but they are, nevertheless, indispensable if we are to introduce moral criteria into our work. It is a measure of their value that economic sociology had so little use for them. For example, Chapter 3 showed how economic sociology could not incorporate the Hawthorne workers' idea of a reasonable day's work as a research goal. Economic sociologists would not dream of setting up a research programme to find out where there was variation from a reasonable day's work and how this variation could be adjusted, perhaps by making all employers recognize they had a social contract with their employees to provide a fair day's pay for a fair day's work. The debilitating effect of economic sociology on research is even more obvious in another example: the sociology of industrial injuries. Here the case for moral evaluation is stark yet sociologists largely neglected to research the area until the pioneering contribution of Nichols (1997) exposed various aspects of economic behaviour to moral evaluation by showing how they were implicated in industrial injury rates.

Only by introducing the idea of evaluating current practice against a moral standard do we find out where practices vary furthest and in this way we begin to develop our critiques. On the basis of these critiques we will be able to make policy recommendations. Some examples of policy prescriptions were drawn from the critiques developed in previous chapters. In Chapter 7 a critique of the use of migrants to provide cheap labour led to support for the setting of a minimum wage and regularizing the position of illegal migrants. More generally, a critique of the relationship between work and family life suggested a new sensibility was needed to replace the sentiment that common sense undermined and displaced. Governments could support this sensibility with the right sort of policies but some governments had pursued policies which made it impossible to generate this sensibility. For example, it was argued that governments should compel employees to take parental leave rather than making this a matter of individual choice (and sometimes a matter over which employers exercised a veto). It was also suggested that some governments were actually making matters worse by placing work and economic rationality at the heart of every policy, from welfare to education.

The sociology of economic behaviour should be working towards policy prescriptions like these rather than, as economic sociology has so often done, pretending we can advise corporations and countries on the secret of success. Sociology has no expert role in helping managers to manage better, firms to compete better, governments to capitalize on comparative advantage, or individuals to invest in their human capital. The pursuit of the knowledge needed to play this role leads to self-delusion and the only role that economic sociology has played was the one it did not understand: it helped to shore up, and sometimes even construct, the status quo (Shenhav, 1999). The sociology of economic behaviour was not invented so that we could keep things as they are.

A renascent sociology of economic behaviour will not be well received by those who benefit most from the current disposition of values in society and also have the biggest psychological (and even spiritual) investment in it. They have told themselves that accumulation, hard work, consumption, and being at the centre of the whirlwind of innovation, creative destruction and rising productivity are the only reality. They think any other belief is ridiculous and it is perhaps their fear of being thought ridiculous that is the greatest obstacle to their acceptance of a critique of economic behaviour. It is not their fear of having nothing to do, or having to do without the material things they are already bored with, that makes them so fearful. Most of all they fear being ridiculed for saying they have found something to believe in. Perhaps this was also Max Weber's fear and the source of the original impulse to create economic sociology. Perhaps, but this no longer matters.

247

NOTES

1 Arguably the only reason Goffman found himself remarking on the significance of everyday politeness was because it was on the way out – to be replaced, if at all, by the synthetic alternative. In this respect it is perhaps instructive that Goffman found inspiration in fieldwork in the remote, and at that time quite traditional, Western Isles of Scotland.

2 A similar mistake was made later in respect of other narcotics (Fevre, 2000b).

3 Although she recognized the way this morality served capitalism's purposes,

Casey (1995) argued that it was the organic product of the working class.

4 Although I am sure there is still plenty of room for healthy disagreement between us, I am enormously grateful to Bill Jordan for encouraging me to clarify my thinking on this and related matters.

5 It is worth bearing in mind that André Gorz once wondered whether HRM would provide the opportunity for 'the colonization ... of non-economic aspirations by economic rationality ... or ... an autonomization of non-quantifiable, extra-economic values, to such an extent that these will restrict the rights of economic logic in order to impose their own claims' (1989: 60).

bibliography

Abreu, A.R. de P., Beynon, H. and Ramalho, J.R. (2000) '"The dream factory": VW's modular production system in Resende, Brazil', *Work, Employment and Society*, 14 (2): 265–82.

Adkins, L. (1995) *Gendered Work: Sexuality, Family and the Labour Market*. London: Routledge.

Ainley, P. (1991) *Young People Leaving Home*. London: Cassell.

Andreski, S. (1972) *Social Science as Sorcery*. London: Deutsch.

Anthony, P. (1977) *The Ideology of Work*. London: Tavistock.

Antikainen, A., Houtsonen, J. Kauppila, J. and Houtelin, N. (1996) *Living in a Learning Society: Life–histories, Identities and Education*. London: Falmer Press.

Apple, M. (1997) 'The New Technology: is it part of the solution or part of the problem in education?', in G.E. Hawisher and C. Selfe (eds), *Literacy, Technology and Society: Confronting the Issues*. Upper Saddle River, NJ: Prentice Hall.

Archer, M. (2000) 'Homo economicus, Homo sociologicus and Homo sentiens', in M.S. Archer and J.Q. Tritter (eds), *Rational Choice Theory: Resisting Colonization*. London: Routledge.

Ascher, K. (1987) *The Politics of Privatisation: Contracting out the Public Services*. London: Macmillan.

Ashton, D. and Green, F. (1996) *Education, Training and the Global Economy*. Cheltenham: Edward Elgar.

Atkinson, J. (1984) Flexibility, Uncertainty and Manpower Management (IMS Report No. 89). Brighton: Institute for Manpower Studies.

Bach, S. (1999) 'Europe', in S. Bach, L. Bordogna, G. Della Rocca and D. Winchester, *Public Service Employment Relations in Europe: Transformation, Modernisation or Inertia?* London: Routledge.

Banks, M. et al. (1992) *Careers and Identities*. Milton Keynes: Open University Press.

Baran, P. and Sweezy, P. (1966) *Monopoly Capital*. New York: Monthly Review Press.

Barbour, B. (ed.) (1979) *Benjamin Franklin: A Collection of Critical Essays*. Englewood Cliffs, NJ: Prentice Hall.

Barley, S. and Kunda, G. (1992) 'Design and devotion: surges of rational and normative ideologies of control', *Administrative Science Quarterly*, 37: 363–99, reprinted in K. Grint (ed.), *Work and Society*. Cambridge: Polity. pp. 303–42.

Barry, M. (1998) 'Introduction', in M. Barry and C. Hallett (eds), *Social Exclusion and Social Work*. Dorchester: Russell House.

Batchelor, R. (1994) *Henry Ford: Mass Production, Modernism and Design*. Manchester: Manchester University Press.

Batenburg, R. and de Witte, M. (2001) 'Underemployment in the Netherlands: how the Dutch "Poldermodel" failed to close the education–jobs gap', *Work, Employment and Society*, 15 (1): 73–94.

Bates, I. and Riseborough, G. (eds) (1993) *Youth and Inequality*. Buckingham: Open University Press.

Bauman, Z. (1989) *Modernity and the Holocaust*. Ithaca, NY: Cornell University Press.

Bauman, Z. (1991) *Modernity and Ambivalence*. Cambridge: Polity Press.

Bauman, Z. (1993) *Postmodern Ethics*. Oxford: Blackwell.

Bauman, Z. (1998) *Work, Consumerism and the New Poor*. Buckingham: Open University Press.

Bauman, Z. (2000) 'Foreword', in R. Fevre, *The Demoralization of Western Culture*. London: Continuum.

Bauman, Z. (2001) *The Individualized Society*. Cambridge: Polity.

Beck, U. (1992) *The Risk Society, Towards a New Modernity*. London: Sage.

Beck, U. and Beck-Gernsheim, E. (2001) *Individualization*. London: Sage.

Becker, G.S. (1967) 'Investment in human capital: a theoretical analysis', *Journal of Political Economy*, 70, supplement to October issue: 529–549.

Becker, G.S. (1975) *Human Capital: A Theoretical and Empirical Analysis*. Chicago: University of Chicago Press.

Becker, G.S. (1976) *The Economic Approach to Human Behaviour*. Chicago: University of Chicago Press.

Becker, H. (1963) *Outsiders*. New York: Free Press.

Beder, S. (2000) *Selling the Work Ethic: From Puritan Pulpit to Corporate PR*. London: Zed Books.

Beechey, V. (1987) *Unequal Work*. London: Verso.

Bell, D. (1976) *The Coming of Post-Industrial Society*. Harmondsworth: Penguin.

Bell, D. (1979) *The Cultural Contradictions of Capitalism*. London: Heinemann.

Bellah, R., Madsen, R., Sullivan, W., Swidler, A. and Tipton, S. (1985) *Habits of the Heart: Individualism and Commitment in American Life*. Berkeley, CA: University of California Press.

Bendix, R. (1956) *Work and Authority in Industry*. New York: Harper and Row.

Berg, I., with Gorelick, S. (1971) *Education and Jobs: The Great Training Robbery*. Boston: Beacon Press.

Berg, I. et al. (1979) *Managers and Work Reform: A Limited Engagement*. New York: Free Press.

Berg, M. (1985) *The Age of Manufactures*. Oxford: Basil Blackwell.

Berlin, I. (1969) *Four Essays on Liberty*. Oxford: Oxford University Press.

Beynon, H. (1974) *Working for Ford*. Harmondsworth: Penguin.

Beynon, H. (1997) 'The changing practices of work', in R. Brown (ed.), *The Changing Shape of Work*. London: Macmillan.

Blackburn, R. and Mann, M. (1979) *The Working Class in the Labour Market*. London: Macmillan.

Blanchflower, D. and Oswald, A. (1994) *The Wage Curve*. Cambridge, MA: MIT Press.

Blau, P. (1964) *Exchange and Power in Social Life*. New York: John Wiley.

Blau, P. and Duncan, O.D. (1967) *The American Occupational Structure*. New York: John Wiley.

Blumberg, P. (1968) *Industrial Democracy: The Sociology of Participation*. London: Constable.

Bohning, W.R. and Maillat, D. (1974) *Effects of the Employment of Foreign Workers*. Paris: OECD.

Bond, S. and Sales, J. (2001) 'Household work in the UK: an analysis of the British Household Panel Survey 1994', *Work, Employment and Society*, 15 (2): 233–50.

Bourdieu, P. (1986) *Distinction: A Social Critique of the Judgement of Taste*. London: Routledge.

Bourdieu, P. (1988) *Homo Academicus*. Stanford, CA: Stanford University Press.

Bourdieu, P. (2000) *Pascalian Meditations*. Cambridge: Polity Press.

Bowen, J. and Basch, J. (1992) 'Strategies for creating customer–oriented organizations', in R. Teare and M. Olsen (eds), *International Hospitality Management: A Corporate*

Strategy in Practice. London: Pitman.

Bowring, F. (2000) 'Social exclusion: limitations of the debate', *Critical Social Policy*, 20 (3): 307–30.

Bowring, F. (2002) 'Post-Fordism and the end of work', *Futures*, 34: 159–72.

Brandth, B. and Kvande, E. (2001) 'Flexible work and flexible fathers', *Work, Employment and Society*, 15 (2): 251–67.

Braverman, H. (1974) *Labor and Monopoly Capital*. New York: Monthly Review Press.

Brown, A. (1996) 'Whither the Dual System: pressures for change and prospects for the future of vocational education and training in Germany', paper presented to the ESRC Symposium on Comparative Skill Formation Processes, Bristol, 28–9 May.

Brown, P. (1990) 'The "Third Wave": education and the ideology of parentocracy', *British Journal of Sociology of Education*, 11 (1): 65–85.

Brown, P. (1995) 'Cultural capital and social exclusion: some observations on recent trends in education, employment and the labour market', *Work, Employment and Society*, 9: 29–51.

Brown, P. (2000) 'The globalisation of positional competition?', *Sociology*, 34 (4): 633–53.

Brown, P. and Hesketh, A. with Williams, S. (forthcoming, 2004) *The Mis-Management of Talent: Employability, Competition and Careers in the Knowledge-Driven Economy*. Oxford: Oxford University Press.

Brown, P. and Lauder, H. (1996) 'Education, globalisation and economic development', *Journal of Education Policy*, 11: 1–24.

Brown, P. and Lauder, H. (2001) *Capitalism and Social Progress*. London: Palgrave.

Brown, P. and Scase, R. (1994) *Higher Education and Corporate Realities*. London: UCL Press.

Brusco, S. (1982) 'The Emilian model: productive disintegration and social integration', *Cambridge Journal of Economics*, 6 (2): 167–84.

Burawoy, M. (1979) *Manufacturing Consent*. Chicago: University of Chicago Press.

Burawoy, M. (1983) 'Between the labor process and the state: the changing face of factory regimes under advanced capitalism', *American Sociological Review*, 48: 587–605.

Burge, A., Trottman, C. and Francis, H. (1998) In a Class of their Own: Adult Learning and the South Wales Mining Community 1900–1939, (Working Paper No. 14, Patterns of Participation in Adult Education and Training). Cardiff: School of Education, Cardiff University.

Burns, T. and Stalker, G.M. (1961) *The Management of Innovation*. London: Tavistock.

Burt, R.S. (1992) *Structural Holes: The Social Structure of Competition*. Cambridge, MA: Harvard University Press.

Bynner, J. (1989) Transition to Work: Results from a Longitudinal Study of Young People in Four British Labour Markets (ESRC 16–19 Initiative Occasional Papers, 4). London: City University.

Calhoun, C. (1982) *The Question of Class Struggle*. Chicago: University of Chicago Press.

Callon, M. (1998) *The Laws of the Markets*. Oxford: Blackwell.

Cameron, K. and Whetten, D. (eds) (1983) *Organizational Effectiveness: A Comparison of Multiple Models*. New York: Academic Press.

Campbell C. (1987) *The Romantic Ethic and the Spirit of Modern Consumerism*. Oxford: Blackwell.

Carnevale, A.P. and Rose, S.J. (1998) *Education for What? The New Office Economy*. Washington, DC: Educational Testing Service.

Carter, S. (1991) *Reflections of an Affirmative Action Baby*. New York: Basic Books.

Casey, C. (1995) *Work, Self and Society*. London: Routledge.

Casey, C. (2002) '"New Age" religions and identity at work', in M. Dent and

S. Whitehead (eds), *Managing Professional Identities: Knowledge, Performativity and the 'New' Professional*. London: Routledge.

Castells, M. (1996/7) *The Information Age (vol. 1: The Rise of the Network Society; vol. 2: The Power of Identity; vol. 3: The End of the Millennium)*. Malden, MA: Blackwell.

Castles, S. and Kosack, G. (1973) *Immigrant Workers and the Class Structure*. Oxford: Oxford University Press, for the Institute of Race Relations.

Child, J. (1969) *British Management Thought*. London: George Allen and Unwin.

Clapham, J.H. (1907) *The Woollen and Worsted Industries*. London: Methuen.

Clegg, H.A., Fox, A. and Thompson, A.F. (1964) *A History of British Trade Unions Since 1889*. Oxford: Clarendon Press.

Coates, D. (1994) *The Question of UK Decline*. New York: Harvester Wheatsheaf.

Coffield, F. (1999) 'Breaking the consensus: lifelong learning as social control', *British Educational Research Journal*, 25 (4): 479–99.

Coleman, J. (1990) *The Foundations of Social Theory*. Cambridge, MA: Harvard University Press.

Collins, R. (1979) *The Credential Society*. New York: Academic Press.

Collinson, D. (1994) 'Strategies of resistance: power, knowledge and subjectivity in the workplace', in J. Jermier, D. Knights and W.R. Nord (eds), *Resistance and Power in Organizations*. London: Routledge.

Collinson, D., Knights, D. and Collinson, M. (1990) *Managing to Discriminate*. London: Routledge.

Cooke, P. and Morgan, K. (1998) *The Associational Economy: Firms, Regions and Innovation*. Oxford: Oxford University Press.

Cooley, C.H. (1913) 'The sphere of pecuniary valuation', *American Journal of Sociology*, 19: 188–203.

Copley, F. (1923) *Frederick Winslow Taylor: Father of Scientific Management*. New York: Harper and Row.

Corrigan, P.R.D.C. (1977) 'Feudal relics of capitalist monuments?' *Sociology*, 11: 435–66.

Coser. L. (1974) *Greedy Institutions: Patterns of Undivided Commitment*. New York: Free Press.

Crompton, R. and Birkelund, G.E. (2000) 'Employment and caring in British and Norwegian banking: an exploration through individual careers', *Work, Employment and Society*, 14 (2): 331–52.

Crompton, R. and Harris, F. (1998) 'Gender relations and employment: the impact of occupation', *Work, Employment and Society*, 12 (2): 297–315.

Cutler, T. (1992) 'Vocational training and British economic performance: a further instalment of the British labour problem', *Work Employment and Society*, 6: 161–84.

Dahrendorf, R. (1958) *Class and Class Conflict in Industrial Society*. Stanford, CA: Stanford University Press.

Davies, P. (1987) *A.J. Cook*. Manchester: Manchester University Press.

Davis, J. (1972) 'Gifts and the UK economy', *Man*, 7 (1): 408–31.

Davis, J. (1973) 'Forms and norms: the economy of social relations', *Man*, 8 (2): 159–76.

Davis, J. (1992) *Exchange*. Buckingham: Open University Press.

Davis, K. and Moore, W.E. (1945) 'Some principles of stratification', *American Sociological Review*, 10: 242–9.

Deal, T. and Kennedy, A. (1982) *Corporate Cultures*. Harmondsworth: Penguin.

Deetz, S. (1992) 'Disciplinary power in the modern corporation', in M. Alvesson and H. Wilmott (eds), *Critical Management Studies*, London: Sage, pp. 21–45; reprinted in K. Grint (ed.), *Work and Society*. Cambridge: Polity, pp. 142–62.

Dent, M. and Whitehead, S. (eds) (2002) *Managing Professional Identities: Knowledge, Performativity and the 'New' Professionals*. London: Routledge.

Devine, F., Britton, J., Mellor, R. and Halfpenny, P. (2000) 'Professional careers in Manchester's business and financial sector', *Work, Employment and Society*, 14 (3): 521–40.

Dex, S., Willis, J., Paterson, R. and Sheppard, E. (2000) 'Freelance workers and contract uncertainty: the effects of contractual changes in the television industry', *Work Employment and Society*, 14 (2): 283–305.

DfEE (1995) *Training Statistics*. London: HMSO.

Dickens, P. (1996) *Reconstructing Nature: Alienation, Emancipation and the Division of Labour*. London: Routledge.

Dickinson, J. (1995) 'The role of beliefs about the fairness of wages differentials in wage setting', *People Management*, November,.

Dickinson, J. and Sell–Trujillo, L. (1996) 'Explanations for pay differentials: rhetoric or social representations?', in C. Roland–Lévy (ed.), Social and Economic Representations, 2 (Proceedings of the International Association for Economic Psychology). Paris: Université René Descartes. p. 1139.

Doeringer, P.B. (1986) 'Internal labor markets and noncompeting groups', *American Economic Review* ('Papers and Proceedings'), 76: 48–52.

Doeringer, P.B. and Piore, M.J. (1971) *Internal Labor Markets and Manpower Analysis*. Lexington, MA: D.C. Heath.

Doogan, K. (2001) 'Insecurity and long–term employment', *Work, Employment and Society*, 15 (3): 419–41.

Dore, R. (1973) *British Factory, Japanese Factory: The Origins of Diversity in Industrial Relations*. London: Allen and Unwin.

Dore, R. (1976) *The Diploma Disease: Education, Qualification and Development*. London: Allen and Unwin.

Driver, C. (1970) *Tory Radical: The Life of Richard Oastler*. New York: Octagon Books.

du Bois-Reymond, M. and Walther, A. (1999) 'Learning between want and must: contradictions of the learning society', in A. Walther and B. Stauber (eds), *Lifelong Learning in Europe: Differences and Divisions, vol. 2*. Tübingen: Neuling Verlag.

Du Gay, P. (1996) *Consumption and Identity at Work*. London: Sage.

Du Gay, P. and Salaman, G. (1992) 'The cult(ure) of the customer', *Journal of Management Studies*, 29 (5): 615–33, reprinted in K. Grint (ed.), *Work and Society*. Cambridge: Polity, pp. 76–93.

Dunne, G.A. (1998) '"Pioneers behind our own front doors": towards greater balance in the organisation of work in partnerships', *Work, Employment and Society*, 12 (2): 273–95.

Durkheim, E. (1893/1964) *The Division of Labor in Society*. New York: Free Press.

Durkheim, E. (1897/1952) *Suicide*. London: Routledge.

Durkheim, E. (1991) *Professional Ethics and Civic Morals*. London: Routledge.

Edwards, J. (1987) *Positive Discrimination, Social Justice and Social Policy*. London: Tavistock.

Edwards, J. (1995) *When Race Counts: The Morality of Racial Preference in Britain and America*. London: Routledge.

Edwards, R.C. (1979) *The Contested Terrain: The Transformation of the Workplace in the Twentieth Century*. London: Heinemann.

Edwards, R.C., Reich, M. and Gordon, D.M. (1975) *Labour Market Segmentation*. Lexington, MA: D.C. Heath.

Ekins, P. and Max–Neef, M. (eds) (1993) *Real–life Economics: Understanding Wealth Creation*. London: Routledge.

Elster, J. (1985) *Making Sense of Marx*. Cambridge: Cambridge University Press.

Employment Department Group (1994) *Training in Britain: A Guide*. London: HMSO.

253

Engels, F. (1845/1958) *The Condition of the Working Class in England*. Oxford: Basil Blackwell.

Epstein, C.F., Seron, C., Oglensky, B. and Saute, R. (1999) *The Part-time Paradox*. New York: Routledge.

Erickson, C. (1957) *American Industry and the European Immigrant 1860–1888*. Cambridge, MA: Harvard University Press.

Erickson, R. and Goldthorpe, J.H. (1992) *The Constant Flux: A Study of Class Mobility in Industrial Societies*. Oxford: Clarendon Press.

Esping–Andersen, G. (1999) *Social Foundations of Postindustrial Economies*. Oxford: Oxford University Press.

Esping–Andersen, G. (2000) 'Interview on postindustrialism and the future of the welfare state', *Work, Employment and Society*, 14 (4): 757–69.

Etzioni, A. (1961) *A Comparative Analysis of Complex Organizations*. Glencoe, IL: Free Press.

Etzioni, A. (1988) *The Moral Dimension*. New York: Free Press.

Exworthy, M. and Halford, S. (eds) (1999) *Professionals and the New Managerialism in the Public Sector*. Buckingham: Open University Press.

Faist, T. (2000) *The Volume and Dynamics of International Migration and Transnational Social Spaces*. Oxford: Oxford University Press.

Farnham, D. and Horton, S. (eds) (1993) *Managing the New Public Services*. London: Macmillan.

Featherman, D., Jones F. and Hauser, R. (1975) 'Assumptions of social mobility research in the US: the case of occupational status', *Social Science Research*, 4: 329–60.

Fernandez Kelly, M.P. (1995) 'Social and cultural capital in the urban ghetto: implications for the economic sociology of migration', in A. Portes (ed.), *The Economic Sociology of Immigration*. New York: Russell Sage Foundation.

Fevre, R. (1984) *Cheap Labour and Racial Discrimination*. Aldershot: Gower.

Fevre, R. (1985) 'Racial discrimination and competition in British trade unions', *Ethnic and Racial Studies*, 8 (4): 563–80.

Fevre, R. (1986) 'Contract work in the recession', in K. Purcell et al. (eds), *The Changing Experience of Employment*. London: Macmillan.

Fevre, R. (1987) 'Redundancy and the labour market: the role of "readaption" benefits', in R.M. Lee (ed.), *Redundancy, Layoffs and Plant Closures*, London: Croom Helm.

Fevre, R. (1989) *Wales is Closed*. Nottingham: Spokesman.

Fevre, R. (1990) 'Sub/contracting and industrial development', in S. Kendrick et al. (eds), *Interpreting the Past, Understanding the Present*. Basingstoke: Macmillan.

Fevre, R. (1991) 'The growth of alternatives to full–time and permanent employment in the United Kingdom', in P. Brown and R. Scase (eds), *Poor Work*. Milton Keynes: Open University Press.

Fevre, R. (1992) *The Sociology of Labour Markets*. Hemel Hempstead: Harvester Wheatsheaf.

Fevre, R. (1998) 'Labour migration and freedom of movement in the European Union: social exclusion and economic development', *International Planning Studies*, 3 (1): 75–92.

Fevre, R. (2000a) 'Socialising social capital: identity, the transition to work and economic development', in S. Baron, J. Field and T. Schuller (eds), *Social Capital: Critical Perspectives*. Oxford: Oxford University Press.

Fevre, R. (2000b) *The Demoralization of Western Culture: Social Theory and the Dilemmas of Modern Living*. London: Continuum.

Fevre, R., Borland, J. and Denney, D. (1997) 'Class, status and party in the analysis of nationalism: lessons from Max Weber', *Nations and Nationalism*, 3 (4): 559–77.

Fevre, R., Gorard, S. and Rees, G. (2000) 'Necessary and unnecessary learning: the acquisition of knowledge and "skills" in and outside employment in South Wales in the twentieth century', in F. Coffield (ed.), *The Necessity of Informal Learning.* Bristol: Policy Press.

Fevre, R., Rees, G. and Gorard, S. (1999) 'Some sociological alternatives to human capital theory and their implications for research on post-compulsory education and training', *Journal of Education and Work*, 12 (2): 117–40.

Fielden, J. (1836/1969) *The Curse of the Factory System.* London: Frank Cass.

Filby, M. (1992) '"The figures, the personalities and the bums": service work and sexuality', Work, *Employment and Society*, 6 (1): 23–42.

Fine, B. (2001) *Social Capital versus Social Theory: Political Economy and Social Science at the Turn of the Millennium.* London: Routledge.

Fine, B. and Green, F. (2000) 'Economics, social capital, and the colonization of the social sciences', in S. Baron, J. Field and T. Schuller (eds), *Social Capital: Critical Perspectives.* Oxford: Oxford University Press.

Folgero, I. and Fjeldstad, I. (1995) 'On duty – off guard: cultural norms and sexual harassment in service organisations', *Organization Studies*, 16 (2): 299–313.

Foucault, M. (1988a) 'Technologies of the Self', in L.H. Martin, H. Gutman and P.H. Hutton (eds), *Technologies of the Self.* London: Tavistock.

Foucault, M. (1988b) 'The political technology of individuals', in L.H. Martin, H. Gutman and P.H. Hutton (eds), *Technologies of the Self.* London: Tavistock.

Frank, A.G. (1998) *ReOrient: Global Economy in the Asian Age.* Berkeley, CA: University of California Press.

Fraser, N. (1989) *Unruly Practices: Power, Discourse and Gender in Contemporary Social Theory.* Minneapolis, MN: University of Minnesota Press.

Fraser, N. (1999) 'Social justice in the age of identity politics: redistribution, recognition and participation', in L. Ray and A. Sayer (eds), *Culture and Economy after the Cultural Turn.* London: Sage.

Freedman, M. (1976) *Labor Markets: Segments and Shelters.* Montclair, NJ: Allanheld Osmun and Co.

Friedland, R. and Robertson, A. (eds) (1990) *Beyond the Marketplace: Rethinking Economy and Society.* New York: Aldine de Gruyter.

Friedman, A. (1977) *Industry and Labour.* Basingstoke: Macmillan.

Friedmann, G. (1955) *Industrial Society: The Emergence of the Human Problems of Automation.* Glencoe, IL: Free Press.

Frobel, R., Heinrichs, J., Kreye, D. (1980) *The New International Division of Labour*, Cambridge: Cambridge University Press/Paris: Editions de la Maison des Sciences de l'Homme.

Fukuyama, F. (1995) *Trust: The Social Virtues and the Creation of Prosperity.* New York: Free Press.

Fukuyama, F. (1999) *The Great Disruption: Human Nature and the Reconstitution of Social Order.* New York: Free Press.

Gallie, D. (1978) *In Search of the New Working Class.* Cambridge: Cambridge University Press.

Garrahan, P. and Stewart, P. (1992) *The Nissan Enigma.* London: Mansell.

Giddens, A. (1984) *The Constitution of Society: An Outline of the Theory of Structuration.* Cambridge: Polity Press.

Gilbert, D., Guerrier, Y. and Guy, J. (1994) 'Sexual harassment issues in the hospitality industry', *International Journal of Contemporary Hospitality Management*, 10 (2): 179–202.

Gillespie, R. (1991) *Manufacturing Knowledge: A History of the Hawthorne Experiments.* Cambridge: Cambridge University Press.

Ginn, J., Arber, S., Brannen, J., Dale, A., Dex, S., Elias, P., Moss, P., Pahl, J., Roberts, C. and Rubery, J. (1996) 'Feminist fallacies: a reply to Hakim on women's employment', *British Journal of Sociology*, 47 (1): 167–77.

Ginn, J. and Sandell, J. (1997) 'Balancing home and employment: stress reported by social services staff', *Work, Employment and Society*, 11 (3): 413–34.

Giuffre, P. and Williams, C. (1994) 'Boundary lines: labelling sexual harassment in restaurants', *Gender and Society*, 8 (3): 374–401.

Goffman, E. (1959) *The Presentation of Self in Everyday Life*. Garden City, NY: Doubleday & Co.

Goffman, E. (1961) *Asylums*. Garden City, NY: Doubleday & Co.

Goldthorpe, J. (1978) 'The current inflation: towards a sociological account', in F. Hirsch and J. Goldthorpe (eds), *The Political Economy of Inflation*. London: Martin Robertson.

Goldthorpe, J. (1996) 'The uses of history in sociology: reflections on some recent tendencies', in M. Bulmer and A.M. Rees (eds), *Citizenship Today: The Contemporary Relevance of T.H. Marshall*. London: UCL Press.

Goldthorpe, J., Llewellyn, C. and Payne, C. (1987) *Social Mobility and Class Structure in Modern Britain*. Oxford: Oxford University Press.

Gonyea, J.G. and Googins, B.K. (1996) 'The restructuring of work and family in the United States: a new challenge for American corporations', in S. Lewis and J. Lewis (eds), *The Work-Family Challenge: Rethinking Employment*. London: Sage.

Gorard, S., Rees, G. and Fevre, R. (1999) 'Patterns of participation in lifelong learning: do families make a difference?', *British Educational Research Journal*, 25 (4): 517–32.

Gorard, S., Rees, G., Fevre, R. and Furlong, J. (1998a) 'Learning trajectories: travelling towards a learning society?', *International Journal of Lifelong Education*, 17 (6): 400–10.

Gorard, S., Rees, G., Fevre, R. and Furlong, J. (1998b) 'The two components of a new learning society', *Journal of Vocational Education and Training*, 50 (1): 5–19.

Gordon, D.M. (1972) *Theories of Poverty and Unemployment*. Lexington, MA: D.C. Heath.

Gorz, A. (1989) *Critique of Economic Reason*. London: Verso.

Gorz, A. (1999) *Reclaiming Work: Beyond the Wage-based Society*. Cambridge: Polity Press.

Gramsci, A. (1971) *Selections from the Prison Notebooks*. London: Lawrence and Wishart.

Granovetter, M. (1985) 'Economic action and social structure: the problem of embeddedness', *American Journal of Sociology*, 78: 481–510.

Granovetter, M. (1990) 'The old and the new economic sociology', in R. Friedland and A. Robertson (eds), *Beyond the Marketplace*. New York: Aldine de Gruyter. pp. 89–112.

Greenhalgh, C. and Mavrotas, G. (1994) 'Workforce training in the Thatcher era: market forces and market failures', in R. McNabb and K. Whitfield (eds), *The Market for Training*. Aldershot: Avebury.

Greenhalgh, C. and Stewart, M. (1987) 'The effects and determinants of training', *Oxford Bulletin of Economics and Statistics*, 49 (2): 171–90.

Grimshaw, D., Ward, K.G., Rubery, J. and Beynon, H. (2001) 'Organisations and the transformation of the internal labour market', *Work, Employment and Society*, 15 (1): 25–54.

Grint, K. (1995) *Management: A Sociological Introduction*. Oxford: Polity Press.

Griswold, C. (1999) *Adam Smith and the Virtues of Enlightenment*. Cambridge: Cambridge University Press.

Grugulis, I., Dundon, T. and Wilkinson, A. (2000) 'Cultural control and the "culture manager": employment practices in a consultancy', *Work, Employment and Society*, 14 (1): 97–116.

Guerrier, Y. and Adib, A.S. (2000) '"No, we don't provide that service": the harassment of hotel employees by customers', *Work, Employment and Society*, 14 (4): 689–705.

Hakim, C. (1991) 'Grateful slaves and self–made women: fact and fantasy in women's work orientations', *European Sociological Review*, 7 (2): 101–21.

Hakim, C. (1995) 'Five feminist myths about women's employment', *British Journal of Sociology*, 46 (3): 429–55.

Hakim, C. (1996) *Key Issues in Women's Work: Female Heterogeneity and the Polarisation of Women's Employment*. London: Athlone.

Hales, C. (2000) 'Management and empowerment programmes', *Work, Employment and Society*, 14 (3): 501–19.

Hall, E. (1993) 'Smiling, deferring and flirting: doing gender by giving "good service"', *Work and Occupations*, 20 (4): 452–71.

Hall, S. and Jacques, M. (1989) *New Times: The Changing Face of Politics in the 1990s*. London: Lawrence and Wishart.

Halsey, A.H., Heath, A.F. and Ridge, J.M. (1980) *Origins and Destinations*. Oxford: Clarendon Press.

Halsey, A.H., Lauder, H., Brown, P. and Wells, A.S. (eds) (1997) *Education: Culture, Economy and Society*, Oxford: Oxford University Press.

Hansen, M.N. (2001) 'Closure in an open profession: the impact of social origin on the educational and occupational success of graduates of law in Norway', *Work, Employment and Society*, 15 (3): 489–510.

Haraszti, M. (1977) *A Worker in a Worker's State*. Harmondsworth: Penguin.

Hardy, C., Phillips, N. and Lawrwnce, T. (2000) 'Distinguishing trust and power in interorganizational relations: forms and façades of trust', in C.L. Lane and R. Bachmann (eds), *Trust Within and Between Organizations*. Oxford: Oxford University Press.

Harley, B. (1999) 'The myth of empowerment: work organisation, hierarchy and employee autonomy in contemporary Australian workplaces', *Work, Employment and Society*, 13 (1): 41–66.

Harrigan, K. (1985) *Strategic Flexibility: A Management Guide to Changing Times*. Lexington, MA: D.C. Heath.

Harrison, R. (1993) 'Disaffection and access', in J. Calder (ed.), *Disaffection and Diversity: Overcoming Barriers to Adult Learning*. London: Falmer.

Hartmann, H. (1979) 'Capitalism, patriarchy and job segregation by sex', in Z. Eisenstein (ed.), *Capitalist Patriarchy and the Case for Socialist Feminism*. New York: Monthly Review Press.

Hay, D. and Morris, M. (1991) *Industrial Economics and Organisation*. Oxford: Oxford University Press.

Hayes, R. and Abernathy, W. (1980) 'Managing our way to economic decline', *Harvard Business Review*, July/August: 67–77.

Hechter, M. (1987) *Principles of Group Solidarity*. Berkeley, CA: University of California Press.

Hendricks, G. and Ludeman, K. (1997) *The Corporate Mystic*. New York: Bantam.

Herrnstein, R. and Murray, C. (1996) *The Bell Curve: Intelligence and Class Structure in American Life*. New York: Free Press.

Hertz, N. (2001) *The Silent Takeover: Global Capitalism and the Death of Democracy*. London: Heinemann.

Hill, E. (2001) 'Women in the Indian informal economy: collective strategies for work life improvement and development', *Work, Employment and Society*, 15 (3): 443–64.

Hill, S. (1995) 'From quality circles to total quality management', in A. Wilkinson and H. Wilmott (eds), *Making Quality Critical*. London: Routledge.

Himmelfarb, G. (1995) *The De-Moralization of Society: From Victorian Values to Modern Values*. New York: Alfred Knopf.

Hirsch, F. (1977) *Social Limits to Growth*. London: Routledge and Kegan Paul.

Hochschild, A. (1983) *The Managed Heart: The Commercialization of Human Feeling*. Berkeley, CA: University of California Press.

Hochschild, A. (1989) *The Second Shift: Working Parents and the Revolution at Home*. New York: Avon Books.

Hochschild, A. (1997) *The Time Bind: When Work Becomes Home and Home Becomes Work*. New York: Metropolitan Books.

Hodson, R. (2001) *Dignity at Work*. Cambridge: Cambridge University Press.

Holden, C. (1999) 'Globalisation, social exclusion and Labour's new work ethic', *Critical Social Policy*, 19 (4): 529–38.

Homans, G.C. (1950) *The Human Group*. New York: Harcourt, Brace and World.

Homans, G.C. (1961) *Social Behaviour: Its Elementary Forms*. New York: Harcourt, Brace and World.

Honneth, A. (1995) *The Struggle for Recognition*. Cambridge: Polity Press.

Honneth, A. (1997) 'Recognition and moral obligation', *Social Research*, 64 (1): 16–35.

Hopfl, H. (1992) 'The making of the corporate acolyte: some thoughts on charismatic leadership and the reality of organizational commitment', *Journal of Management Studies*, 2 (1): 23–33.

Hopfl, H. (1993) 'Culture and commitment in British Airways', in D. Gowlder, K. Legge and C. Legge (eds), *Case Studies in Organisational Behaviour*. London: Paul Chapman Publishing.

Hudson, P. (1981) 'Proto-industrialisation: the case of the West Riding wool textile industry in the eighteenth and nineteenth centuries', *History Workshop*, 12: 34–61.

Hughes, K.D. and Tadic, V. (1998) '"Something to deal with": customer sexual harassment and women's retail service work in Canada', *Gender, Work and Organization*, 5 (4): 207–19.

Hurstfield, J. (1987a) 'A route to inefficiency: compulsory contracting', *Low Pay Review*, 29.

Hurstfield, J. (1987b) 'The tender trap: the effects of the Local Government Bill', *Low Pay Review*, 31.

Hutton, W. (1996) *The State We're In*. London: Vintage.

International Labour Organisation (2001) *Yearbook of Labour Statistics*, 60th edition. Geneva: ILO.

Jackson, B. and Marsden, D. (1962) *Education and the Working Class*. London: Routledge and Kegan Paul.

Jackson, M. (2001) 'Non-meritocratic job requirements and the reproduction of class inequality: an investigation', *Work, Employment and Society*, 15 (3): 619–30.

Jahoda, M., Lazarsfeld, P. and Zeisel, H. (1972) *Marienthal: The Sociography of an Unemployed Community* (English translation). London: Tavistock.

Jenkins, R. (1984) 'Acceptability, suitability and the search for the habituated worker: how ethnic minorities and women lose out', *International Journal of Social Economics*, 11 (7): 65–75.

Jenkins, R. (1986) *Racism and Recruitment*. Cambridge: Cambridge University Press.

Jewson, N. and Mason, D. (1986) 'Modes of discrimination in the recruitment process: formalisation, fairness and efficiency', *Sociology*, 20: 43–63.

Johnson, D.H. and Makepeace, G.H. (1997) 'Occupational advantage in the eighties: an analysis of the lifetime earnings of men', *Work, Employment and Society*, 11 (3): 4101–11.

Johnson, G. (1992) 'Managing strategic change: strategy, culture and action', *Long Range Planning*, 24 (1): 28–36.

Jones, B. (1996) 'Why workers can't be commodities: the social construction of labour markets', in R. Crompton, D. Gallie and K. Purcell (eds), *Changing Forms of Employment*. London: Routledge.

258

Jones, B. (2000) 'The money or the principle', *Work, Employment and Society*, 14 (1): 191–200.

Jones, C., Taylor, G. and Nickson, D. (1997) 'Whatever it takes? Managing empowered workers in an international hotel chain', *Work, Employment and Society*, 11 (3): 541–54.

Jordan, W. (1982) *Mass Unemployment and the Future of Britain*. Oxford: Basil Blackwell.

Jordan, W. (2002) 'Demoralization, exit and mobility', paper presented to the Conference on Demoralization: Morality, Authority and Power, 5–6 April, Cardiff University.

Kahveci, E., Nichols, T. and Sugur, N. (1996) 'The shoe-shine boys of Izmir', in E. Kahveci, T. Nichols and N. Sugur (eds), *Work and Occupation in Modern Turkey*. London: Mansell.

Keep, E. (1989) 'Corporate training strategies: the vital component?', in J. Storey (ed.), *New Perspectives on Human Resource Management*. London: Routledge.

Keep. E. (1997) ' "There's no such thing as society ..." : some problems with an individual approach to creating a learning society', *Journal of Education Policy*, 12 (6): 457–71.

Kelvin, P. and Jarrett, J.E. (1985) *Unemployment: Its Social Psychological Effects*. Cambridge: Cambridge University Press.

Kenyon, P. (1972) *Textiles: A Protection Racket*. London: World Development Movement.

Kirkpatrick, I. and Martinez–Lucio, M. (1995) 'The uses of "quality" in the British government's reform of the public sector', in I. Kirkpatrick and M. Martinez-Lucio (eds), *The Politics of Quality in the Public Sector*. London: Routledge.

Kirkpatrick, I. and Martinez-Lucio, M. (1996) 'Introduction: the contract state and the future of public management', *Public Administration*, 74 (1): 1–8.

Klein, N. (2001) *No Logo*. London: Flamingo.

Knights, D. and McCabe, D. (1998) 'Dreams and designs on strategy: a critical analysis of TQM and Management Control', *Work, Employment and Society*, 12 (3): 433–56.

Knights, D., Murray, F. and Willmott, H. (1993) 'Networking as knowledge work: a study of strategic interorganizational development in the financial services industry', *Journal of Management Studies*, 30 (6): 975–95.

Korczynski, M., Shire, K., Frenkel, S. and Tam, M. (2000) 'Service work and consumer capitalism: customers, control and contradictions', *Work, Employment and Society*, 14 (4): 669–87.

Kunda, G. (1992) *Engineering Culture: Control and Commitment in a High-tech Corporation*. Philadelphia, PA: Temple University Press.

Lamont, M. (1992) *Money, Morals and Manners: The Culture of the French and American Upper-Middle Class*. Chicago: University of Chicago Press.

Lamont, M. (2000) *The Dignity of Working Men: Morality and the Boundaries of Race, Class and Immigration*. New York: Russell Sage / Cambridge, MA: Harvard University Press.

Lane, C.L. and Bachmann, R. (eds) (1998) *Trust Within and Between Organizations*. Oxford: Oxford University Press.

Lane, R. (2000) *The Loss of Happiness in Market Democracies*. New Haven, CT: Yale University Press.

Lankshear, G., Cook, P., Mason, D., Coates, S. and Button, G. (2001) 'Call centre employees' responses to electronic monitoring: some research findings', *Work, Employment and Society*, 15 (3): 595–605.

Lasch, C. (1979) *The Culture of Narcissism: American Life in an Age of Diminishing Expectations*. New York: W.W. Norton.

259

Lee, R. (1996) 'Moral money? LETS and the social construction of local economic geographies in Southeast England', *Environment and Planning A*, 28 (8): 1377–94.

Leidner, R. (1993) *Fast Food Fast Talk: Service Work and the Routinization of Everyday Life*. Berkeley, CA: University of California Press.

Lewis, O. (1965) *La Vida*. New York: Random House.

Lewis, R. (1993) *Leaders and Teachers: Adult Education and the Challenge of Labour in South Wales, 1906–1940*. Cardiff: University of Wales Press.

Lewis, S. (1997) '"Family friendly" employment policies: a route to changing organisational culture or playing about at the margins', *Gender, Work and Organization*, 4 (1): 13–23.

Liddington, J. and Norris, J. (1978) *One Hand Tied Behind Us*. London: Virago.

Littler, C. (1979) 'Internal contract and the transition to modern work systems', in D. Dunkerley and G. Salaman, *International Yearbook of Organisational Studies*. London: Routledge.

Livingstone, D.W. (1998) *The Education-Jobs Gap: Underemployment or Economic Democracy*. Boulder, CO: Westview Press.

MacIntyre, A. (1985) *After Virtue: A Study in Moral Theory*. 2nd edition. London: Duckworth.

Mackenzie, R. (2000) 'Subcontracting and the reregulation of the employment relationship: a case study from the telecommunications industry', *Work, Employment and Society*, 14 (4): 707–26.

Maclagan, P. (1998) *Management and Morality: A Developmental Perspective*. London: Sage.

Madsen, M. (1997) 'The relationship between working life and individualisation: a study amongst Danish trade union members', *Work, Employment and Society*, 11 (2): 197–217.

Mann, J. de L. (1971) *The Cloth Industry in the West of England from 1640 to 1880*. Oxford: Clarendon Press.

Mannheim, K. (1935) *Man and Society in an Age of Reconstruction*. London: Routledge and Kegan Paul.

March, J. and Simon, H.A. (1958) *Organizations*. New York: Wiley.

Marcuse, H. (1964) *One-Dimensional Man*. London: Routledge and Kegan Paul.

Marglin, S. (1974) 'What do bosses do?', *Review of Radical Political Economy*, 6 (2): 60–112.

Marshall, G. (1990) *In Praise of Sociology*. London: Unwin Hyman.

Marshall, G., Swift, A. and Roberts, S. (1997) *Against the Odds: Social Class and Social Justice in Industrial Societies*. Oxford: Clarendon Press.

Marx, K. (1852/1934) *The Eighteenth Brumaire of Louis Bonaparte*. London: Lawrence and Wishart.

Marx, K. (1867–94/1954–9) *Capital, vols 1–3*, London: Lawrence and Wishart.

Marx, K. and Engels, F. (1848/2002) *The Communist Manifesto*. London: Penguin Books.

Mauss, M. (1954) *The Gift*. New York: Norton.

Mayo, E. (1932/1977) *The Human Problems of an Industrial Civilization*. New York: Arno Press.

Mayo, E. (1973) *The Social Problems of an Industrial Civilization*. London: Routledge.

McKee, L., Mauthner, N. and Maclean, C. (2000) '"Family friendly" policies and practices in the oil and gas industry: employers' perspectives', *Work, Employment and Society*, 14 (3): 557–71.

McNabb, R. and Whitfield, K. (1994) *The Market for Training*. Aldershot: Avebury.

Mead, G.H. (1967) *Mind, Self and Society*. Chicago: Chicago University Press.

Melossi, D. and Pavarini, M. (1981) *The Prison and the Factory: Origins of the Penitentiary System*. London: Macmillan.

Mestrovic, S. (1991) *The Coming Fin de Siècle: An Application of Durkheim's Sociology to Modernity and Postmodernity*. London: Routledge.

Mestrovic, S. (1997) *Postemotional Society*. London: Sage.

Michels, R. (1911/1962) *Political Parties*. New York: Collier.

Miles, R. (1987) *Capitalism and Unfree Labour: Anomaly or Necessity?* London: Tavistock.

Miller, D. (1992) 'Deserving jobs', *Philosophical Quarterly*, 42: 161–81.

Miller, P. and Rose, N. (1990) 'Governing economic life', *Economy and Society*, 19: 1–31.

Mills, C.W. (1951) *White Collar*. New York: Oxford University Press.

Mumby, D. and Putnam, L. (1992) 'The politics of emotion: a feminist reading of bounded rationality', *Academy of Management Review*, 17 (3): 465–86.

Murphy, J. (1990) 'A most respectable prejudice: inequality in educational research and policy', *British Journal of Sociology*, 41 (1): 29–53.

Murray, C. (1990) *The Emerging British Underclass*. London: IEA.

Murray, C. (1994) *Losing Ground*. New York: Basic Books.

Neill, M. (1995) 'Computers, thinking and schools in the "new world economic order"', in J. Brook and I. Boal (eds), *Resisting Virtual Life: The Culture and Politics of Information*. San Francisco: City Lights.

Nichols, T. (1969) *Ownership, Control and Ideology*. London: George Allen and Unwin.

Nichols, T. (1986) *The British Worker Question*. London: Routledge and Kegan Paul.

Nichols, T. (1997) *The Sociology of Industrial Injury*. London: Mansell.

Nichols, T. (2001) 'The condition of labour: a retrospect', *Capital and Class*, 75: 185–98.

Nichols, T. and Armstrong, T. (1976) *Workers Divided*. London: Collins.

Nichols, T. and Beynon, H. (1977) *Living with Capitalism*. London: Routledge.

Nichols, T. and O'Connell Davidson, J. (1993) 'Privatisation and economism: an investigation amongst "producers" in two privatised public utilities in Britain', *Sociological Review*, 41 (4): 707–30.

Nichols, T., Sugur, N., Demir, E. and Kasapoglu, A. (1998) 'Privatisation in Turkey: employees' views on privatisation in the Turkish cement industry, and some comparisons with Britain', *Work, Employment and Society*, 12 (1): 1–23.

Offe, C. and Heinze, R. (1992) *Beyond Employment: Time, Work and the Informal Economy*. Cambridge: Polity Press.

Ohmae, K. (1983) *The Mind of the Strategist*. New York: Penguin.

Olsen, M. (1965) *The Logic of Collective Action*. Cambridge, MA: Harvard University Press.

O'Neill, J. (1998) *The Market. Ethics, Knowledge and Politics*. London: Routledge.

Ouchi, W. (1981) *Theory Z: How American Business Can Meet the Japanese Challenge*. Reading, MA: Addison-Wesley.

Park, A. (1994) *Individuals' Commitment to Lifelong Learning: Individual Attitudes*. London: Employment Department.

Parker, M. (2000) *Organisational Culture and Identity*. London: Sage.

Parker, M. (2002) *Against Management*. Cambridge: Polity Press.

Parkin, F. (1979) *Marxism and Class Theory: A Bourgeois Critique*. London: Tavistock.

Parsons, T. (1947/1964) 'Introduction', in M. Weber, *The Theory of Social and Economic Organisation*. New York: Free Press.

Parsons, T. (1949) *The Structure of Social Action*. New York: Free Press.

Parsons, T. (1951) *The Social System*. London: Routledge.

Parsons, T. and Smelser, N.J. (1956) *Economy and Society: A Study in the Integration of Economic and Social Theory*. London: Routledge.

Pattison, S. (1997) *The Faith of the Managers: When Management Becomes Religion*.

London: Cassell.

Perlow, L.A. (1997) *Finding Time: How Corporations, Individuals and Families Can Benefit from New Work Practices.* Ithaca, NY: Cornell University Press.

Peters, T. (1987) *Thriving on Chaos.* Basingstoke: Macmillan.

Peters, T. and Austin, N. (1985) *A Passion for Excellence: The Leadership Difference.* London: Collins.

Peters, T. and Waterman, R. (1982) *In Search of Excellence: Lessons from America's Best-run Companies.* London: Harper and Row.

Petersen, A. and Willig, R.(2002) 'An interview with Axel Honneth: the role of sociology in the theory of recognition', *European Journal of Social Theory,* 5 (2): 265–70.

Pinchbeck, I. (1930) *Women Workers and the Industrial Revolution.* London: Routledge.

Piore, M.J. and Sabel, C. (1984) *The Second Industrial Divide.* New York. Basic Books.

Polanyi, K. (1944/1957) *The Great Transformation.* Boston: Beacon Press.

Polanyi, K., Arensberg, C. and Pearson, H. (1957) *Trade and Market in Early Empires.* New Yourk: Free Press.

Pollard, S. (1965) *The Genesis of Modern Management: A Study of the Industrial Revolution in Great Britain.* London: Edward Arnold.

Pollert, A. (1988) 'Dismantling "flexibility"', *Capital and Class,* 34: 42–75.

Pollert, A. (ed.) (1991) *Farewell to Flexibility.* Oxford: Basil Blackwell.

Portes, A. (1995a) 'Economic sociology and the sociology of immigration: a conceptual overview', in A. Portes (ed.), *The Economic Sociology of Immigration.* New York: Russell Sage Foundation.

Portes, A. (ed.) (1995b) *The Economic Sociology of Immigration.* New York: Russell Sage Foundation.

Portes, A. (1998) 'Social capital: its origins and applications in modern sociology', *Annual Review of Sociology,* 24: 1–24.

Powell, W.W. and DiMaggio, P.J. (eds) (1991) *The New Institutionalism in Organizational Analysis.* Chicago: University of Chicago Press.

Powell, W.W. and Smith-Doerr, L. (1994) 'Networks and economic life', in N. Smelser and R. Swedberg (eds), *The Handbook of Economic Sociology,* Princeton, NJ: Princeton University Press.

Power, M. (1997) *The Audit Society.* Oxford: Oxford University Press.

Prandy, K. (1998) 'Class and continuity in social reproduction: an empirical investigation', *Sociological Review,* 46 (2): 340–64.

Prandy, K. and Bottero, W. (2000) 'Social reproduction and mobility in Britain and Ireland in the nineteenth and early twentieth centuries', *Sociology,* 34 (2): 265–81.

Przeworski, A. (1980) 'Material bases of consent: economics and politics in a hegemonic system', *Political Power and Social Theory,* 1: 21–66.

Pugh, D. and Hickson, D. (1976) *Organizational Structure and its Context.* Westmead: Saxon House.

Putnam, R. (1995a) 'Bowling alone: America's declining social capital', *Journal of Democracy,* 6 (1): 65–78.

Putnam, R. (1995b) 'Tuning in, tuning out: the strange disappearance of social capital in America', *PS: Political Science and Politics,* 28 (4): 664–83.

Putnam, R., with Leonardi, R. and Nanetti, R. (1993) *Making Democracy Work: Civic Traditions in Modern Italy.* Princeton, NJ: Princeton University Press.

Rainwater, L. (1970) *Behind Ghetto Walls.* New York: Aldine.

Rees, G., Fevre, R., Furlong, J. and Gorard, S. (1997) 'History, place and the learning society: towards a sociology of lifetime learning', *Journal of Education Policy,* 12 (6): 485–97.

Reich, R. (1991) *The Work of Nations.* London: Simon and Schuster.

Riesman, D. (1950) *The Lonely Crowd.* New Haven, CT: Yale University Press.

Ritzer, G. (1993) *The MacDonaldization of Society*. London: Sage.

Roethlisberger, F.J. and Dickson, W.J. (1939) *Management and the Worker*. Cambridge, MA: Harvard University Press.

Roker, D. (1993) 'Gaining the edge', in I. Bates and G. Riseborough (eds), *Youth and Inequality*. Buckingham: Open University Press.

Rose, M. (1988) *Industrial Behaviour*. Harmondsworth: Penguin.

Rose, N. (1989) *Governing the Soul: The Shaping of the Private Self*. London: Routledge.

Rosenthal, P., Hill, S. and Peccei, R. (1997) 'Checking out service: evaluating excellence, HRM and TQM', *Work, Employment and Society*, 11 (3): 481–503.

Rostow, W.W. (1960) *The Stages of Economic Growth*. Cambridge: Cambridge University Press.

Russell, B. (1932/1999) 'In praise of idleness', originally printed in Harper's Magazine (October 1932), reprinted in K. Thomas (ed.) *The Oxford Book of Work*. Oxford: Oxford University Press.

Sabel, C. (1982) *Work and Politics*. Cambridge: Cambridge University Press.

Samuel, R. (1977) 'The workshop of the world', *History Workshop*, 3: 6–72.

Sassen, S. (1988) *Cities in a World Economy*. Thousand Oaks, CA: Pine Forge Press.

Saunders, P. (1990) *Social Class and Stratification*. London: Routledge.

Saunders, P. (1995) 'Might Britain be a meritocracy?', *Sociology*, 29: 23–41.

Saunders, P. (1997) 'Social mobility in Britain: an empirical evaluation of two competing explanations', *Sociology*, 31: 261–88.

Savage, M. et al. (1992) *Property, Bureaucracy and Culture: Middle Class Formation in Contemporary Britain*. London: Routledge.

Sayer, A. (2000a) 'Moral economy and political economy', *Studies in Political Economy*, 6 (1): 79–104.

Sayer, A. (2000b) 'Equality and moral economy', paper presented to the Tenth Annual Conference of the Equality Studies Centre, University College Dublin.

Sayles, R. (1958) *The Behaviour of Industrial Work Groups*. New York: John Wiley.

Schremmer, E. (1976) 'The textile industry in Southern Germany 1750–1850', *Textile History*, 7: 60–89.

Schuller, T. (1996) *Building Social Capital: Steps towards a Learning Society* (Occasional Papers Series, No. 11). Edinburgh: Centre for Continuing Education, University of Edinburgh.

Schultz, T.H. (1961) 'Investment in human capital', *American Economic Review*, L1: 1–17.

Schumacher, E.F. (1979) *Good Work*. London: Jonathan Cape.

Scott, B. (1998) *The Sexual Harassment of Women in the Workplace, 1600–1993*. Jefferson, NC: McFarland.

Scott, J. (1976) The Moral Economy of the Peasant. New Haven, CT: Yale University Press.

Scott, W.G. (1985) 'Organizational revolution: an end to managerial orthodoxy', *Administration and Society*, 17: 149–70.

Selwyn, N. and Gorard, S. (2002) *The Information Age: Technology, Learning and Exclusion in Wales*. Cardiff: University of Wales Press.

Sennett, R. (1998) *The Corrosion of Character*. New York: W.W. Norton.

Serrin, W. (1973) *The Company and the Union*. New York: Alfred Knopf.

Seyfang, G. (2001) 'Working for the fenland dollar: an evaluation of local exchange trading schemes as an informal employment strategy to tackle social exclusion', *Work, Employment and Society*, 15 (3): 581–93.

Shenhav, Y. (1999) *Manufacturing Rationality*. Oxford: Oxford University Press.

Siltanen, J. (1994) *Locating Gender: Occupational Segregation, Wages and Domestic Responsibilities*. London: UCL Press.

Simmel, G. (1900/1990) *The Philosophy of Money*, edited by D. Frisby. London: Routledge.

Simmel, G. (1902–3/1950) *The Sociology of Georg Simmel* (originally published 1908), edited by K.H. Wolff. New York: Free Press.

Simmel, G. (1904/1971) *On Individuality and Social Forms*, edited by D.N. Levine. Chicago: University of Chicago Press.

Smelser, N. and Swedberg, R. (eds) (1994) *The Handbook of Economic Sociology*, Princeton, NJ: Princeton University Press.

Smith, A. (1976a) *An Inquiry into the Nature and Causes of the Wealth of Nations*. Oxford: Clarendon Press.

Smith, A. (1976b) *The Theory of Moral Sentiments*. Oxford: Clarendon Press.

Sorokin, P. (1959) *Social and Cultural Mobility*. New York: Free Press.

Sosteric, M. (1996) 'Keeping women in and out of line: sexual harassment and occupational segregation', *Work, Employment and Society*, 10 (2): 297–318.

Sowell, T. (1990) *Preferential Policies: An International Perspective*. New York: Morrow.

Spencer, D.A. (2000) 'Braverman and the contribution of labour process analysis to the critique of the capitalist production: twenty–five years on', *Work, Employment and Society*, 14 (2): 223–43.

Spencer, D.A. (forthcoming) 'The demise of radical political economics? An essay on the evolution of a theory of capitalist production', *Cambridge Journal of Economics*.

Stivers, R. (1994) *The Culture of Cynicism: American Morality in Decline*. Cambridge, MA: Blackwell.

Stivers, R. (1999) *Technology as Magic*. London: Continuum.

Storey, J. (1992) *Developments in the Management of Human Resources*. Oxford: Blackwell.

Storey, J. (ed.) (1995) *Human Resource Management: A Critical Text*. London: Routledge.

Storey, J. and Harrison, A. (1999) 'Coping with world class manufacturing', *Work, Employment and Society*, 13 (4): 643–64.

Strathdee, R. (2001) 'Changes in social capital and school-to-work transitions', *Work, Employment and Society*, 15 (2): 311–26.

Streeck, W. (1987) 'The uncertainties of management in the management of uncertainty: employers, labour relations and industrial adjustment in the 1980s', *Work, Employment and Society*, 1 (3): 281–308.

Streeck, W. (1989) 'Skills and the limits of neo-liberalism: the enterprise of the future as a place of learning', *Work, Employment and Society*, 3 (1): 89–104.

Swedberg, R. (1986) 'Economic sociology: past and present', *Current Sociology*, 35 (1): 1–22.

Swedberg, R. (ed.) (1993) *Explorations in Economic Sociology*. New York: Russell Sage Foundation.

Taylor, F.W. (1911/1972) *Principles of Scientific Management*. Westport, CT: Greenwood Press.

Taylor, S. and Spencer, L. (1994) *Individuals' Attitudes: Individual Commitment to Lifetime Learning, Report on Qualitative Phase*, (Employment Department, Research Series No. 31, July).

Taylor, S. and Tyler, M. (2000) 'Emotional labour and sexual difference in the airline industry', *Work, Employment and Society*, 14 (1): 77–95.

ten Bos, R. (2000) *Fashion and Utopia in Management Thinking*. Amsterdam: John Benjamins.

Thompson, E.P. (1971) 'The moral economy of the English crowd in the eighteenth century', *Past and Present*, 50: 553–72.

Thompson, E.P. (1974) *The Making of the English Working Class*.

Harmondsworth: Penguin.

Thompson, E.P. (1976) 'On history, sociology and historical relevance', *British Journal of Sociology*, 27 (3): 387–402.

Thompson, P. (1983) *The Nature of Work*. London: Macmillan.

Thorpe, E. (1973) 'The taken-for-granted reference: an empirical examination', *Sociology*, 7 (3): 361–76.

Townley, B. (1994) *Reframing Human Resource Management: Power, Ethics and the Subject at Work*. London: Sage.

Trist, E. and Bamforth, K. (1951) 'Some psychological and social consequences of the longwall methods of coal–getting', *Human Relations*, 4: 3–38.

Trompenaars, F. and Hampden-Turner, C. (1997) *Riding the Waves of Culture*. London: Nicholas Brealey.

Turnbull, P. and Wass, V. (1999) 'Redundancy and paradox of job insecurity', in E. Heery and J. Salmon (eds), *The Insecure Workforce*. London: Routledge.

Ure, A. (1835/1967) *The Philosophy of Manufactures*. New York: Kelley.

Vroom, V. (1964) *Work and Motivation*. New York: Wiley.

Waddington, D., Parry, D. and Critcher, C. (1998) 'Keeping the red flag flying? A comparative study of two worker takeovers in the British coal mining industry, 1992–1997', *Work, Employment and Society*, 12 (2): 317–49.

Wajcman, J. (1998) *Managing Like a Man*. Cambridge: Polity.

Walby, S. (1986) *Patriarchy at Work: Patriarchal and Capitalist Relations in Employment*. Cambridge: Polity Press.

Walby, S. (ed.) (1988) *Gender Segregation at Work*. Milton Keynes: Open University Press.

Walby, S. (1990) *Theorising Patriarchy*. Oxford: Basil Blackwell.

Walby, S. (1997) *Gender Transformations*. London: Routledge.

Walker, W. (1979) *Juteopolis*. Edinburgh: Scottish Academic Press.

Wallis, E., Winterton, J. and Winterton, R. (2000) 'Subcontracting in the privatised coal industry', *Work, Employment and Society*, 14 (4): 727–42.

Weber, M. (1904–5/1958) *The Protestant Ethic and the Spirit of Capitalism*. New York: Charles Scribner's Sons.

Weber, M. (1968) *Economy and Society*, G. Roth and C. Wittich (eds), New York: Bedminster Press.

Weber, M. (1981) *General Economic History*. New Brunswick, NJ: Transaction Books.

Weber, M. (1989) 'The national state and economic policy' (inaugural lecture, Freiburg, May 1895), in K. Tribe (ed.), *Reading Weber*. London: Routledge.

Wheen, F. (1999) *Karl Marx*. London: Fourth Estate.

Williams, K., Haslam, C. and William, J. (1987) 'The end of mass production?', *Economy and Society*, 6 (3): 404–38.

Williamson, O. (1975) *Markets and Hierarchies*. New York: Free Press.

Williamson, O. (1985) *The Economic Institutions of Capitalism*. New York: Free Press.

Willis, P. (1977) *Learning to Labour*. Farnborough: Saxon House.

Winch, P. (1990) *The Idea of Social Science*, 2nd edition. London: Routledge.

Windebank, J. (2001) 'Dual-earner couples in Britain and France: gender divisions of domestic labour and parenting work in different states', *Work, Employment and Society*, 15 (2): 269–90.

Wing, C. (1967) *The Evils of the Factory System*. London: Frank Cass.

Winner, L. (1994) 'Three paradoxes of the Information Age', in G. Bender and T. Druckrey (eds), *Culture on the Brink: Ideologies of Technology*. Seattle: Bay Press.

Wolfe, A. (1989) *Whose Keeper? Social Science and Moral Obligation*. Berkeley, CA: University of California Press.

Wood, S. (ed.) (1982) *The Degradation of Work?* London: Routledge.

Woodward, J. (1958) *Management and Technology*. London: HMSO.

Woodward, J. (1965) *Industrial Organisation: Theory and Practice*. London: Oxford University Press.

Woolcock, M. (1998) 'Social capital and economic development: toward a theoretical synthesis and policy framework', *Theory and Society*, 27 (1): 15–208.

Woolcock, M. (2000) *Using Social Capital: Getting the Social Relations Right in the Theory and Practice of Economic Development*. Princeton, NJ: Princeton University Press.

Zukin, S. and DiMaggio, P. (eds) (1990) *Structures of Capital*. Cambridge: Cambridge University Press.

index